introduction to project management

project management

one small step for the project manager

Rory Burke

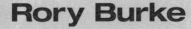
cosmic MBA series

email: rory@burkepublishing.com
web site: www.burkepublishing.com

Introduction to Project Management

Rory Burke

ISBN: 0-9582 733-3-2

Published: 2007

Distributors: UK: rory@burkepublishing.com

USA: Partners Book Distributing, email: partnersbk@aol.com

South Africa: Blue Weaver Marketing, email: orders@blueweaver.co.za

Australia: Thames and Hudson, email: orders@thaust.com.au

DTP: Sandra Burke

Cover Design: Simon Larkin

Sketches: Buddy Mendis, Michael Glasswell

Printer: Everbest, HK / China

Production notes: Page size (168 x 244 mm), Body Text (Minion Pro, 11 pt), Chapter Headings (Helvetica, bold, 60 pt), Subheadings (Helvetica, bold, 11 pt), Software InDesign, Photoshop, Illustrator, CorelDRAW, PC and Mac notebook computers.

Dedicated ....to Mike, Mags, Amy and Jemma, thank you for the entertainment in the City of Gold!

Content

Foreword

Author's Note

Chapter 1	**Introduction to Project Management**	**14**
	1. What is a Project?	16
	2. What is Project Management?	18
	3. Types of Projects	19
	4. Management-by-Projects	21
	5. General Management	22
	6. Project Management Process	24
	7. Project Lifecycle	25
	8. Role of the Project Manager	26
	9. Project Management Environment	27
	10. Project Management Environment	27
	11. Benefits of Project Management	27
Chapter 2	**History of Project Management**	**30**
	1. Project Management Techniques	31
	2. Program Evaluation and Review Techniques (PERT)	32
	3. Project Organisation Structures	34
	4. Project Management Triangle	35
	5. History of Project Management Computing	36
Chapter 3	**Project Management Standards**	**38**
Chapter 4	**Project Lifecycle**	**44**
	1. Project Lifecycle (4 phases)	45
	2. House Extension Project Lifecycle (4 phases)	47
	3. Input, Process, Output	48
	4. Overlap Between Phases (fast tracking)	50
	5. Level of Effort	51
	6. Level of Influence vs Cost of Changes	52
	7. Product Lifecycle	53
Chapter 5	**Feasibility Study**	**58**
	1. Feasibility Study Initiation	58
	2. Stakeholders Analysis	59
	3. Define the Client's Needs	62
	4. Project Viability Check	63
	5. Internal Project Constraints	64
	6. Internal Corporate Constraints	66
	7. External Constraints	67
	8. Evaluate Options and Alternatives	68
	9. Feasibility Study Summary Template	69

Chapter 6	**Project Planning and Control Cycle**................................	**70**
	1. Project Planning Steps..	71
	2. Project Control Cycle..	77
	3. Reporting Frequency..	79
	4. Planning and Control Spiral..................................	80
Chapter 7	**Scope Management**...	**82**
	1. Project Initiation...	83
	2. Scope Planning...	85
	3. Scope Definition...	85
	4. Scope verification...	85
	5. Scope Change Control..	86
	6. Project Closeout..	93
Chapter 8	**Work Breakdown Structure**..	**96**
	1. Purpose of the WBS..	97
	2. WBS Structure...	98
	3. Methods of Subdivision..	100
	4. Activity List..	103
	5. Checklists..	104
	6. WBS Templates...	105
	7. The Numbering System...	106
	8. Cost Breakdown Structure (Estimating)...............	107
Chapter 9	**Estimating Techniques**..	**108**
	1. Direct Costs..	109
	2. Indirect Costs...	110
	3. Fixed and Variable Costs......................................	110
	4. Labour Costs...	111
	5. Procurement Costs..	112
	6. Unit Rates...	113
	7. Estimating Format (top down/bottom up).............	114
Chapter 10	**Project Risk Management**...	**116**
	1. Risk Management Model.......................................	117
	2. Define Objectives...	119
	3. Risk Identification..	122
	4. Risk Quantification..	123
	5. Risk Response...	126
	6. Risk Control...	127
Chapter 11	**Critical Path Method**...	**128**
	1. Network Diagram..	129
	2. Definition of an Activity.......................................	130
	3. Logical Relationships..	131
	4. How to Draw the Logical Relationships................	132
	5. Activity Duration..	133
	6. Definition of an Event..	133
	7. Calendar / Work Pattern.......................................	133
	8. Activity Logic..	134
	9. Critical Path Method Steps...................................	135
	10. Forward Pass...	136
	11. Backward Pass...	137
	12. Activity Float...	138

Chapter 12	**Gantt Charts**		**140**
	1. How to Draw a Gantt Chart		141
	2. Tabular Reports		142
	3. Activity Float		143
	4. Hammocks		144
	5. Events, Keydates and Milestones		145
	6. Revised Gantt Chart		146
	7. Rolling Horizon Gantt Chart		148
Chapter 13	**Procurement Schedule**		**150**
	1. Procurement Cycle		151
	2. Procurement Schedule		155
	3. Expediting		156
Chapter 14	**Resources**		**158**
	1. Resource Estimating		159
	2. Resource Histogram		160
	3. Resource Smoothing		162
	4. Time-Limited Resource Scheduling		164
	5. Resource-Limited Resource Scheduling		165
	6. How to Increase Resources		166
	7. Reduce Resources		166
	8. Resource Planning and Control		167
Chapter 15	**Project Accounts**		**168**
	1. Cashflow Statement		169
	2. Cashflow Timing		171
	3. Cost Distribution		172
	4. How to Draw an Expense S Curve		174
Chapter 16	**Project Control**		**176**
	1. Control Cycle		177
	2. Scope of Control		177
	3. Data Capture		180
	4. How to Apply project Control		183
Chapter 17	**Earned Value**		**184**
	1. Earned Value Terminology		185
	2. Earned Value Graph		187
	3. Earned Value Table		188
	4. project Control		189
	5. Client's View of Earned Value		189
	6. Earned Value Reporting		189
	7. Earned Value Example		190
Chapter 18	**Quality Management**		**192**
	1. Quality Definitions		193
	2. Quality Control		195
	3. Quality Control Plan (QCP)		196
Chapter 19	**Communication**		**198**
	1. Communication Theory		200
	2. Communication Plan		203
	3. Project Information and Control System		205
	4. Project Reporting		206
	5. Document Control		208

Chapter 20	**Project Meetings**		**212**
	1. How to Prepare a Meeting		214
	2. Handover Meeting		217
	3. Project Progress Meetings		219
	4. Brainstorming Workshops		220
Chapter 21	**Project Organisation Structures**		**222**
	1. Functional Organisation Structure		223
	2. Matrix Organisation Structure		225
	3. Job Description		228
	4. Responsibility-Authority Gap		230
Chapter 22	**Project Teams**		**232**
	1. Purpose of Project Teams		234
	2. Individuals Purpose for Team Membership		235
	3. Benefits of Teams		235
	4. Team Size		236
	5. Why Teams Win		237
	6. Why Teams Fail		238
	7. Role of Project Manager		238
Chapter 23	**Managing Small Projects**		**240**
	1. Define Small Projects		241
	2. Managing Small Projects		243
	3. Product Lifecycle		244
	4. Small Business Management		246
Chapter 24	**Project Management Office**		**248**
	1. Site Office		249
	2. Matrix Organisation Structure		250
	3. Centre of Excellence		251
	4. Management-by-Projects		256
	5. Mobile Project office		256
Chapter 25	**Event Management**		**258**
	1. What is an Event?		259
	2. Project Management Techniques		260

Appendix 1 - Solutions

Further Reading

Glossary

Index

Cosmic MBA Series

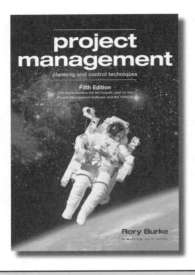

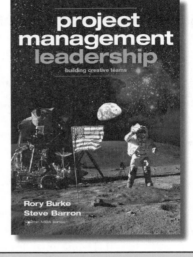

Project Management 5ed
ISBN 0-9582 733-1-6
Project Management BOK
Project Lifecycle
Feasibility Study
Planning and Control Cycle
Scope Management
Estimating Techniques
Risk Management
CPM
Gantt Charts
Procurement Management
Resource Management
Project Control
Earned Value
Communication / Meetings
OBS / Matrix

Project Management Leadership
ISBN 0-9582 733-5-9
Leadership Styles
Team Creation
Team Development Phases
Team Dynamics
Delegation
Problem Solving
Decision Making
Creativity and Innovation
Negotiation
Conflict Resolution
Communication Theory
Team Meetings
OBS/Matrix
Outdoor Teambuilding

Cosmic MBA Series

Project Management Entrepreneur
ISBN 0-9582 733-2-4
Levels of Entrepreneurship
Entrepreneur BOK
Small Business Management Skills
Product Lifecycle
Creating a New Venture
PM Entrepreneur Traits
Problem Solving
Risk Management
Networking
Business Plan
Gantt Charts
Procurement Management
Resource Management
Quality Control Plan
Project Teams

Entrepreneurs Toolkit
ISBN 0-9582 391-4-2

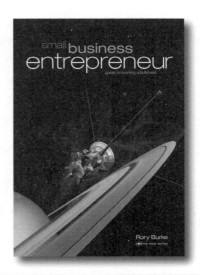

Small Business Entrepreneur
ISBN 0-9582 391-6-9

Foreword

If you are looking at this book you are probably looking for something that will introduce you to the world of managing projects. Perhaps you are an engineer who is working to deadlines and budgets, a team member who has to mentor and report project performance, or an entrepreneur starting a new venture. Whoever you are, I hope this introduction to project management will start your journey into a world of projects that will present some surprises, challenge some perceptions and lead you to some places you never knew existed!

Firstly, you will need to learn a new language because the world of projects has its own lingo. You will be introduced to breakdowns that are helpful, risks that can be avoided and plans that deliver results. You will learn techniques that convert data into information and how to present information in a meaningful manner that provides insight into what is going on in your project. The project world is a world of uncertainty but also a world of meaning. If there is a name for this project world, it would probably be *"Planet Organize"*. Project management is principally about organizing and its language, techniques and behaviours exist to provide order in an uncertain world.

You can work through the content of this book and learn all about the techniques and how to apply them. I am sorry to say it is likely this will not be sufficient to be a good project manager. If you want to be a juggler, could you claim to be able to juggle after reading a book? Of course not! To be able to juggle you need to be able to throw balls (for example) in the air and be able to catch them. The only way to do this is to practice throwing and catching (please don't try that just now, especially with this book), maybe starting with one item and progressing to more as your skill progresses.

It is the same with projects. Reading this book is just the start. You need to try out the techniques on your projects, possibly one at a time. Try out one technique that helps to solve an immediate problem, then try another. Over time you will collect a number of tools for your project management toolbox. A carpenter generally uses only one tool at a time. However, throwing things in the air one at a time does not make a juggler. The real skill of a project manager is getting the techniques to work together in concert, each one feeding information to the others until the project is a result of *"joined up"* organizing. This is not a mission impossible but the result of having a go and persistence in trying out the techniques until they work for you.

There is one last use of the juggling metaphor that I would like to leave with you. One of the key skills of the juggler is not about knowing where the balls ARE, but rather where they WILL BE. The hands of the juggler need to be ready to catch the ball at the end of its trajectory, not in mid air. The project management techniques help a similar prediction about where the project work is heading and helps to consider consequences of action.

So, like the juggler, you need to keep your balls in the air, think about where they are going to be and, most importantly, try not to drop one!

I wish you well in your journey into project management.

Steve Barron
Lancaster University
Director of the Executive MSc in
Project Management

"...the project management juggler!..."

Author's Note

Introduction to Project Management – getting started has been written as a broad based introduction to the field of project management. This book will outline all the key project management principles, tools and techniques and show how they can be used to manage your projects.

This book is ideal for managers entering the field of project management who need a solid platform of techniques from which to manage small projects or sub-projects with a limited scope of work, limited number of resources and a small budget.

This book is also ideal for **project team members** who need to understand the basic principles of project management so that they can support the project manager and carryout the project administration function within the project management office (PMO). As a team member this may involve gathering and processing project data, monitoring and reporting project progress, administrating scope change control, administrating documentation control and expediting progress.

With deregulation and privatization large companies and government departments have been forced to become more competitive and more customer focused. One way of achieving this is to package their work as many small projects which can be effectively managed as projects through a project management office. Combine this with products becoming more technically complex, with shorter durations and tighter budgets, hence there is another reason for companies to adopt project management to plan and control their scope of work.

As the use of projects becomes more pervasive, so more managers are entering the field of project management. Their success will be helped by their ability to develop and apply a comprehensive toolkit of planning and control techniques - as a mechanic works with a bag of tools, so the project manager works with a computer producing organisation charts, work breakdown structures, Gantt charts, resource histograms and cashflow statements.

This book is structured in line with the PMBOK's nine knowledge areas, the APM bok, the Australian competency standards, and the South African unit standards for project management (numbers 120372, 120376, 120381, 120384, 120387, 120382). This book also explains the planning and control techniques used by the project management software. These standards form the corner stones of project management and will help you ringfence what you need to know.

This book includes plenty of worked examples and exercises, together with an Instructor's Manual which can be downloaded from *(www. knowledgezone.net)*.

Special thanks to Annemie Willemse for her educational input, and Steve Barron for his inspirational foreword.

Rory Burke
Burke Publishing
www.burkepublishing.com

Interview at the BBC

1

Introduction to Project Management

Learning Outcomes

After reading this chapter, you should be able to;

Define project management

Define management-by-projects

List the benefits of project management

Outline the role of the project manager and team members

Explain the difference between project management and general management

Introduction to Project Management – features the management of small projects and project administration, and offers a structured approach to getting started. The purpose of this book is to introduce the latest project management techniques used to manage a range of projects. These techniques are used by the planning software and are referred to in the PMI's Project Management Body of Knowledge (PMBOK), the APM's body of knowledge (bok), and the SA unit standards.

This broad based introduction to project management is ideal for managers who are new to project management and who are managing small projects or sub-projects and need information, knowledge and skills to get started.

This book is also written for project team members who need to understand the special techniques of project management so that they can support the project manager and run the project management office (PMO) administration. As a team member this may involve gathering and processing project data, monitoring and reporting project progress, administrating scope change control, administrating documentation control and expediting progress.

Projects have traditionally been managed through a classic functional hierarchical type organisation structure but, with the increase of multi-disciplines, multi-departments, multi-companies and multi-national projects, there has been a trend towards the following;

- project teams
- management-by-projects
- matrix organisation structures.

These organisation structures empower all levels of the company and help to make the project team members feel more responsible and motivated to achieve their goals. As the project manager is the single point of responsibility, it is the project manager's responsibility to set up a management structure which meets the needs of the project, the needs of the organisation, the needs of the stakeholders and the needs of the individuals working on the project (see figure 1.1).

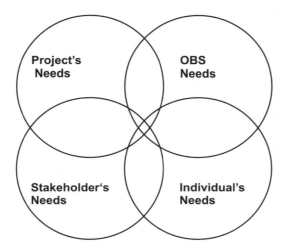

Figure 1.1: Intersecting Needs – shows the project's needs, the OBS's needs, the stakeholders' needs and the individuals needs as intersecting circles

1. What is a Project?

The main difference between project management and other management disciplines relates to the definition of a project and what the project intends to deliver for the client and stakeholders.

> **DEFINITION**
>
> The Project Management Institute's (PMI) guide to the project management body of knowledge (PMBOK) defines a project as; *'.... a temporary endeavour undertaken to create a unique product or service (outcome or result). Temporary means that every project has a definite end. Unique means that the product or service is different in some distinguishing way from all similar products or services.'*

Some of the special features of a project include;

Start and Finish	A project has a clear start and finish.
Lifecycle	A project has a beginning and an end, with a number of distinct phases in between.
Schedule and Timeline	Projects are often time-limited. This means they must finish by a certain date.
Budget	Projects have a clear budget, often broken down to a budget per work package.
Non-Repetitive	Activities are essentially unique and non-repetitive.
Resources	Resources may be sourced from different functional departments and need to be co-ordinated.
Single Point of Responsibility	The project manager, project leader or project entrepreneur are responsible for the whole project.
Teams	Project teams are formed to complete the project.

Traditionally projects were associated with construction, petro-chemical and defence type projects, but in recent years most proactive industries (particularly IT), businesses and government departments have re-structured their work as projects. Consider the following different types of projects:

Construction Project	Designing and constructing a building, a bridge or a power station.
Product Development Project	Designing and testing a new product – a prototype car or a washing machine.
Advertising and Marketing Project	Launching and promoting a new product.
IT Project, or Computer Upgrade Project	Designing and implementing a new computer system which includes new hardware and software.
Human Resource Project	Designing and implementing a new organisation structure.
Office Project	Moving office, implementing new management systems.
Quality Management Project	Planning and conducting an audit.
Disaster Recovery Project	Limiting the damage to the business and loss of information caused by fires, floods or any type of accident.
Maintenance Project	Repairing and maintaining equipment.
Sports Project or Event Management	Managing a rugby tour to New Zealand, managing the London Olympics.
Entertainment Project or Event Management	Organising the Rolling Stones or Robbie Williams' world tour.
Travel Project	Planning an overseas business trip or holiday.
Fashion Show	Planning a fashion show of the latest designer fashions.
Domestic Project or Event Management	Planning a wedding or 40th birthday party.
Training and Education Project	Developing a new course.
Social Project	Building a heritage centre.
Police Project	Managing terrorism.
Aid Project	Providing basic infrastructure to remote villages.

Table 1.1: Types of Projects – shows the different types of projects

Within the context of this book a project may be defined as implementing a change, event, solution, or a new venture which uses a range of special project management techniques to plan and control the scope of work in order to deliver a product to satisfy the client's and stakeholders' needs and expectations.

2. What is Project Management

DEFINITION

Project management is defined by the PMBOK as; '..... *the application of knowledge, skills, tools and techniques to project activities in order to meet stakeholders needs and expectations from a project.*'

In other words the project team must do whatever is required to make the project happen - one could not have a wider all encompassing job description!

This definition clearly identifies that the purpose of the project is to meet the stakeholders' needs and expectations. It is, therefore, a fundamental requirement for the project team to establish who are the stakeholders (besides the client) and analyse their needs and expectations to define, at the outset, the project's scope of work and objectives (this will be developed in the *Feasibility Study* chapter).

The discipline of project management can also be described in terms of its component processes, conveniently defined by the PMI (PMBOK) as nine knowledge areas:

- Scope
- Quality
- Risk

- Time
- HRM
- Procurement

- Cost
- Communication
- Integration

These nine knowledge areas are defined in the *Project Management Standards* chapter.

DEFINITION

The APM bok defines project management as; '....*the most efficient way of introducing change. .... achieved by:*
- ....*defining what has to be accomplished, generally in terms of time, cost, and various technical and quality performance parameters;*
- ....*developing a plan to achieve these and then working this plan, ensuring that progress is maintained in line with these objectives;*
- ....*using appropriate project management techniques and tools to plan, monitor and maintain progress;*
- ....*employing persons skilled in project management - including normally a project manager - who are given* [single] *responsibility for introducing the change and are accountable for its successful accomplishment.*'

Companies performing projects will generally subdivide their projects into several phases or stages to provide better management control. Collectively these project phases are called the project lifecycle. Along with the project lifecycle the other special project management techniques which form part of the project management integration process are:

- Work breakdown structure (WBS)
- Critical path method (CPM)
- Resource smoothing
- Earned value
- Configuration control.

3. Types of Projects

Projects range in type, size, scope, cost and time from mega international projects costing millions of dollars and implemented over many years, to small domestic projects with a small budget and taking just a few hours to complete. Projects can also be grouped – it is becoming popular for large companies that have many small projects, to adopt a management-by-projects approach where all their projects are channelled through a project office.

Another way of classifying projects is by focusing on the clarity of the objectives and the development of the project management processes and tools. The following model and text is developed from Obeng, Frigenti and Comninos (2002).

Fog Type	Fog-type projects can be described as walking in thick fog. On these type of projects, the project participants and stakeholders are not sure what is to be achieved or how it is to be carried out.
Movie Type	Movie-type projects are projects where participants and stakeholders have a high degree of certainty of how the project is to be carried out, but not what is to be delivered.
Quest Type	Quest-type projects are also known as semi-closed projects. On Quest projects, the project participants and stakeholders have a high degree of certainty of what should be done, but they are not sure of how to achieve it.
Painting by Numbers	Painting by numbers projects are known as closed projects. The project participants and most of the stakeholders have a high degree of certainty about what is to be done and how to achieve it.

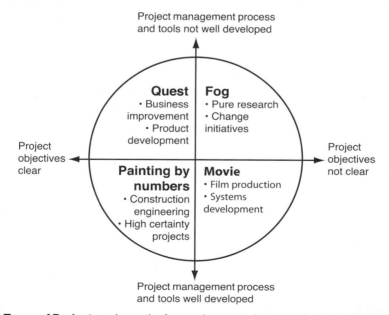

Figure 1.2: Types of Projects – shows the four project types in terms of project objectives (clear / not clear), and project management processes and tools (well developed / not well developed)

As a project develops it can move from one state to another; for example, the early stages of a business improvement project could be described as a 'fog project' as the organisation knows it needs to improve performance but is not sure exactly where to focus its attention. As the project emerges from the fog into clarity, targets for improvement are set, moving the project into a 'quest' state, but the best approach to achieve the project is not yet clear. As the project progressively elaborates, the design and implementation details emerge which, when sufficiently clear, lead to the 'painting by numbers' state. During the implementation the project is predominantly in the 'painting by numbers' state, although it may at times need to revert back to 'quest' or 'fog' if unforeseen factors arise.

Project type (description by Obeng)	General description	Project Process	Project Tools	Management approach
Fog **Pure research** **Change initiatives** **First-time projects**	We are not sure where we are going, or how to get there	Not well understood	Not well developed	Proceed with caution one step at a time. Focus on the next beacon and carefully move towards it. Having reached a beacon, the path to the next beacon becomes clear through the fog.
Movie **Film production** **Systems development**	We are not sure what our final destination will be. Once we have some idea we will know how to get there	Well understood	Well developed	Because the project management and production processes are well known, avoid spending too much time on definition and planning. It is better to concentrate on finding a good product (script), and the project process will be easily managed.
Quest **Business improvement** **Project development**	We know what our destination is, but we are not entirely sure how to get there	Not well understood	Not necessarily well developed	These projects require considerable research in the project initiation and definition phase, so a picture can be built up of a means and an approach required to achieve the final outcome. Care should be taken not to get into too much detailed planning and design, but rather progressively elaborate the project. This project type usually requires considerable buy-in from the performing organisation as well as important stakeholders.
Painting by Numbers **Construction and engineering** **Similar projects done in the past**	We know what our destination is We are confident of getting there	Very well understood	Very well developed	Painting by Numbers projects are complex, and tend to be large and involve many parties. As time and costs are predictable, the challenge is to deliver within tight financial, time and specification constraints. Diligent application of process and workflow is critical to success.

4. Management-by-Projects

Many organisations are changing the way they manage their work. Instead of the work being done as the resources become available (resource limited), the work is being packaged as scheduled projects, and the resources adjusted to suit the work schedule as time-limited projects.

This management-by-projects approach has been used in engineering, construction, aerospace and defence for many years, and now we see other organisations buying into the process; pharmaceutical, medical, telecommunications, software development, systems development, energy, manufacturing, fashion, travel, education and service organisations.

To achieve a flexible workforce which can adjust its availability to meet the workload (not the other way round), companies are increasingly having to outsource their work to many small entrepreneurial type companies and contractors. For example, a telecom company would deal directly with their clients and log the jobs. This work (new connections, repairs or maintenance) would then be outsourced to private contractors for an immediate response. This way the telecom companies can vary their workforce to meet the workload and not have to permanently employ a large workforce on stand-by.

To manage a large number of small projects, companies are using a project office management (PMO) approach where the project office captures the work, initiates the project and assigns the work to a department or contractor. This way the clients can be advised more accurately when the work will be done, so they in turn can plan their workload. The management-by-projects approach encourages:

- organisation flexibility
- decentralised management accountability, responsibility and empowerment
- a holistic view of problems
- a goal-orientated problem solution process
- a direct costing giving better planning and control.

There are profound changes happening in the job market. **Time Magazine**; '...*full-time, full-year workers are no longer as dominant as they were. There is more self-employment, more part-time employment and the beginnings of what might be called task employment*'. I would call this short term project employment. Therefore, for the employer and employee to make the most of the new employment patterns a working understanding of management-by-projects and project team dynamics is essential.

Programme Management: The APM bok defines Programme Management as: '*.... the management of a collection of projects related to some extent to achieve a common objective*'. This could be a multi-disciplined project like a heritage site, or a sports stadium which is subdivided into many minor sub-projects. The key feature is many inter-related small projects to achieve a common goal.

Portfolio Management: The APM bok defines Portfolio Management on the other hand as: '....*the management of a number of projects that do not share a common objective*'. This would apply to the project management office (PMO) using a management-by-projects approach to manage a number of unrelated projects. For example, a city council projects department will have many unrelated small projects; fix a street light, fill a pothole, or repair a park bench.

Entrepreneur Projects: Creating a new venture, particularly the implementation phase has all the characteristics of a small project which should benefit from project management skills. In fact, it can be argued that most projects are initiated by an entrepreneur's creative and innovative skills and their ability to spot marketable opportunities.

5. General Management

Although this book is about project management, the successful project manager and team member must also be competent in a wide range of general management skills:

- leadership
- communication
- organising
- staffing
- team building
- planning
- instructing
- co-ordinating
- implementing
- monitoring
- controlling.

General management also includes a number of support disciplines:

- computer systems and electronic filing
- legal contracts
- personnel and human resources
- sales and marketing
- accounts and salaries.

The project manager would obviously not be expected to be an expert in all these fields but, for a project to be successful, all these areas may need to be addressed at one time or another. It is the project manager's responsibility to delegate the work to a team member or outsource as required.

Technical Management: The technical aspects of the project also need to be managed. The technical skills refer to the technical knowledge you need to design and make the product. Every profession has its unique range of technical skills and as an apprentice you will be shown the ropes and learn 'the trade'. Training courses will help you 'fast track' up the learning curve. This is your opportunity to get a broad based grounding in all the technical aspects of your trade, and acquire plenty of relevant work experience. On smaller projects the project manager may be expected to be the technical expert as well as the project manager. In fact, early on in your career you will probably not be appointed as project manager unless you are a technical expert in your field.

Two other management styles to consider with respect to project management are production management and process management.

Production Management: Although projects are deemed to be unique, in reality many projects contain similar activities. For example, if your project includes manufacturing 100 similar items it could be more efficient to set-up a jig (former or mould) and make all the items at the same time rather than making them one at a time as you need them (additional storage accepted). The project manager should, therefore, always be looking for ways of using production management techniques embedded in the project.

Process Management: Process management is used to manage products which flow from one process to another. For example, in wine making the grapes are crushed, fermented, blended and bottled in batches. The same manufacturing process applies to chemical plants and refineries. Process management techniques are unlikely to be as useful to the project manager as production management techniques, however, in a petro-chemical plant, where process management techniques are used, they might also use a management-by-projects approach.

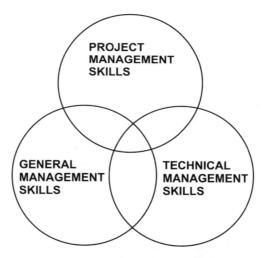

Figure 1.3: Intersecting Management Skills – shows project management, general management and technical management skills

6. Project Management Process

> **DEFINITION**
>
> The PMBOK states that project management is accomplished through processes. The PMBOK defines a process as: '....*a set of interrelated actions and activities that are performed to achieve a pre-specified set of products, results or services.*'

The project management process can be subdivided into five key processes which are linked by the results they produce - the outcome from one process is often the input to another process.

Initiating Process	The initiating process starts the project – this would usually include the project charter and feasibility study.
Planning Process	The planning process selects and develops the best courses of action to attain the objectives that the project was undertaken to achieve.
Execution Process	The execution processes integrates, instructs and co-ordinates people and resources to implement and carry out the management plan and make-it-happen.
Controlling Process	The controlling process ensures the project objectives are met by monitoring and measuring progress regularly to identify any variances from the management plan so that corrective action can be taken as necessary.
Closing process	The closing process formally accepts the project and brings it to an orderly end. This involves commissioning the product and handing it over to the client for operation.

Table 1.2: Project Management Processes – shows the five key project management processes

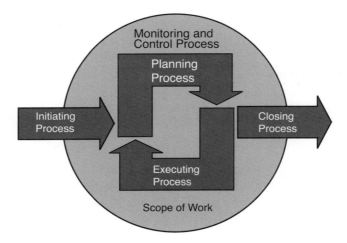

Figure 1.4: Project Management Process – shows the relationship between the five project management processes developed from the PMBOK

7. Project Lifecycle

The project lifecycle and the PMBOK are excellent models to explain the major processes and activities required to manage a project. The project lifecycle outlines the project as four sequential phases, and the PMBOK outlines the processes as nine knowledge areas. Figure 1.5 shows the integration of these two models.

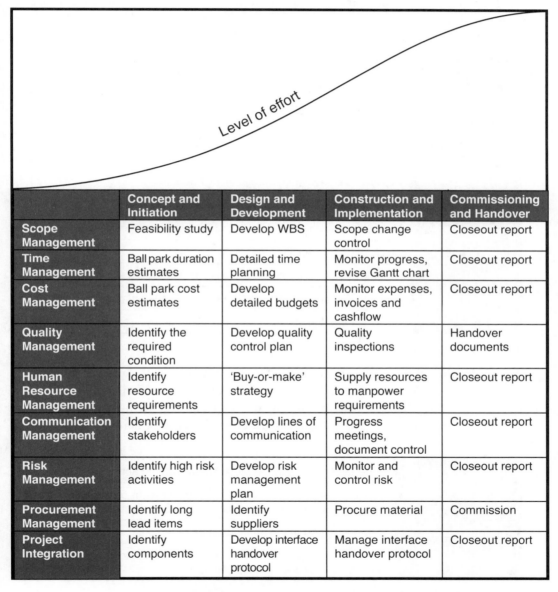

	Concept and Initiation	Design and Development	Construction and Implementation	Commissioning and Handover
Scope Management	Feasibility study	Develop WBS	Scope change control	Closeout report
Time Management	Ball park duration estimates	Detailed time planning	Monitor progress, revise Gantt chart	Closeout report
Cost Management	Ball park cost estimates	Develop detailed budgets	Monitor expenses, invoices and cashflow	Closeout report
Quality Management	Identify the required condition	Develop quality control plan	Quality inspections	Handover documents
Human Resource Management	Identify resource requirements	'Buy-or-make' strategy	Supply resources to manpower requirements	Closeout report
Communication Management	Identify stakeholders	Develop lines of communication	Progress meetings, document control	Closeout report
Risk Management	Identify high risk activities	Develop risk management plan	Monitor and control risk	Closeout report
Procurement Management	Identify long lead items	Identify suppliers	Procure material	Commission
Project Integration	Identify components	Develop interface handover protocol	Manage interface handover protocol	Closeout report

Figure 1.5: Project Lifecycle PMBOK Interface – shows a number of the key planning and control techniques

8. Role of the Project Manager

Experience has shown that the selection of the project manager is a key appointment which can influence the success or failure of the project. As the single point of responsibility, it is the project manager who integrates and co-ordinates all the contributions from stakeholders and guides them to successfully complete the project.

The role of the project manager should be outlined in the project charter (see *Scope Management* chapter) along with the purpose of the project. Consider the following lists of desirable attributes:

Team Creation	Ability to select and develop an operational team from a standing start.
Leadership	Leadership skills and management ability.
Problem-Solving	Ability to anticipate problems, solve problems and make decisions.
Integration	Ability to integrate the project stakeholders.
Flexibility	Operational flexibility.
Expediting	Ability to plan, expedite and get things done.
Negotiation	Ability to negotiate, persuade and make deals.
Environment	Understand the environment within which the project is being managed.
Control	Ability to review monitor and apply control.
Contract	Ability to administer the contract, the scope of work and scope changes.
Change Control	Ability to manage within an environment of constant change.
Client	Ability to keep the stakeholders and client happy.

Table 1.3: Project Manager's Role

Team Members: Team members play an important role in the management of projects. Their tasks would typically involve; collecting data, processing information, managing scope changes, distributing documentation, organizing meetings and expediting progress – the team members are often the unsung heroes. Their roles usually include;

Support	Undertake or support the project management activities.
Assist	Assist the project manager and/or project team by contributing and participating in planning, execution and control activities.
Administration	Provide support to the administration of a project.
Tools and Techniques	Describe and apply specialized technical methods, tools and techniques to a project to deliver project objectives.

Table 1.4: Team Member's Roles

9. Project Management Environment

The project environment directly influences the project and how it should be managed. Projects are not carried out in a vacuum, they are influenced by a wide range of stakeholders and issues. Consider the following:

- Stakeholders (all interested parties)
- Client / sponsor's requirements
- Your company's organisation structure
- Market requirements
- Competitors products and pricing strategy
- New technology
- Rules and regulations (health and safety)
- Economic cycle.

For project managers to be effective they must have a thorough understanding of the project's environment. The project environment consists of the numerous stakeholders and players that have an input, or are impacted by the project. All must be managed as any one person could derail the project (see *Feasibility Study* chapter).

10. Project Management Software

Today, powerful but inexpensive project management software is readily available for the personal computer. This has essentially moved project management computing away from the data processing department to the project office or project manager's desk. This represents a major shift in the management of information.

Whilst project planning software will certainly help project manager's plan and control their projects, its application will only be effective if the planning and control techniques are clearly understood by the project manager and the project team members. The purpose of this text is therefore to develop these techniques through manual examples and exercises.

11. Benefits of Project Management

The benefits of using a project management approach, obviously follows on from addressing the needs of the project. The project manager is responsible for developing a plan through which the project can be tracked and controlled to ensure the project meets preset objectives. To do this effectively the project manager requires accurate and timely information. This information should be supplied by the planning and control system, which outlines the scope of work and measures performance against the original plan.

Although the planning and control systems will incur additional management costs, it should be appreciated that lack of information could be even more expensive if it leads to poor management decisions, costly mistakes, rework and overruns. Listed in table 1.5 are some of the main benefits associated with a fully integrated project planning and control system:

Client	The project manager is the project's single point of responsibility and the company's representative to the client (and stakeholders). During meetings with the client the planning and control system will provide information about every aspect of the project. Clients prefer to deal with one person – the project manager – who is accountable, responsible and manages the complete project. Client's do not like being passed around like a football!
WBS	The work breakdown structure subdivides the work into manageable work packages and checklists which are easier to estimate, plan, monitor, control and assign to a responsible person.
Estimating	The estimate forms the basis of the project plan.
CPM	Critical path method calculates the activities' start dates, finish dates and float. The activities with zero float form the critical path of activities which determine the duration of the project - delaying a critical activity will delay the project.
Fast Track	Changing the logic and crashing activities enables the project manager to get the product to market before the competition.
Scheduled Gantt	Communicates the what, when and who.
Project Integration	Project integration co-ordinates and integrates the contribution of all the project participants. It limits underlap and overlap of work preventing a doubling up of effort.
Response Time	Timely response on project performance is essential for effective project control. The project planning and control system can adjust the content and frequency of the feedback to address the needs of the project, while the corporate functional systems may be less flexible. Consider the accounts department for example - they generally use a monthly reporting cycle where feedback on invoices may be 4 to 6 weeks behind timenow.
Trends	Projects are best controlled by monitoring the progress trends of time, cost and performance. This information may not be available to the project manager if the trend parameters are derived from a number of different functional sources. The project manager needs to work through a common data base.
Data Capture	If the project progress reporting is based on information supplied by the functional departments, the project manager cannot control the accuracy of this information. The problem here is that it may only become obvious towards the end of the project that the reporting was inaccurate, by which time it may be too late to bring the project back on course in order to meet the project's objectives (see *Project Control* chapter).
Procedures	Planning and control system enables the project manager to develop procedures and work instructions which are tailored to the specific needs of the project.
Quality Management	A quality management system enables the project manager to set up a quality system to manage the project. The quality control plan can be developed to vary the level of inspection and number of hold points to suit the project. Quality audits enable the project manager to inspect management systems within their own company and within the sub-contractor's company.
Closeout Report	The performance of the current project will form the estimating data base for future projects. If this data is not collected by the planning and control system it may be lost forever and you will live to repeat your mistakes.

Table 1.5: Benefits of Project Management

There are many benefits from using a project management approach to managing projects. However, if there is not a culture of managing projects within the company, senior management should consider a softly softly approach as resistance to change could derail future projects.

Key Points:

- The project management body of knowledge (PMBOK) and APM (bok) define project management under a number of knowledge areas.
- Project management has become a recognised profession with international accreditation of its members.
- Many companies are adopting a *management-by-project* approach with the project manager as the *single point of responsibility*.

Exercises:

Discuss how you could use project management techniques to manage your company's work. Your discussion should consider the following:

1. What is project management, and why it is different to other forms of management.
2. Explain how project management can be applied to your company's projects.
3. Outline the role of the project manager.
4. Suggest a small pilot project on which you can develop and prove your project management systems.

Further Reading:

Frigenti, Enzo, and **Comninos**, Dennis, *The Practice of Project Management: a guide to the business - focused approach,* Kogan Page, 2002.

2

History of Project Management

Learning Outcomes

After reading this chapter, you should be able to;

Understand the history of project management

Perform the PERT calculation

Understand the time, cost, quality triangle trade-off

Modern day project management is associated with Henry Gantt's development of the Gantt chart (early 1900s), and special project management techniques developed during the military and aerospace projects of the 1950s and 1960s in America and Britain. It is these special distinctive project management tools and techniques which are used by the body of knowledge, the planning software and developed in this book.

Traditionally the management of projects was considered more of an art than a science, but with the growing number of project management institutions, associations and academic establishments, project management has become more of a science and discipline as accepted practices are captured and formalised in the global body of knowledge and certificate programmes.

Today, rapidly changing technology, fierce competitive markets and a powerful environmental lobby have encouraged companies to change their management systems - in this sink or swim, adopt or die environment, project management and management-by-projects are offering a real solution.

1. Project Management Techniques

Nearly all of the special project management techniques we use today were developed during the 1950s and 1960s by the US defence-aerospace industry (DoD and NASA). This includes program evaluation and review technique (PERT), earned value (EV), configuration management, value engineering and work breakdown structures (WBS). The construction industry also made its contribution to the development of the critical path method (CPM) using network diagrams and resource smoothing - the motivation was scheduling urgency. During this period large scale projects were effectively shielded from the environment, society, and ecology issues. The Apollo space programme and the construction of nuclear power stations typified projects of this period. Some of the key achievements during this period are chronologically listed below:

1950s	Development of PERT and CPM.
1950s	Development of the concept of a single point of responsibility for multi-disciplined projects where one person is made responsible for completing the project. Coupled with this approach came the project team, secondment and resource sharing through a matrix organisation structure.
1960	NASA experiments with matrix organisation structures.
1963	Earned value adopted by the USAF.
1963	Project lifecycle adopted by the USAF.
1963	The US Navy introduces PERT to plan and control hundreds of sub-contractors on the Polaris submarine project.
1964	Configuration management adopted by NASA to review and document proposed changes.
1965	DoD and NASA move from cost-plus contracts towards incentive type contracts such as firm fixed price or cost plus incentive fee.
1965	The mid 1960s saw a dramatic rise in the number of projects in the construction industry that used modern project management techniques.
1965	The TSR-2 (swing-wing bomber) highlighted the problems of concurrency, i.e. starting the development and production before the design was stable. Increasing the scope of work led to cost overrun and delays - eventually the project was cancelled.
1966	A report in 1966 stated that not enough time was spent on front-end definition and preparation (of the project lifecycle); there were wide variations in standards of cost and schedule control, and inadequate control over design changes.
1967	Founding of the International Project Management Association (IPMA) [formerly called the INTERNET].
1969	Project Management Institute (PMI) formed, certification and the PMBOK (1987, 1996, 2000, 2004) were to follow.

2. Program Evaluation and Review Technique (PERT)

In the late 1950s the US Navy set up a development team under Admiral Red Raborn with the Lockheed Aircraft Corporation, and a management consultant Booz Allen & Hamilton, to design PERT as an integrated planning and control system to manage the hundreds of sub-contractors involved in the design, construction and testing of their Polaris Submarine missile system.

The PERT technique was developed to apply a statistical treatment to the possible range of activity time duration. A three time probabilistic model was developed, using pessimistic (p), optimistic (o), and most likely (m) time durations (see figure 2.1). The three time durations were imposed on a normal distribution to calculate the activity's expected time.

In practice one would usually estimate around the most likely time. The optimistic time would be slightly shorter, if everything went better than planned. While the pessimistic time would be extended if everything went worse than planned (late delivery, or a machine breakdown).

The success of the Polaris Submarine project helped to establish the PERT technique in the 1960s as a planning and control tool within many large corporations. At the time the PERT technique was believed to be the main reason the submarine project was so successful, meanwhile CPM was not receiving anywhere near as much recognition even though it also offered a resource allocation and levelling facility.

There were, however, a number of basic problems which reduced PERT's effectiveness and these eventually led to its fall from popularity. Besides the computing limitations, statistical analysis was not generally understood by project managers - they must have been pleased to see the end of standard deviations and confidence limits.

Other features of PERT, however, are seeing a renaissance as the benefits of milestone planning and control is becoming more widely used. By defining the project as a series of milestones, you can simplify the planning and control process at your own level and make your sub-contractors responsible for achieving their milestones. Even with the powerful planning software available today there is still a need to empower an increasingly educated workforce.

The early differences between CPM and PERT have largely disappeared and it is now common to use the two terms interchangeably as a generic name to include the whole planning and control process.

Example 1: Using the PERT equation

Expected time = (o + 4m + p) / 6

o = 6 days

m = 8 days

p = 13 days

T (expected) = 8.5 days

Exercise 2:

o = 12 days

m = 15 days

p = 24 days

What is T (expected)?

See Appendix 1 for solution

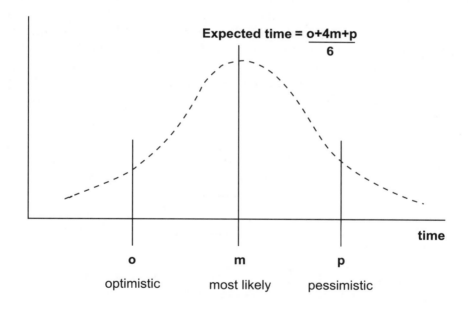

Figure 2.1: PERT – shows the three time probabilistic analysis

3. Project Organisation Structures

Up to the mid 1950s projects tended to be run by companies using the traditional functional hierarchical organisation structure, where the project work would be passed from department to department.

In the 1950s Bechtel was one of the first companies to use a project management organisation structure to manage their oil pipeline project in Canada where responsibility was assigned to an individual operating in a remote location with an autonomous team. This is a good example of an organisation structure with the project manager as the **single point of responsibility** with autonomous authority over a pool of resources. The norm during this time (and still is for many companies) would be for the head of department or functional manager to be responsible for the project as it passed through their department. The project approach is to assign responsibility to one person who would work on the project full-time through the project lifecycle from initiation to completion. In due course, this person was called the **project manager**.

As the project responsibility shifted from the functional managers to the project managers so the functional departments were increasingly seen as a pool of company resources that could be used on any project. This new organisation structure where the project lines of responsibility and authority overlaid the functional lines of responsibility and authority became known as the matrix organisation structure (see the chapter on *Project Organisation Structures*). This enabled companies to work on many projects at the same time, share resources, address scope overlap and underlap, and, most importantly, have one person communicating with the client. Matrix organisation structures were soon to become synonymous with project management (see figure 2.2).

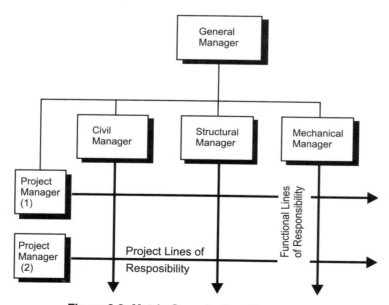

Figure 2.2: Matrix Organisation Structure

4. Project Management Triangle

In the 1980s there was a significant increase in the influence of external stakeholders, the green issue and the CND - this put increasing pressure on project designers to find acceptable solutions for all the stakeholders.

As project management tools and techniques proliferated in the 1960s, were refined in the 1970s, so they were integrated in the 1980s into accepted practices. The integration of time, cost and quality was initially presented as a triangle of balanced requirements - where a change in one parameter could impact the others (see figure 2.3). This was later joined by scope and the organisation breakdown structure (OBS) to indicate that the scope of work was performed through an organisation structure. There was also an increasing awareness of external issues, so the project environment was included (see figure 2.4).

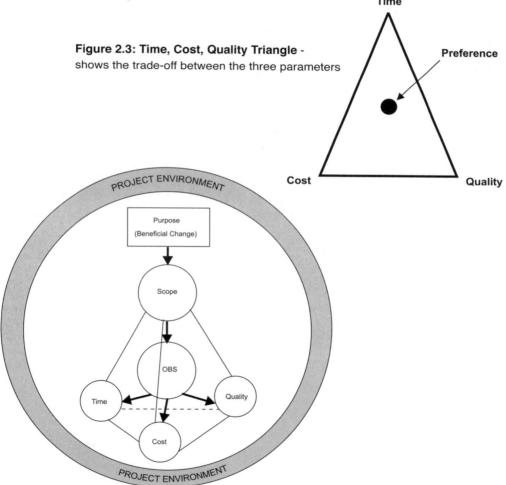

Figure 2.3: Time, Cost, Quality Triangle -
shows the trade-off between the three parameters

Figure 2.4: Project Environment Model – shows that the project manager is encouraged to look at the project's bigger picture and consider all the stakeholder's needs and expectations

5. History of Project Management Computing

The development of schedule Gantt charts, network diagrams and other distinctive project management tools were originally developed for manual calculation. These tools were gradually computerised during the 1960s and 1970s using mini and mainframe computers, but it was the introduction of the personal computer (PC) that ushered in a dramatic explosion and proliferation of project management software. Some of the key dates to note are:

1977	Launch of Apple 11- the first PC.
1979	Launch of VisiCalc, the first spreadsheet - Lotus and Excel were to follow.
1981	Launch of the IBM PC - this established the market standard.
1983	Launch of Harvard Project Manager - the first planning software package.
1990s	Launch of Windows, networks - Internet and email
2000s	Internet broadband, mobile communication for voice and data; development of web site facilities; B2B (business-to-business) procurement; real-time progress reporting.

The introduction of the PC in the late seventies (Apple 11) and the IBM PC (1981) in the early eighties, with accompanying business software, encouraged the growth of project planning software and the use of project management techniques.

The history of PC based project management computing dates back to 1983 with the launch of the **Harvard Project Manager,** a planning software package. Although this may be an isolated event it does reflect the general development of a broad range of management software taking place at the time.

The project management software created two main changes to the manual planning and control process;

1. Change from activity-on-arrow to activity-on-node.

2. Change from departmental planning and control to project planning and control using a common data base.

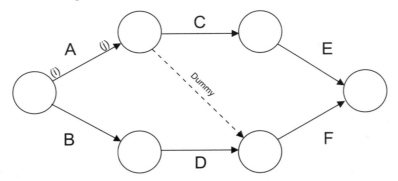

Figure 2.5: Activity-On-Arrow – shows the task's description written on the arrows

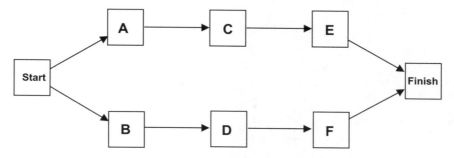

Figure 2.6: Activity-On-Node – shows the task's description written in the boxes

Network diagrams were originally developed as activity-on-arrow. Activity-on-arrow was initially preferred by engineers in the 1960s because it was easier to write the description along the arrow, but with the transition from manual calculations to computer software calculations so the preference changed to activity-on-node. The benefits of activity-on-node: (AON)

- AON offers a number of logical relationships between the activities, such as start-to-start, finish-to-finish and lag. This overcomes the AOA's need for dummy activities.
- The AON also offers a professional presentation, which is generally known today as a network diagram.
- AOA uses a dummy activity to clarify the logic, but it is possible to have a double dummy that is illogical.

There are many other management tools that present information in a box; WBS, OBS and flow charts.

Common Data Base: The change to a common data base was the most significant change, because this moved the planning and control information into the project office. The project team now had full control over all the project related information.

Exercises:

1. Discuss the history of project management and identify where and why project management techniques were developed.
2. Calculate the PERT exercise from section 2 (solution Appendix 1).
3. Discuss how the time, cost, quality triangle trade-off applies to your projects.

3

Project Management Standards

Project managers have traditionally learnt about project management as an extra skill needed to carry out their job. Most project managers would begin their careers in a technical field and as they progressed they would become more involved in the management of their projects. This is when they would develop a need for project management education.

The worldwide trend towards project management has been accompanied by formal project management education and training. There are now many academic and certification programmes available from universities and colleges around the world.

Historically, as the discipline of project management grew and became established, so a number of institutions and associations were formed to represent the project management practitioners with respect to education, professional accreditation, ethics and a body of knowledge.

These project management associations and institutions have formed chapters around the world to encourage and support the development of project management as a profession. These chapters organise regular meetings and newsletters to keep their members informed about project management issues.

The key project management issues are:

- Body of knowledge
- Certification of project managers (PMP)
- Unit standards
- Ethics
- Global forum.

Body of Knowledge: Over the past fifty years a considerable body of knowledge has been built up around project management tools, skills and techniques. This data base of information has been developed into what the Project Management Institute (PMI) call the project management body of knowledge (PMBOK).

DEFINITION

The PMBOK defines body of knowledge as: '... *inclusive term that describes the sum of knowledge within the profession .... and rests with the practitioners and academics that apply and advance it.*'

There are a number of institutions, associations and government bodies around the world which have produced a body of knowledge, unit standards and competency standards – they all have a presence on the Internet:

- Project Management Institute (PMI) [PMBOK]
- Australian Institute of Project Management (AIPM) [Competency Standards]
- International Project Management Association (IPMA)
- Association for Project Management (APM) [bok]
- Association for Construction Project Managers (ACPM)
- Cost Engineering Association of South Africa (CEASA)
- Project Management South Africa (PMSA).

There are a number of recognised standards published by APM, PMI, IPMA, Global Performance Standards for Project Management Personnel, American National Standard Institute, International Standards Organisation, British Standards and the South African National Standards.

The purpose of the body of knowledge is to identify and describe best practices that are applicable to most projects most of the time, for which there is widespread consensus about their value and usefulness. They are also intended to provide a common lexicon and terminology within the profession of project management – locally and internationally. As a developing international profession there is still a need to converge on a common set of terms.

The PMBOK describes project management under the following nine knowledge areas:

Project Scope Management	Project scope management includes the processes required to ensure that the project includes all the work required, and only the work required, to complete the project successfully. It is primarily concerned with defining and controlling what is or what is not included in the project, to meet the sponsors' and stakeholders' goals and objectives. It consists of authorisation, scope planning, scope definition, scope change management and scope verification.
Project Time Management	Project time management includes the process required to ensure timely performance of the project. It consists of activity definition, activity sequencing, duration estimating, establishing the calendar, schedule development and time control.
Project Cost Management	Project cost management includes the process required to ensure that the project is completed within the approved budget. It consists of resource planning, cost estimating, cost budgeting, cashflow and cost control.
Project Quality Management	Project quality management includes the process required to ensure that the project will satisfy the needs for which it was undertaken. It consists of determining the required condition, quality planning, quality assurance and quality control.
Human Resource Management	Human resource management includes the process required to make the most effective use of the people involved with the project. It consists of organisation planning, staff acquisition and team development.
Project Communications Management	Project communications management includes the process required to ensure proper collection and dissemination of project information. It consists of communication planning, information distribution, project meetings, progress reporting and administrative closure.
Project Risk Management	Project risk management includes the process concerned with identifying, analysing, and responding to project risk. It consists of risk identification, risk quantification and impact, response development and risk control.
Project Procurement Management	Project procurement management includes the process required to acquire goods and services from outside the performing project team or organisation. It consists of procurement planning, solicitation planning, solicitation, source selection, contract administration and contract closeout.
Project Integration	Project integration management integrates the three main project management processes of planning, execution and control - where inputs from several knowledge areas are brought together.

Table 3.1: Project Management Knowledge Areas

The body of knowledge can be subdivided into four core elements which determine the **deliverable** objectives of the project:

- Scope
- Time
- Cost
- Quality

The other knowledge areas provide the means of achieving the deliverable objectives, namely:

- Human resources
- Communication
- Risk
- Procurement and contract
- Integration.

APM bok: The APM bok takes a broad approach, subdividing project management into 50 + knowledge areas. This incorporates not only inward focused project management topics (such as planning and control techniques), but also broad topics in which the project is being managed (such as social and ecological environment), as well as specific areas (such as technology, economics and finance, organisation, procurement and people, as well as general management).

As an overall scoping guide, the topics are described in the APM bok at an outline level leaving the details to the texts, listed in their booklist, to explain the working of the knowledge areas (see www.apm.org.uk).

DEFINITION

The APM defines its body of knowledge as:

- '... *a practical document, defining the broad range of knowledge that the discipline of project management encompasses*'.
- '... *as the basis for its various professional development programmes*'.
- '... *representing topics in which practitioners and experts consider professionals in project management should be knowledgeable and competent*'.

Certification of Project Managers (PMP): The certification process offers a means for experienced project managers to gain a formal qualification in project management. There is a trend away from the knowledge based examinations which assess a person's knowledge, towards competence based examinations which assess a person's ability to perform. The PMI's certification is called the Project Management Professional (PMP). There is an increasing recognition of certification and for some projects it is being made a mandatory pre-qualification.

Competence is a mixture of explicit knowledge derived from formal education, tacit knowledge and skills derived from experience. For young professionals, explicit knowledge is more important, but other competencies will become increasingly important as they progress in their careers. The PMI's (PMP) is a single level certificate programme, which measures explicit knowledge directly through a multi-choice test, and tacit knowledge and skill indirectly by assessing the candidate's experience. It is, therefore, aimed at an early to mid-career professional.

The IPMA and AIPM (Australian), on the other hand, have developed a multi-stage programme. At the first stage explicit knowledge is measured directly through a multi-question test. This is aimed at professional managers starting their careers. At the second stage tacit knowledge and skill are measured directly - this is early to mid stage certification, equivalent to PMP.

At the third stage, the programmes measure the performance of senior project managers directly; and IPMA has a fourth stage to measure the performance of project directors.

In Europe the integration of the EU is encouraging a growing number of cross-border projects, which not only require collaboration, but a need to converge on common practices, common legal systems and, not least, a common business language.

Unit Standards: When SAQA (South African Qualifications Authority), the Services SETA, the Project Management Standard Generating Body (SGB) and the PMSA (Project Management Institute of South Africa) worked together to register the Further Education and Training Certificate: Project Management (NQF 4, SAQA ID 50080) and the set of unit standards leading towards this qualification, they utilized locally and internationally recognized best practice and standards in project management. This qualification provides an entry point to further learning for NQF level 5 and above qualifications as well as a international qualifications in Project or General Management.

Code of Ethics: An ethical project management style is one where the project manager is honest, sincere and is able to motivate the team, contractors, suppliers and stakeholders for the best and fairest solution.

Ethics in procurement relates to insuring best value to the public in monetary terms. It insures fairness and, most importantly, deals with conflicts of interest which could influence outcomes and insure accountability.

Global Project Management Forum: Project management has been an international profession for many years, but only recently have the global issues of project management been discussed. The first global project management forum was held in New Orleans in 1995 where 30 countries were represented. Some of the key topics discussed at these forums include:

- What industries or types of projects are the main users of modern project management in your country?
- What industries or areas of application in your country have the greatest need for more or better project management?
- What industries or organisations offer the greatest opportunities for growth of professional project management in your country?

Exercise:

1. Identify the principal bodies of knowledge worldwide and discuss how these relate to your national standard.
2. Discuss how the PMBOKs nine knowledge areas relate to your projects.
3. Discuss how you can achieve your national certification in project management.

Further Reading;

PMI <www.pmi.org>

APM <www.apm.org.uk>

IPMA <www.ipma.ch>

APM <www.apm.org.uk>

Australian AIPM <www.dab.uts.au/aipm/competencystandards/index.html>

South African Qualifications Authority <www.saqa.org.za>

Global PM Forum <www.pmforum.org>

4

Project Lifecycle

Learning Outcomes

After reading this chapter, you should be able to;

Understand how a project can be subdivided into four sequential phases

Appreciate the importance of front end planning to reduce the potential for design changes later in the project

Outline the product lifecycle - from the cradle to the grave

The project lifecycle is one of the special project management techniques for subdividing the scope of work into manageable areas of work. In this case the project lifecycle subdivides the scope of work into four sequential project phases.

DEFINITION

The PMI's guide to the body of knowledge says; '....because projects are unique and involve a certain degree of risk, companies performing projects will generally sub-divide their projects into several project phases to provide better management control. Collectively these project phases are called the project life-cycle.'

A project lifecycle diagram which is often seen on project office notice boards subdivides the project into a number of phases of increasing mismanagement.

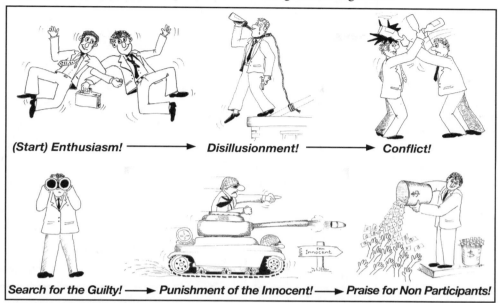

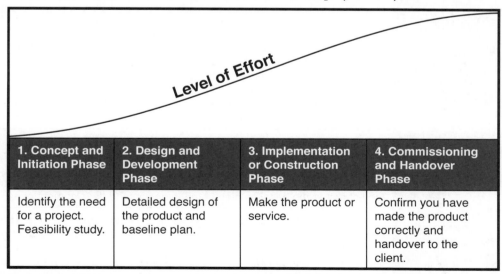

Figure 4.1: Project Lifecycle - shows a lifecycle of mismanagement

1. Project Lifecycle (4 phases)

There is general agreement that most projects pass through four distinct phases, and it is these four phases which form the structure of the project lifecycle:

1. Concept and Initiation Phase	2. Design and Development Phase	3. Implementation or Construction Phase	4. Commissioning and Handover Phase
Identify the need for a project. Feasibility study.	Detailed design of the product and baseline plan.	Make the product or service.	Confirm you have made the product correctly and handover to the client.

Figure 4.2: Project Lifecycle – shows the widely accepted four project phases with its associated level of effort

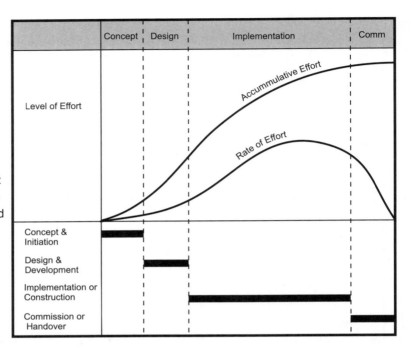

Figure 4.3: Project Lifecycle (generic) – shows the project lifecycle with its associated Gantt chart and level of effort. The typical work associated with each phase is developed in the table below

1. Concept and Initiation Phase	The first phase starts the project by establishing a need or opportunity for the product, facility or service. The start of the project is usually formalized by establishing a **project charter** which gives the project an identity (usually a name and number) so that budgets and responsibilities can be assigned. This is where new ideas and options are considered and tested **(feasibility study and build-method)** to ensure the product can be made and is making the best use of the company's funds and resources. The output from this phase is an understanding of the risks and opportunities of pursuing with the project.
2. Design and Development Phase	On acceptance of the project proposal the project moves into the second phase to design and develop the project. A budget is allocated to produce detailed designs and specifications of the project and to develop detailed scope and planning documents. These all role-up into the **baseline plan**. The **procurement** and **negotiation** for long lead items and contracts would begin in this phase.
3. Implementation or Construction Phase	On acceptance of the baseline plan, the third phase allocates a budget to **implement** the project's baseline plan to make the facility or solve the problem. This is usually the biggest phase of the project in terms of level of effort and expenditure, but in principle this phase should only implement the project as per the baseline plan from the design and development phase.
4. Commissioning and Handover Phase	The fourth and last phase of the project lifecycle confirms the project has been implemented or built to the baseline plan. It uses a range of **inspection** and **testing** techniques to confirm compliance. It runs up and commissions the equipment to confirm everything is working before handing over the facility to the client. This phase may also involve training of the client's personnel. On acceptance by the client the project is terminated and a **closeout report** produced.

2. House Extension Project Lifecycle (4 phases)

A good example of the project lifecycle is to outline how a house extension project passes through the four phases.

Figure 4.4: Project Lifecycle – shows the project lifecycle for a house extension with its associated Gantt chart and level of effort

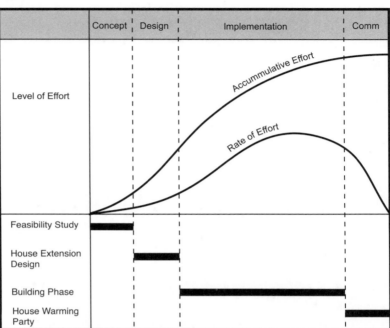

Feasibility Study	House Extension Design	Building Phase	House Warming Party
The desire for a house extension develops into a need. A feasibility study is conducted to consider all the options and alternatives. The output is an outline of the preferred type of house extension and estimated budget.	On acceptance of the feasibility study a detailed design of the house extension is produced, together with a detailed scope of work and planning documents. This includes all the associated planning of schedules, procurement, resources and budgets. Building permission and any long lead items may be bought in this phase.	On acceptance of the design of the house extension detailed baseline plan the contracts are negotiated and let, materials are procured and the construction is project managed. The house extension is built to the detailed plans developed in the previous phase. Changes may be made to the original baseline plan as problems arise or better information is forth coming (for example, the latest bathroom fittings).	On completion the building is inspected and approved by the client and responsible authorities. The house is now ready to be handed over for occupation. A closeout report is produced to learn from the experience and the project is terminated.

3. Input, Process, Output

Each phase of the lifecycle can be further subdivided into the input requirements (documents and approvals), how the information is processed (feasibility study), and the output documentation (baseline plan).

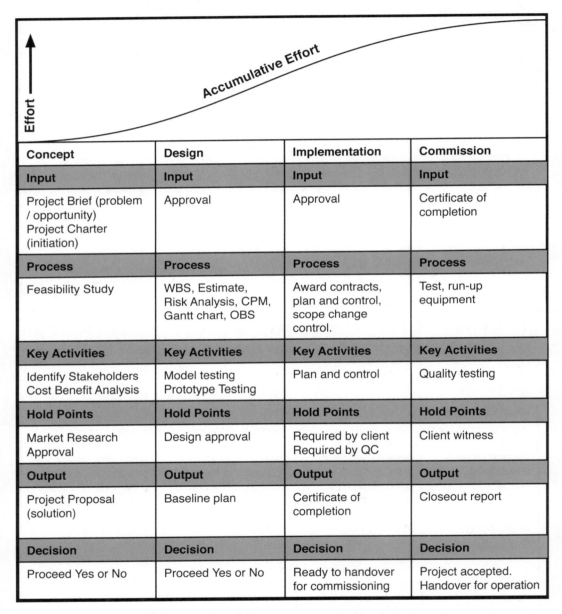

Concept	Design	Implementation	Commission
Input	**Input**	**Input**	**Input**
Project Brief (problem / opportunity) Project Charter (initiation)	Approval	Approval	Certificate of completion
Process	**Process**	**Process**	**Process**
Feasibility Study	WBS, Estimate, Risk Analysis, CPM, Gantt chart, OBS	Award contracts, plan and control, scope change control.	Test, run-up equipment
Key Activities	**Key Activities**	**Key Activities**	**Key Activities**
Identify Stakeholders Cost Benefit Analysis	Model testing Prototype Testing	Plan and control	Quality testing
Hold Points	**Hold Points**	**Hold Points**	**Hold Points**
Market Research Approval	Design approval	Required by client Required by QC	Client witness
Output	**Output**	**Output**	**Output**
Project Proposal (solution)	Baseline plan	Certificate of completion	Closeout report
Decision	**Decision**	**Decision**	**Decision**
Proceed Yes or No	Proceed Yes or No	Ready to handover for commissioning	Project accepted. Handover for operation

Figure 4.5: Project Lifecycle Input, Process, Output – shows the input documents, processes, key activities, hold points, outputs and approvals

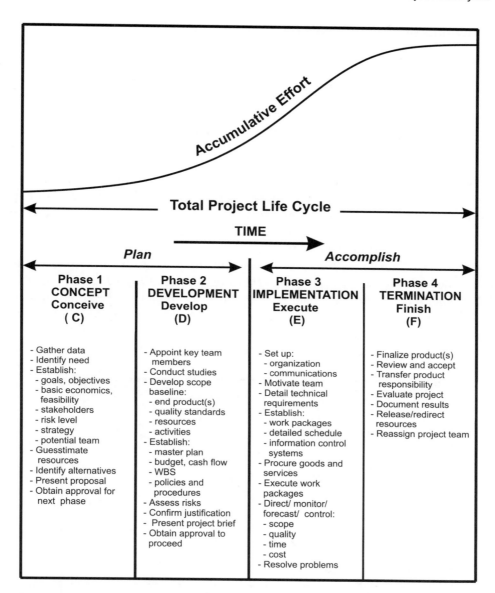

Figure 4.6: Project Lifecycle (generic – developed from PMBOK) - shows a list of the typical activities associated with each phase for a generic project

4. Overlap Between Phases (fast tracking)

The project phases have been shown here in sequence, implying that the concept and initiation phase must be complete before the design and development phase starts. And further the design and development phase must be complete before the implementation and construction starts.

However, in practice there is usually some degree of overlap between the phases, meaning the following phase can start before the preceding phase is totally complete. For example, in the previous section the construction of a house extension may start before the house design is totally complete – if the plans for the foundation, walls and roof are complete and approved the construction can go ahead even though the design of the interior lighting and plumbing may not be complete. This practice is called **fast tracking,** where the deliverables from the preceding phase are progressively approved so that work can start on the next phase.

When fast tracking is practised throughout the project, this will speed up the completion and get your product to market before your competition. This is particularly important for commercial companies operating in a competitive environment where coming second will significantly devalue your product. For example, the Sony Walkman was the first to market with the personal tape recorder, and more recently the Apple iPod was the first to market with the personal downloadable video.

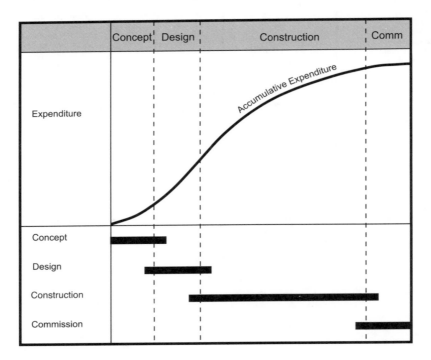

Figure 4.7: Project Lifecycle Overlap – shows the overlap (fast tracking) between phases on a house extension project

5. Level of Effort

The project lifecycle is often presented with its associated level of effort. The level of effort gives an indication of the amount of activity or work being performed during each phase. This could be any parameter that flows through the project, but it is most commonly expressed as manhours or expenditure. These parameters can be presented as a line graph of level of expenditure per day (or unit of time) and the accumulated expenditure (or S curve). See the *Project Accounts* chapter for details on how to draw the S curve.

The level of effort profile, see Figure 4.7, clearly shows a slow build-up of effort during the initial phases as the project is being considered, designed and developed. The build-up of effort accelerates during the implementation phase to a maximum as the work faces are opened-up and resources assigned, before a sharp decline as the work is completed and commissioned and the project draws to a close.

From this curve one would naturally assume that the greatest level of effort occurs during the implementation phase when most of the effort is applied and most of the costs are incurred. It would then be logical to assume that this is the most important phase determining the success of the project - this is after all where the product or facility is made or service provided. Certainly the tools and techniques developed in the 1960's (PERT, CPM, WBS, resource histograms, etc.) were all focusing on this implementation phase. But if we consider the difference between efficiency and effectiveness, efficiency is performing the activities as quickly as possible, while effectiveness is doing the right activity. This distinction could paint a different picture – see the next section which discusses the potential to add value.

6. Level of Influence vs Cost of Changes (front-end importance)

In the 1960's and 1970's project management tools and techniques tended to focus on the implementation and construction phase of the project lifecycle which certainly accounted for the greatest level of effort where the majority of the expenses were incurred. In the 80's the emphasis was beginning to shift and focused more on the initial front-end of the project where the selection and design decisions were made. This is where the stakeholder's needs were analysed, feasibility studies conducted, build methods established, value management encouraged, risk management assessed and the product designed and developed.

It is now acknowledged that the initial phases offer the greatest potential to add value to the product whereas the implementation phase, even though it has the greatest expenditure, should do no more than implement the work as designed. Further, the cost of making any changes due to design errors, unforeseen rules, the client changing the scope and incorporating new technology, were recognised as becoming increasingly more expensive as the project progressed through the lifecycle.

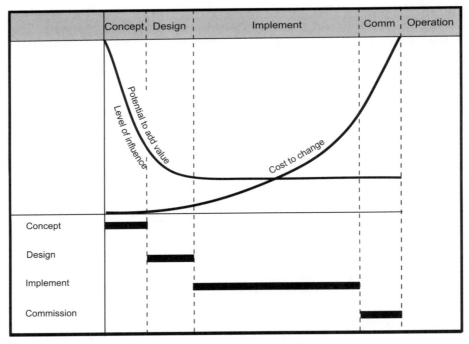

Figure 4.8: Potential to Add Value vs Cost of Changes – shows the potential to add value reducing as the project progresses. It also shows the associated cost of changes increasing as the project progresses

As technology projects become more complex, with fierce competition between rivals, so the importance of getting the design right at the outset became essential. It can be extremely expensive to make design changes during the implementation phase, far better (and less expensive) to make your design changes during the early stages of the project.

For example, on a house extension project the cost of changing the arrangement of the extension during the design phase would only be the cost of reproducing a number of drawings. But, changing the position of the walls after they have been built would lead to additional costs of labour and materials, and a longer construction period.

This understanding has rightly encouraged project managers to spend more time and effort model and prototype testing during the concept and design phases, to make sure the design is stable, before moving into the implementation phase where the changes will be much more expensive.

The stakeholders level of design influence, or potential to add value to the project reduces as the project progresses. As the design develops, so design freezes must be imposed progressively for the other aspects of the design to progress. For example, in the house extension the arrangement of the rooms must be frozen before the built-in cupboards and other fittings can be designed.

This is clearly illustrated in figure 4.8 where the level of influence and cost of changes are plotted against the project lifecycle. At the outset of the project the potential for adding value and cost savings are at there highest, but steadily reduces as the project progresses - loosely mirroring this curve are the associated costs of any changes. The financial encouragement is, therefore, to spend proportionally more time and effort during the initial phases to get the design right before implementation.

7. Product Lifecycle

The classic project lifecycle only considers the project from concept to handover. However, if the project was to set up a business, build a facility, build a factory, a computer system or sports stadium then (looking at the project from the client's perspective) the efficient operation of the facility and the return on investment should also be considered. To look at the wider picture we use what is termed the **product lifecycle**, which considers the facility from the cradle to the grave (figure 4.9).

This view highlights why design decisions made during the initial phases can have a large impact during later phases of the lifecycle even though the phases may be many years away and the facility may even be operated by another company. It is important to look at the project as a whole, from conception to disposal, to ensure that all the interrelated activities are identified. Seemingly simple decisions made during the initial phases of the project (for example, equipment selection and access) could have a major impact on future equipment maintenance, upgrading and disposal.

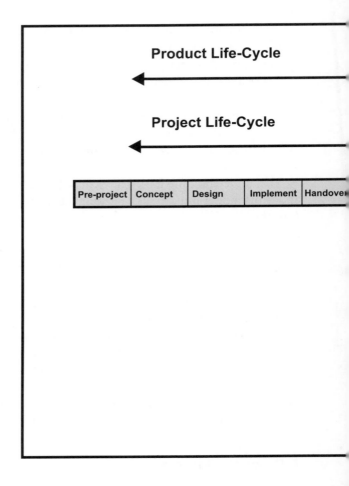

Figure 4.9: Product Lifecycle
– shows the bigger picture from the idea, to implementation, to operation, and finally to disposal

Pre-Project Phase: Projects usually evolve from the work environment or market within which a company operates. There is usually some entrepreneurial event which triggers the project, consider the following:

- Your R&D generates new ideas, innovation and creativity
- Upgrade a system (computer system) to take advantage of new technology
- Market research identifies market changes
- Responding to your competitor's new product
- Expand your facilities to meet increased demand
- Output from quality circles, improving efficiency and effectiveness
- Disaster recovery, accident, or cyclone damage.

Managing the pre-project environment is important for a company's long term survival in a changing world.

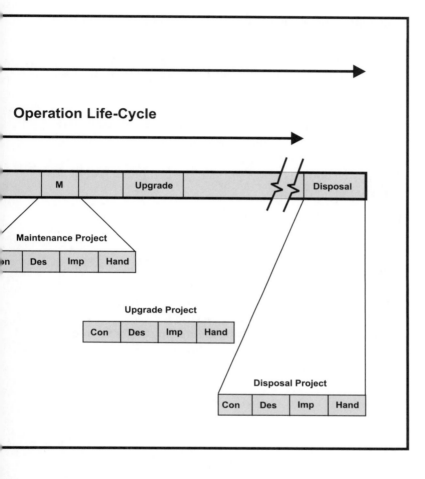

Operation Phase: Although the operation phase may be the whole purpose of the project, it usually falls outside the project manager's sphere of influence. However, with new ventures, the entrepreneur, project manager and small business manager may all be the same person. Within the operational phase there are a number of mini projects;

- Maintenance
- Up-grade and expansion
- Disposal.

Maintenance Phase: Almost all products have to be maintained as per the manufacturers maintenance schedule. The maintenance phases are embedded in the operation phase to keep the facility operational and running efficiently. Ease of maintenance, minimum impact on production and time out of commission are important considerations.

Up-Grade, Half-Life Refit and Expansion Phase: At some point the facility will require a major overhaul, refit, up-grade, or expansion to keep it running efficiently and competitively. New technology, competition, market requirements, rules and regulations are all factors influencing the up-grade. Consider managing the up-grade as a mini project. These type of projects are characterised by tight time scales and working round the clock to get the facility up and running again.

Ease of up-grade or expansion is a consideration that should have been considered and allowed for in the initial design. Any company working in a high technology environment will be well aware of the short lifecycle of their products. Up-grades and the ability to accommodate new technology are essential if the computer system, for example, is going to respond to the market place.

Decommission and Disposal: The final part of the product lifecycle is decommissioning and disposing of the facility. This may mean listing (IPO) or selling the facility or company and so end the company's involvement.

Depending on the product, disposal may mean a trip to the scrap heap, or a more involved decommissioning process. For example, as people become more aware of the environment, if a product contains any substances which could have a negative impact on the environment the disposal may be an elaborate procedure.

The disposal phase for some projects may actually be the starting phase for another project. For example, the removal of an old computer system may be the first activity of installing a new computer system.

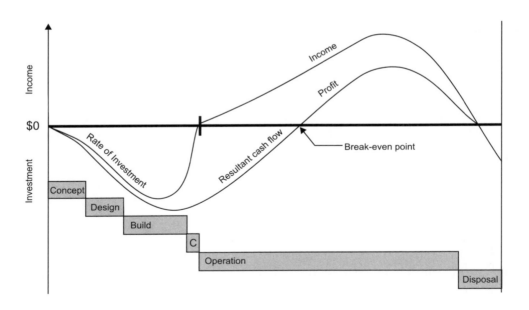

Figure 4.10: Lifecycle Costing – shows the breakeven point

Lifecycle Costing: Projects are often implemented to provide a facility or to manufacture a product which will give the client a return on their investment or an income stream. By looking at the bigger picture the designers are able to trade-off the cost of making the product with the cost of maintenance, up-grading, expansion and disposal over the life of the facility. For example, these considerations would apply to a toll road or a toll bridge which gains its income from the people using the facility. One of the measures of risk and success is reaching the breakeven point as shown in the figure 4.10.

Exercise:

1. Discuss how the project management process can be used to manage your company's projects.
2. Discuss how your projects can be subdivided into four sequential phases.
3. Discuss how front-end planning will reduce the potential for design changes later on in your projects.
4. Discuss the product lifecycle of your product.

5

Feasibility Study

Learning Outcomes

After reading this chapter, you should be able to;

Understand the purpose of the feasibility study

Conduct a stakeholders' analysis

Identify your clients needs and expectations

Conduct a viability and build-method check on the project

Consider alternative options

Identify further opportunities

Ideas, needs and problems crystallize into projects in different ways. The process of project formulation varies in different companies and on different types of projects. Whichever way your new venture or project develops there should at some point be a feasibility study to not only ensure the project is feasible, but also ensure the venture is making the best use of the company's resources.

1. Feasibility Study Initiation

The lead up to the feasibility study is the formalizing of the new venture or project with the **project charter.** The project charter outlines the purpose of the project and what the project is meant to achieve. Likewise the feasibility study should be formalized with requirements and boundaries:

- Who is responsible?
- Project brief outlining the situation
- Who should be involved (stakeholders)?
- Level of detail
- Budget for the feasibility study
- Report back date.

At this point you have only made the decision to proceed with the feasibility study, the decision to proceed with the design phase and implementing the project will be made later - presumably based on the feasibility study.

2. Stakeholder Analysis

The purpose of the stakeholder analysis is to determine the needs and expectations of all the stakeholders. Project stakeholders are organisations or people (both internal and external) who are either actively involved in the project, or whose interests are impacted by the project being implemented (during and/or after implementation).

It is obviously in the project manager's interests to identify all the stakeholders and determine their needs and expectations so these can be integrated with the new venture or project's objectives. The project manager should create an environment where the stakeholders are encouraged to contribute their skills and knowledge as this may be useful to the success of the venture. Consider the following types of stakeholders:

- Those who are actively involved in the new venture or project
- Those whose interests are impacted by the new venture while it is being implemented
- Those whose interests are impacted after the new venture has been implemented
- Those who could have an impact on the new venture, e.g. the Green lobby.

Consider the following headings for stakeholders:

Originator	The originator is the entrepreneur who suggests the innovative idea or spots the opportunity.
Owner	The owner is the person, department or company whose strategic plan creates the need for the new venture or project.
Sponsor	The sponsor is the company or client who authorises expenditure for the new venture - this could be an internal client.
Users	Users are the people who will operate the facility on behalf of the owner. For example, the crew of a ferry.
Project Team	The project team members plan, organise, implement and control the work of the contractors.
Senior Management	Senior management are the people within your company who you need to support your project because they control the company's resources.
Function Managers	Functional managers within your company supply the workforce for your project.
Boss	Your boss, the person you report to, can play an important role in establishing your working environment.
Colleagues	Although your colleagues may not be working on your project, indirectly, they can supply useful information and offer moral peer support.
Contractors	The contractors are outside companies or people who perform work on your new venture or project. This would also include outsourced work.
Suppliers	Suppliers, vendors and plant hire are the companies who supply materials and equipment for your project. They also have a wealth of experience.

Support Companies	Support companies provide goods and services to enable the facility or product to be manufactured. For example, the suppliers of telephones, electricity, the postal service and even the corner shop.
Admin	The company's administration keeps the wheels of information turning.
Finance	The banks, venture capital and any other source of finance.
Supply Chain	The distributors and retailers are the supply chain and outlets that will sell the products.
Customers	Customers are the people who receive and pay for the benefit of using the product. For example, we are all customers for electricity and telephones.
Networking Organisations	The Chamber of Commerce, Business Clubs, Golf Clubs, and Yacht Clubs are all examples of organizations where people meet and useful contacts can be made.

Table 5.1: Project Stakeholders

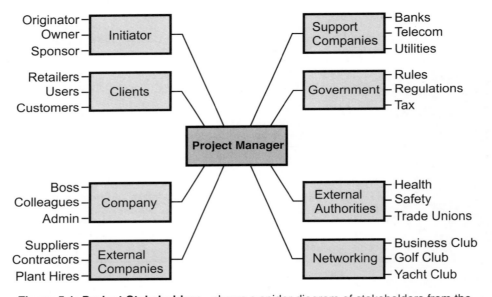

Figure 5.1: Project Stakeholders - shows a spider diagram of stakeholders from the project manager's perspective (source: *Entrepreneurs Toolkit*, **Burke**)

There are other external stakeholders who may not be directly involved with the project, but can influence the outcome:

- Regulatory authorities - health and safety.
- Trade unions.
- Special interest groups (environmentalists) who represent the society at large.
- Lobby groups.
- Government agencies and media outlets.

Stakeholders can be subdivided into those who are only interested in the outcomes of the project, and those who are only interested in the project while it is being implemented. For example, a car manufacturer may be only interested in the manufacturing phase of making a car, while a car hire company will only be interested in the operational phase of hiring the car.

Stakeholders can be further classified into those who are positively impacted by the project and those who are negatively impacted by the project. In this situation, can those positively impacted compensate those negatively impacted parties? For example, a mobile phone tower would benefit the mobile phone users in the area. But can the mobile phone operators (and users) compensate the people who have to live in the vicinity of the mobile phone tower?

Some stakeholders will support the project, while others will oppose the project. It is important to address those who oppose and discuss their fears, because it is these stakeholders that could derail your project. Some of their concerns may be valid and with some flexibility could be accommodated. At the end of the day you may not be able to please all your stakeholders. In this conflicting environment you will need to establish the priority of your stakeholders' needs and make your decisions accordingly.

Project:	Car Hire					
Complied By:						
Stakeholder	Interested in project phase	Interested in operation phase	Positively impacted	Negatively impacted	Supporters	Opposers
Manufacturer	Yes	No	Yes	No	Yes	No
Car hire	No	Yes	Yes	No	Yes	No
Travellers	No	Yes	Yes	No	Yes	No
Competition	No	Yes	No	Yes	No	Yes
Petrol stations	No	Yes	Yes	No	Yes	No

Table 5.2: Summary Table of Stakeholders Interests - shows how a range of stakeholders could respond to your project and product

It is the project manager's responsibility to **network** to build coalitions with the various stakeholders on the new venture or project. Project managers must negotiate authority, power and influence to move the project forward; the success of any project depends on the project manager's ability to build a strong team among internal and external players.

3. Define the Client's Needs

The starting point for a new venture or project is usually to address a problem, need, or entrepreneurial opportunity which may be internal or external to the company. The sponsor may start a project to implement a change, make a product, enter a new market or solve a problem. The evolution of a need from something quite vague to something tangible that serves as the basis of a project plan is the project manager's challenge. The needs may be structured as:

Functions	The product must carry out a certain function at a predefined rate.	**Priority**
Environment	The product must operate in a specific environment (summer / winter conditions).	
Life Span	The product must have a working life of so many years.	
Budget	The project's budget must not exceed $ x.	
Efficiency	The product must be energy efficient. For example, a car would quantify this requirement as miles per gallon.	
Spec	The ergonomics must be consistent with the latest accepted practice.	
Risk	The product must achieve reliability requirements. These may be quantified as mean time between failures (MTBF).	
Maintenance	Ease of maintenance and repair must be incorporated into the design. For example, you do not want to have to dismantle the car to replace the cam belt.	
Redundancy	A predetermined level of system redundancy and interchangeable parts must be achieved.	
Standards	The project must meet certain specifications and standards (BS, ABS, DIN).	
Regulations	The product must meet statuary health and safety regulations.	
Local Content	The product must be manufactured with a predefined value of local content. For example, certain countries require their cars to have 25% local content by value.	
Manpower	The operational requirements must achieve predetermined manpower levels and automation.	
Expansion	The product must be flexible and provide opportunities for future expansion and up-grade. For example, a computer must have expansion slots.	
Schedule	The project must be operational by a predefined date. For example, a holiday product in time for the summer season.	
Quality	The product must be manufactured by approved and accredited suppliers, if necessary pre-qualified by an audit.	

Table 5.3: Stakeholder's Needs Analysis – shows a column for ranking by their priority

Many of the above items may be mutually exclusive, which means there will have to be a trade-off and a priority list. For example, it is generally not possible for a car to achieve both maximum power and maximum fuel efficiency. These items of conflict need to be discussed and resolved during the early stages of the project, with all decisions recorded to form the basis of the design philosophy. This key document must be structured in such a way as to facilitate an audit trail of the decisions. If the field of the project is highly specialised the client may employ consultants and specialists to assist in defining the scope and specifications.

4. Project Viability Check

The client may also need assistance in checking the viability of the proposal. Will the product technically and commercially be fit for the purpose and the market? Has the client kept away from wish lists and pipe dreams? These questions will form the basis of the client's feasibility study. Contractors and suppliers as a specialist in the field of the product, can have a valuable input. Consider:

Location	The impact location has on the project. Can the logistic requirements during the project and subsequent operation be met through existing roads, ports and airports?
Environment	How the environment will impact on the product. For example, a hotel in a hot country will require air-conditioning for a five star rating. Consider how the product will impact on the environment - will the product deplete the ozone layer?
Optimum Size	Calculate the optimum size of the end product. Economies of size are not always a straight line extrapolation, but pass through plateaus of optimum production. For example, if you buy a machine that can produce 1000 items a day, is it worth buying two machines for orders of only 1100 items per day?
Fashion	Are the aesthetics and style commensurate with modern day fashions?
Target Market	Define the target market. Who will buy the product? These questions can be quantified by market research.
Demand	Assess the market supply and demand curve. What is the demand for the product now and the forecast demand in the future? What share of the demand does the client hope to achieve?
Competition	Assess the competition from other players in the market. How do you think they will react to your product and pricing strategy?
Clouseout	Review previous closeout reports to gain knowledge of what went right and identify any problem areas.

Table 5.4: Project Viability Check

At the outset of the project it may not be possible to answer all of these questions. The unanswered questions will, however, indicate areas that need more information to gain a better understanding of the project and reduce risk.

5. Internal Project Constraints

The internal project constraints relate directly to the scope of the project and ask basic questions about the product.

Feasibility	Can the product physically be made? (see build-method).
Technology Transfer	Does the company have the technology? If not, can the technology be acquired through a technology transfer, if so with whom?
Best Time	Should the project start now with the present technology or delayed until new and better technology is available?
Risk	How big is the new technology component? Too many new and untested components will increase the risk and uncertainty.
Design Freeze	At what point in the design and development should a design freeze be imposed?
Facilities	Is there sufficient space and facilities available to make the product?
Resources	Can the human resources be trained up to the required level of ability, or should contractors be employed?
Multi-Projects	The multi-project resource analysis will consider the impact other projects will have on the supply of internal resources. For example, if your company is running other projects will there be sufficient resources available?
Machines	Are special machines and equipment required? If yes, can these be sub-contracted out or procured?
Transport	Are there special transport requirements? Can the product be transported in one piece, or does it need to be broken down and assembled on site? For example, if a yacht is built inland and transported by road to sea are there any low bridges in the way?
Management	Are there any new management systems to be introduced, will they be compatible with existing systems they interface with?
Budget	Can the project be completed within the budget?
Quality	What is the quality assurance requirement? For example, is accreditation to ISO 9000 required? Is the present quality system sufficient?
Specs	Can the company meet the specifications?
Procedures	Are there company and project procedures in place? If not is there time to develop them?
Project Office	Is the project office set up? Has the project manager been appointed, the project team selected, the office space allocated and the office equipment installed?
Schedule	Can the project meet the client's completion date and any intermediate key dates?

Penalties	Can the company accept the time penalties?
Risk	Is the project risk and uncertainty acceptable?
Terms	Can the company accept the terms and conditions outlined in the contract document?

Table 5.5: Internal Project Constraints

Build-Method: The build-method is an important part of the feasibility study because it asks the hard questions about the product; what, when, who and how? The build-method supplements the CPM and the Gantt chart which are the documents normally associated with outlining the logical sequence of work. The build-method talks the reader through the various operations by asking the following type of questions;

What	What machines and equipment will be used and where will they be positioned?
Where	Where will the work be manufactured? Will it be outsourced?
How	How will the work be carried out?
Responsibility	What departments or persons will be responsible?
Where	Where will the materials and components be stored?
Inspect	Who will inspect the product, and how?
Transport	What transport will be used to move the materials and finished product - road, rail, air?

Table 5.6: Build-Method – shows the what, where and how

Many of these build-method items may be discussed formally or informally, in meetings or conversations. The aim of the build-method is to capture all the relevant points into one coherent document which can be agreed by the stakeholders and signed off. This will help to ensure that all the stakeholders (particularly the client, contractors and suppliers), work to one build-method.

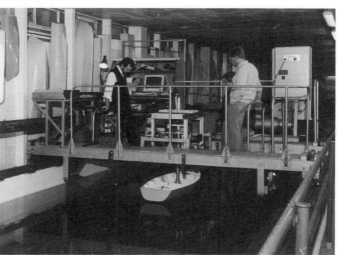

Photo: Model Testing at Solent University - shows how model testing is used to reduce design risks

6. Internal Corporate Constraints

The company itself may impose further quasi constraints on the project. Corporate policy and strategy usually relates to long term issues which indirectly (and unintentionally) may impose limitations on the project.

Financial Objectives	The financial selection criteria may be based on corporate requirements expressed as; payback period, breakeven point and return on investment.
Cashflow	The company may wish the project to maintain a positive cashflow.
Marketing	The company may wish to diversify its products and enter new markets. The new venture may be to implement the technology transfer for the company to operate in a new venture. The project may be a lost leader to enter a new market.
Estimating	Due to a down turn in the economy, the company's main priority may be to keep the workforce together. The lower the bid the greater the probability of being awarded the next contract. The lowest a company can bid is to cover variable costs, with the fixed costs being written-off.
Partner	The company may wish to take on a partner who has previous experience in the field of the project (technology transfer) and also take on a partner to spread the risk.
Industrial Relations	Industrial unrest is often caused by conflict over pay and working conditions. The project manager may have little power to influence these conditions.
Exports	The company may influence the estimate in an effort to acquire exports to enter new markets or take advantage of export incentives.

Table 5.7: Internal Corporate Constraints

Where these company objectives are in conflict with project objectives the company objectives usually take preference. This could lead to increased project costs which must be included in the budget.

7. External Constraints

External constraints are imposed by parties outside the company and the project's sphere of influence. Many of these constraints will not be negotiable.

Regulations	National and international laws and regulations - right of way, planning permission, licenses, permits.
Procurement	Material and component delivery lead times.
Contractors	Limited number of sub-contractors who can do the work.
Resources	Resources are unavailable outside the company due to other large projects in the economy. For example, it is difficult to find carpenters after floods or storm damage, and welders while there are offshore projects and sports stadiums being built.
Transportation	Logistic constraints, availability of transportation.
Currency	Availability of foreign currency and currency fluctuations.
Market	Market forces influence the supply and demand curve of a product.
Environment	Environmental issues, Government legislation and pressure group activities, for example, Green Peace and CND. The nuclear, chemical, mining and transport industries have been particularly impacted in the past.
Climate	Climatic conditions, rain, wind, heat and humidity.
Political	Political unrest.
Insurance	Risks.
Local Restrictions	A construction site in a residential area, may not be allowed to work a night shift because of the noise pollution.

Table 5.8: External Constraints

Consider collating all the constraints into one summary table;

	Project:			
	Complied By:		**Date:**	
WBS	**Description**	**Internal Project Constraints**	**Internal Corporate Constraints**	**External Constraints**
1001	Technical	Need new computer		
1002	Budget		Need to make 15% profit	
1003	Regulation			Health and Safety

Table 5.9: Summary Table of Constraints – shows a template to capture and present constraints

These headings should not be seen as comprehensive, but as the forerunner of a company checklist that ensures all the necessary questions are asked, which in turn should reduce the level of risk and uncertainty.

8. Evaluate Options and Alternatives

Having identified the client's needs and the constraints (project, internal and external), the next step is to consider alternative ways of producing the product. Consider the following questions;

Time	Can the project be completed quicker?
Cost	Can the budget be reduced?
Quality	Can the product be made to a lower level of quality which is acceptable to the client but more cost effective and quicker to produce?
Resources	Can the work be automated to reduce the manpower requirement?
Technology	Has the latest technology been considered?
Design	Is there a simpler design configuration?
Materials	Can cheaper materials be used?
Equipment	Has the use of different equipment and machines been considered?
Build-Method	Is there a simpler build-method?
Trade-off	Has the trade-off between cost, delivery schedule and technical performance been quantified?
Management	Have alternative management systems been considered?

Table 5.10: Options and Alternatives

To help structure all the options and alternative suggestions, set-up a summary template which links in with the WBS.

Project:		
Complied By:		
WBS	Description	Alternatives and Options
2001	Design	Use carbon fibre to reduce weight
2002	Manufacture	Outsource manufacturing to China to reduce costs
2003	Transport	Use airfreight for fast delivery

Table 5.11: Table of Options and Alternatives

The technical definition should aid the direct comparison between options and alternatives. With a machine, for example, the capital costs should be compared with the operating costs. Although this process should be on-going during the project, the design freeze would usually signal the end of this phase. Once the manufacturing phase starts the emphasis would shift to considering manufacturing alternatives.

9. Feasibility Study Summary Template

After you have considered all the separate areas of the feasibility study, consider producing one summary template which gathers together all the main findings. Summary documents give you an overall picture of the project and should make it easier to highlight areas of concern, and the areas of opportunity.

	Project:			
	Complied By:		Date:	
WBS	**Idea**	**Stakeholders Needs**	**Constraints**	**Alternatives**
1000	Design a website	Clients in the tourist market	1 GB host site	Other providers
2000	Build yacht	Bluewater cruising	Comply with Category 1 requirements	Different materials; GRP, Steel, Timber
3000	Your project???			

Table 5.12: Feasibility Study Summary Template

Exercise:

1. Discuss the purpose of a feasibility study in a project environment.
2. Apply the feasibility study framework to your project(s).
3. Identify all your stakeholders and assess their needs and expectations.
4. Check the viability of the project (include the build-method).
5. Produce the feasibility study summary template to give an overview of your project.

6

Planning and Control Cycle

Learning Outcomes

After reading this chapter, you should be able to;

Understand how the baseline plan is compiled

List the main components of the baseline plan

Understand how the control plan is compiled

List the main components of the control

Adjust the reporting frequency to suit the needs of the project

A plan must answer the standard questions what, why, when, where, who, how to and how much, leaving as little as possible to the guesswork of those responsible for project execution.

DEFINITION

The PMBOK defines project integration management as: '... *the process required to ensure that the various elements of the project are properly co-ordinated.'*

DEFINITION

The APM bok defines strategic management as: '... *provides the overall integrative framework for managing the project efficiently and effectively.'*

The planning and control cycle integrates all the special project management planning tools and techniques to produce a coherent series of documents which combines to form the project's baseline plan. And once the project has started, these special tools and techniques are used to monitor and control the project's performance.

This chapter will outline how the various project management tools and techniques discussed in this book relate to each other and how project management integration involves making trade-offs between competing objectives and alternatives in order to meet the stakeholders requirements. It is important to appreciate how a change in one parameter will impact other parameters. For example, a resource overload on a critical activity will delay the completion of the project even though the equipment and materials are available.

The planning of the planning and control cycle is an important part of the planning process because it not only establishes what is to be done (baseline plan), but it also outlines how the work will be authorised, monitored and controlled. It prompts the planner to ask questions (what, why, when, where, who, how to and how much), leaving as little as possible to the guesswork of those responsible for project execution. This in turn increases awareness amongst the team members and stakeholders, it helps to solve problems, and strives for decisions based on consensus.

This planning process communicates information to the stakeholders encouraging them to participate in the process and obliges them to 'sign-on' and pledge their support. When plans are drawn up by those who are going to implement them they should be more obliged (committed) to complete the work as planned. Conversely, if people are not involved in the planning process this may lead to plans being misinterpreted, people may drag their heels, even ignore the plans altogether. The behaviour side of project management is an important component of the planning process.

1. Project Planning Steps

Although the planning steps are outlined here as a sequence of discrete operations, in practice other factors may influence the sequence, and there will almost certainly be a number of iterations, compromises and trade-offs before achieving an optimum plan (see figures 6.1 and 6.2).

Project Evolution: New creative ideas and opportunities evolve and develop in many different ways. The trigger may be an automatic response to a problem or equipment failure; or it may be the identification of a commercial opportunity, technology driven upgrade, or an entrepreneur spotting a gap in the market for a new product.

Project Charter: The project charter is a document which officially formalises the existence of a project which gives the project an identity (name and number) so that budgets and responsibilities can be assigned. The project charter should outline the purpose of the project, the beneficial changes and key objectives, together with the means of achieving them. (see the *Scope Management* chapter).

Project Brief: The project brief outlines the situation - what product or facility is required, or what problem is to be solved.

Project Proposal: The project proposal outlines how the project manager proposes to respond to the project brief.

Feasibility Study: The feasibility study analyses the project charter, project brief and project proposal. It offers a structured approach for identifying the stakeholders and assessing their needs. It reviews closeout reports, together with investigating other options and alternatives to support the new venture's business viability (see the *Feasibility Study* chapter).

Build-Method: The build-method outlines how the product will be assembled or implemented. For example, on a house extension project it considers the position of the scaffolding and ladders, and the storage of the materials. On an IT project it considers how to remove old equipment and install new equipment with the minimum impact on the company's operation.

Scope Management: Scope management defines what work the project includes and, just as importantly, what work is not included in order to meet the stated objectives. On an engineering project, for example, the scope of work would be developed into a list of drawings, bill of materials (BOM) and specifications. Scope management also includes a closeout report to document achievement and problems so the company can learn from the experience.

Execution Strategy: The project's execution strategy considers the buy-or-make decision. If part of the project is to be purchased, this becomes a procurement issue. If part of the project is made in-house this becomes a resource issue. The execution strategy considers the availability of resources and the benefits of outsourcing work.

Contract: The contract outlines the terms and conditions of the agreement.

Work Breakdown Structure (WBS): The WBS is one of the key scope management tools used to subdivide the scope of work into manageable work packages which are easier to estimate, plan, assign and control (see the *WBS* chapter).

Estimating: All the plans are underpinned by an estimate of what will happen. The accuracy of the planning is therefore directly dependent on the accuracy of the estimate. The *Estimating Techniques* chapter outlines a number of estimating techniques which are quick and accurate.

Risk Management Plan: The risk management function includes the process of identifying, analysing, and responding to project risk and opportunities (see the *Project Risk Management* chapter).

Organisation Breakdown Structure (OBS): The OBS and responsibility matrix links the WBS work packages to the company, department, project team or person who is responsible for performing the work (see the *Gantt Charts* chapter for diagram).

Critical Path Method (CPM): The CPM uses a network diagram to present the work packages and activities in a logical sequence of work which is developed from the build-method and other constraints (internal and external). Activity durations and work calendars are estimated, while the availability of procurement, resources and funds are initially assumed. The CPM time analysis (forward pass and backward pass) calculates the activities early start, early finish, late start, late finish, float and the critical path (see the *CPM* chapter). This information is often presented in an activity table and a schedule Gantt chart.

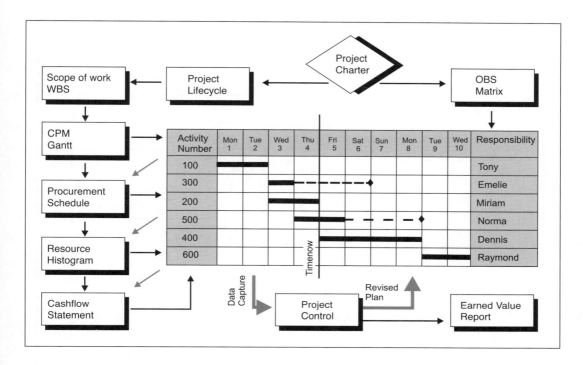

Figure 6.1: Planning and Control Cycle – shows how a number of the different topics are linked. Starting with the project charter which formalised the project, the left side develops the scope of work, and the right side links the work to a person or department performing the work. This is a suggested sequence – first develop the WBS, then the CPM and Gantt chart, then identify procurement long lead items, then identify resource overloads, then consider the project's cashflow – all these components could delay work on the project. Once the project has started monitor progress with respect to; logic, remaining duration, late deliveries, under-resourced, cost-to-compete and earned value

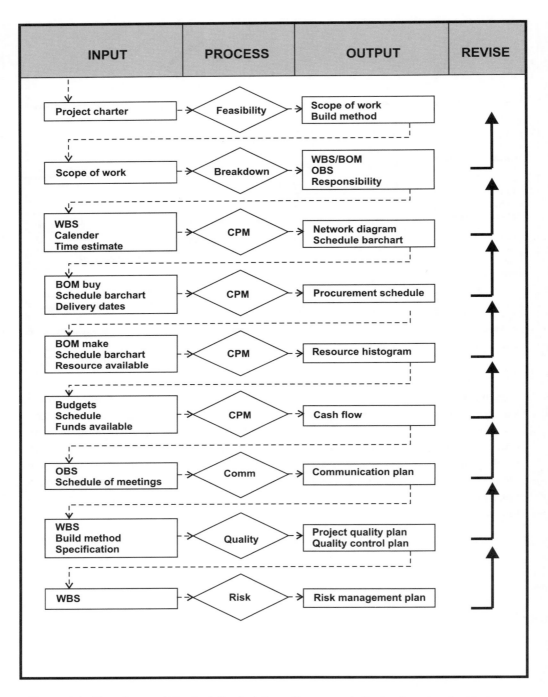

Figure 6.2: Planning and Control Cycle (alternative presentation) - shows embedded input-process-output operations within the planning and control cycle

Schedule Gantt Chart: The schedule Gantt chart is one of the best documents used for communicating schedule information. It enables the project participants to see *'at a glance'* what is happening. It is easy to walk through the sequencing of the project's work. The planning structure can be further simplified by focusing on hammocks, milestones and rolling horizons (see the *Gantt Charts* chapter).

Procurement Schedule: The execution strategy *'buy-or-make'* decision determines if the work is a procurement issue or a resource issue. The procurement function is to supply all the bought-in items at the best price to meet the project schedule. However, long lead items need to be identified early on so that they can be ordered early, or the associated activity will have to be delayed by revising the schedule Gantt chart (see the *Procurement Schedule* chapter).

Resource Histogram: The resource function is to supply a skilled workforce, machines and equipment to complete the work as outlined in the schedule Gantt chart. The manpower process forecasts and compares the resource loading with resources availability. Resource overloads, or resource underloads need to accommodate both project and company requirements. The resource smoothing needs to consider other company projects and outside contractors before revising the scheduled Gantt chart (see the *Resource Planning* chapter). The resources can be integrated with time to produce a manpower 'S' curve which forms the baseline plan for the earned value calculation.

Budgets and Project Cashflow: The project accounting process not only establishes and assigns budgets to all the work packages, but also determines the project's cashflow. There may be cashflow constraints restricting the supply of funds which will require the scheduled Gantt chart to be revised (see the *Project Accounts* chapter). The costs can be integrated with time to produce the planned value (PV) which forms the baseline plan for the earned value calculation.

Project Quality Plan: The project quality plan outlines a quality management system (quality assurance and quality control), which is designed to guide and enable the project to meet the required condition. This may include pre-qualifying project personnel and suppliers, developing procedures, quality inspections and quality documentation – all under the umbrella of total quality management (TQM) (see the *Quality Management* chapter).

Communication Plan: The project communication plan includes the process required to ensure proper collection, storage and dissemination of project information. It consists of communication planning documents, information distribution (lines of communication), a schedule of project meetings, progress reporting and administrative closeout (see the *Project Communication* chapter).

Baseline Plan (Project Plan): The baseline plan may be considered as a portfolio of documents and policies which outlines how to achieve the project's objectives. The level of detail and accuracy will depend on the project phase and complexity. The baseline plan should be a coherent document to guide the project through the execution and project control cycle.

Baseline Plan Checklist				
Project Name:		Date Raised:		
	Document Number	SOW included	SOW excluded	Risk
Project Charter:				
Project Brief:				
Project Proposal:				
Feasibility Study:				
Build-Method:				
Scope Management:				
Execution Strategy:				
Contract:				
WBS:				
Estimating:				
Risk Management Plan:				
OBS:				
Responsibility Matrix:				
Project Team:				
CPM:				
Gantt Chart:				
Procurement Schedule:				
Resource Plan:				
Project Budget:				
Cashflow Plan:				
Quality Control Plan:				
Communication Plan:				

Table 6.1: Baseline Plan – shows all the project management topics to be considered in a suggested sequence. Additional columns can be added to identify the scope of work (SOW) included, and the SOW excluded. It is also advisable to add a risk column to highlight areas of high risk which need to be addressed

2. Project Control Cycle

The project control cycle is presented as a sequence of steps to guide the project to a successful completion. The baseline plan is the starting point for project control as it outlines a plan for managing the project. Once the project starts you can be sure things will deviate; be it late deliveries, sickness, absenteeism, or scope creep (scope of work increasing). The project control cycle monitors project performance and compares it against the baseline plan - it also includes a mechanism for incorporating scope changes.

Work Authorisation: As the single point of responsibility the project manager is responsible for delegating and authorising the scope of work. The issuing of instructions to the appointed contractors and other responsible parties signals the start of the execution phase of the project. The methods for authorising work, reporting and applying control should be discussed and agreed at the handover meeting so that all parties know how the project will be managed. A record of all decisions and instructions should be kept in the project office to provide an audit trail.

Issuing Instructions: The issuing of instructions is the first step in the control cycle (see the *Project Control* chapter). Work authorisation must ensure that the full scope of work is authorised to the responsible person(s), this is often achieved through a job card system.

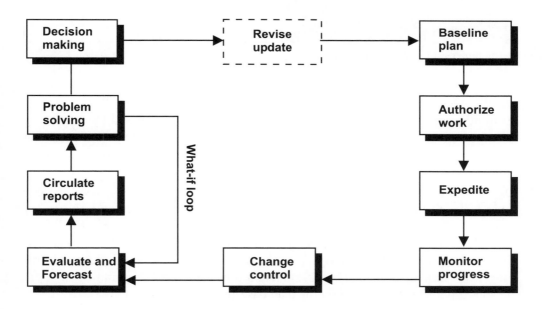

Figure 6.3: Project Control Cycle – shows the flow of work instructions, incorporating scope changes, monitoring progress, comparing planned with actual performance, and the decision-making process to take correction action – then the control cycle starts again

Expedite: Once instructions, job cards, orders and contracts have been issued, project expediting takes a proactive approach to make the work happen. This involves the follow up function (usually by a team member) to confirm that: orders have been received by the contractor or supplier, materials have been procured, skilled labour is available, work has started as planned and the schedule completion dates will be achieved. Any variances should be reported through the data capture system to the responsible stakeholders.

Tracking and Monitoring Progress: The data capture system records the progress and current status of all the work packages and activities. The accuracy of the data capture has a direct bearing on the accuracy of all the subsequent reports (project status, trends and forecast).

Problem-Solving: The problem-solving function generates a number of feasible solutions and opportunities for consideration.

Change Control: The change control function ensures that all changes to the scope of work are captured and approved by the designated people before being incorporated in the baseline plan and communicated through the document control system. As the project is implemented there will be changes to the scope which need to be considered, approved and authorised. These would tend to be authorised by issuing a revised document, typical examples include:

Scope Change	Issue revised drawing
Planning Change	Issue revised schedule
Build-method Change	Issue revised build-method statement
Cost Change	Issue revised budget

Table 6.2: Table of Change Control

Change control is also concerned with influencing the factors which create changes to ensure that any changes are beneficial (see the *Scope Management* chapter).

Evaluation and Forecasting: The project's performance is analysed by comparing actual progress against planned progress within the CPM model and extrapolating trends to forecast the project's position in the future (see the *Project Control* and *Earned Value* chapters).

Decision-Making: The decision-making function collates information and suggestions and decides on an appropriate corrective course of action which commits the necessary resources. One of the main management functions is to make decisions which have the collective support of the team members and stakeholders. In fact, it may be argued that the sole purpose of generating information is to make decisions. The lessons learnt must be documented in an agreed format and time frame and communicated to the person responsible for the estimating data base and closeout report.

Revise Baseline Plan: If there are any changes within the project the baseline plan must be revised to reflect the current scope of work and incorporate any corrective action. By saving the old baseline plan an audit trail of changes can be archived. The control cycle is now complete and the next cycle will authorise the changes and corrective action.

Project:		
Complied By:		Date:
Project Control Plan		
Baseline Plan:		
Issue Instructions:		
Job Cards:		
Expedite:		
Measure Progress:		
Change Control:		
Evaluate and Forecast:		
Problem-Solving:		
Decision-Making:		
Revise Baseline Plan:		

Table 6.3: Project Control Plan – shows the main project management topics of the control plan

3. Reporting Frequency

The frequency of the reporting cycle should reflect the needs of the project, short reporting periods, when there is a high level of change and uncertainty in the project, or long periods when there is little or no change. For example, during project start up and during the commissioning phase the reporting cycle may be reduced to daily or even hourly, while under normal conditions the reporting cycle is usually weekly or monthly.

As a rule of thumb, the reporting cycle should leave sufficient time to implement corrective action to bring any project deviation back on course without delaying any of the critical activities.

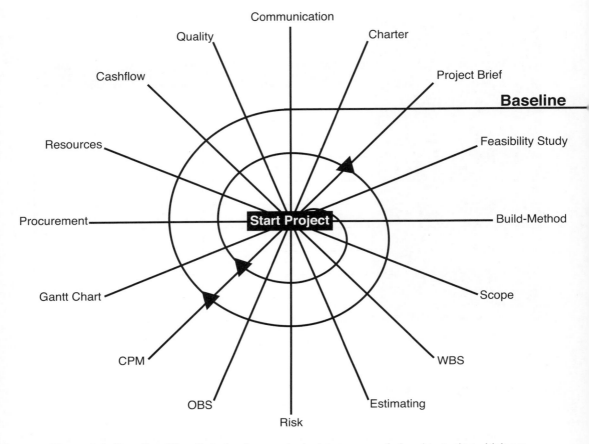

Figure 6.4: Baseline Plan Spiral - shows a typical sequence of planning topics which are repeated iteratively until an optimum baseline plan is achieved

4. Planning and Control Spiral

The planning and control spiral shows a suggested sequence of discreet operations which are repeated iteratively until an optimum baseline plan is achieved. This is a more accurate presentation of how we think compared to a straight forward flow chart of one operation after the other.

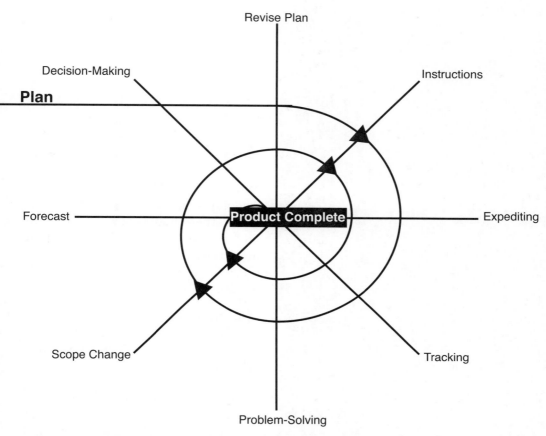

Figure 6.5: Control Spiral - shows a typical sequence of control topics which are repeated every reporting cycle

Exercise:

1. Develop a baseline plan for your project. Show how you name and number your documents.
2. Develop a control plan for your project. Show how you name and number your documents.
3. How do you determine the frequency of the reporting cycle?

7

Scope Management

Learning Outcomes

After reading this chapter, you should be able to;

Explain the reason for scope management techniques in a project environment

Explain the scope change control process

Compile a project closeout report

Effective scope management is one of the key factors determining project success. Failure to accurately interpret the client's needs or problems will produce a misleading definition of the scope of work. And if this causes rework and additional effort, there may be implications for project time, cost and quality. Therefore, project success will be self-limiting if the project's scope of work is not adequately defined.

> **DEFINITION**
>
> The PMBOK defines scope management as; '... *the processes required to ensure that the project includes all the work required, and only the work required, to complete the project successfully. It is primarily concerned with defining and controlling what is or not included in the project.*'

> **DEFINITION**
>
> The APM bok defines scope management as; '... *defining the scope of the project and breaking this into manageable pieces of work.*'

These two definitions have highlighted three main features of scope management;

- Quantify what is included and what is excluded to complete the project (See *WBS* chapter).

- Control scope changes (Scope change control management).

- Subdivide the scope of work into manageable work packages (See *WBS* chapter).

1. Project Initiation

Project initiation focuses on how to start a project. The PMBOK defines project initiation as *'... the process of formally recognising that a new project exists, or that an existing project should continue into its next phase* [of the project lifecycle]'.

Projects by definition have a start and finish. For a contracting company the start could be an invitation to tender, or the award of contract. However, for the client the start of a project may not be so clear. Some projects may evolve as the embryo of an entrepreneurial idea as it responds to market changes and new technology, or the project may respond to an entrepreneur spotting a marketable opportunity. For example, the Apple iPod responded to people in the market wanting to download music – Apple quickly responded and beat the competition to the market.

At some point the company needs to formally recognize the existence of a project with a project charter. It is important to distinguish between wishful thinking whims and innovative ideas that could significantly benefit the company. The project brief, project proposal and project charter are often used interchangeably. If a distinction is required consider using the following definitions.

Project Brief: The project brief is a statement of the situation, outlining the problem or opportunity. For example, an AA survey on your car gives a statement of its condition, or a marine survey of a fishing vessel gives a structured inspection of its actual condition and how it operates.

Project Brief	
Number:	Date Raised:
Compiled By:	
Statement: (outline the situation of the problem or opportunity)	
Propeller shaft bent causing vibration and excessive wear on the bearings.	

Table 7.1: Project Brief

Project Proposal: The project proposal is in response to the project brief. It outlines a solution to the problem, or a way of making the most of the identified opportunity. For example, the survey of a fishing vessel may have highlighted problems with the propeller shaft. The proposal outlines how to dock the vessel and replace the shaft.

Project Proposal	
Number:	Date Raised:
Compiled By:	
Statement: (outline how to respond to the project brief)	
Dock the fishing vessel and replace the propeller shaft.	

Table 7.2: Project Proposal

Project Charter: Also called terms of reference, or project mission, officially acknowledges the existence and start of the project. The project charter will give the project a name and a number and formally add it to the company's register of projects. The project charter outlines the purpose of the project and what it is meant to achieve. It assigns a project manager and a budget to take the project a step further – this may be to conduct a feasibility study.

Project Charter	
	Date Raised:
Number:	Project Name:
Compiled By:	Approved By:
Project Description: (refer to the associated project brief and project proposal). Outline how you WILL respond to the problem or opportunity.	

Table 7.3: Project Charter – shows the official recognition of the project

The project charter should be a tightly worded document outlining what is to be done and the boundaries of the project. For example, the project could be to write a fashion book for the academic market, 200 pages, colour, sell for $40, project managed (editor) by Mark Wordsworth, and be ready for the beginning of the academic year.

Unless the aims of the project can be precisely defined in a few short words it could imply that you are not exactly clear what you want to achieve. The project charter should also include:

- The background to the project
- The key assumptions
- The business and other needs
- The scope of work
- Identifying key activities, budgets and dates
- Comments on how the project is to be managed
- The role of the project manager (responsibility and authority) and reporting structure.

The project charter essentially formalises the project and should be documented and signed off.

2. Scope Planning

DEFINITION

The PMBOK defines scope planning as; *'... the process of developing a written scope statement as the basis for future project decisions including, in particular, the criteria used to determine if the project or phase has been completed successfully.'*

The scope planning outlines the project philosophy which:

- Defines the boundary of the project and confirms common understanding of the project scope amongst the stakeholders.
- Forms the basis of agreement between client and contractor by identifying both the project objectives and major deliverables.
- Is a guide and constraint for the configuration management process influencing change control.

Scope planning develops a written statement which acts as the basis for future decisions and establishes criteria for the completion of an activity, completion of a project phase, or the completion of the project itself. As the project progresses, the scope statement may need to be revised or refined to reflect changes to the scope of the project.

3. Scope Definition

DEFINITION

The PMBOK defines scope definition as; *'... subdividing the major project deliverables into smaller, more manageable components ...'*

The scope definition outlines the content of the project and a method to identify all the items of work that are required to be carried out to complete the project and, by implication, the activities which are not included in the project (see *WBS* chapter).

4. Scope Verification

DEFINITION

The PMBOK defines scope verification as; *'....the process of formalising acceptance of the project scope by the stakeholders....'*

The following table shows how scope verification can be related to the phases of the project lifecycle.

1. Concept	Approve the feasibility study
2. Design	Approve the detailed design and the baseline plan
3. Implementation	Approve all changes and the product is ready for commissioning
4. Commissioning	Commission and test - confirm the product is ready for handover.

These controls are essential to establish the required condition before implementation, and after implementation to confirm the required condition has been achieved.

5. Scope Change Control

All projects are subjected to scope changes at some time or another during their lifecycle. The scope change control system, or configuration management is a system designed to effectively manage the change of scope process. Configuration management is the process of identifying and managing change to the deliverables and other work products as they evolve through the project lifecycle. It helps ensure that the proposed changes are necessary, appropriate and that the integrity of the system is maintained. For example, during the extension of your house you may see some interesting bathroom fittings you want to include. The configuration process will ensure the different fittings can be attached to the existing pipe work and they atheistically complement the new design.

DEFINITION
The PMBOK defines scope change control as:

(a) *Influencing the factors which create scope changes to ensure that changes are beneficial* [to the project].

(b) *Determining that a scope change has occurred.*

(c) *Managing the actual changes when and if they occur.*

The project manager (project team) are responsible for setting-up a system to monitor, evaluate and approve all the changes (by the designated experts) before the changes are incorporated in the baseline plan. This will ensure that the baseline plan always reflects the current status of the project. Change control is also concerned with influencing the factors which create changes to ensure that changes are beneficial. The scope change approval system should be agreed by all stakeholders at the outset and confirmed at the handover meeting. The configuration management system offers:

Procedure	A change control system which formally documents a procedure defining the steps by which official project documents may be changed.
Authority	Lists only people who have the authority to make changes to the scope of work, in both the client and contractor organisations.
Communicates	A current and up-to-date description of the product. Updates and communicates the status of any change requests.
Traceability	Traceability of previous baseline configurations. This includes a record and an audit trail of approved changes.
Monitor	A framework to monitor, evaluate and update the scope baseline to accommodate any scope changes. This will ensure the baseline always reflects the current status of the project.
Emergency	Automatic approval for emergency situations.

The project lifecycle clearly outlines two aspects of the configuration management system which have a similar scope change approval system, but different budgetary structures:

- Scope design and development
- Scope changes

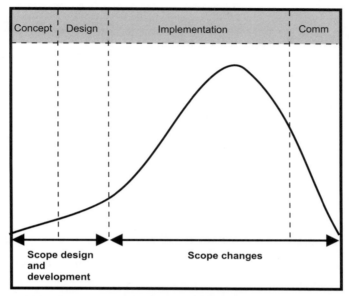

Figure 7.1: Scope Changes – shows the scope changes during the design and development phases, and separately, the scope changes during the implementation and commissioning phases

Scope Design and Development: During the design and development phase, the project brief and project proposal are developed into detailed design drawings and specifications. The configuration management process is used to guide the design and development process to produce a scope baseline. The configuration management system formalises the design management process by capturing all the proposed scope developments. Before the scope baseline is revised these developments must be quantified, assessed, verified, integrated and approved by the authorised people. Only then will the scope baseline be updated. The financial implications of these scope approvals is part of the project's design and development budget.

Scope Change Control System: Once the project starts any scope changes now fall under the scope change control system. These scope changes will need to go through a similar system of approval against the design philosophy, but now the changes may impact on contractual time and budget agreements. If a change falls within the project proposal, this will be considered as a design development. However, if the change falls outside the proposal framework then the change will be considered additional to contract and may attract a time extension and additional costs. This is why it is most important to establish a comprehensive proposal (scope planning) as a basis to allocate the cost of these changes.

It is important, particularly on complex projects, that any scope changes are only approved by the nominated technical experts. This will not only prevent scope changes by non-experts, but also ensure that all implications of the proposed changes have been considered. The control system should allow for scope changes to be initiated by any project stakeholders. Consider the following (figure 7.2):

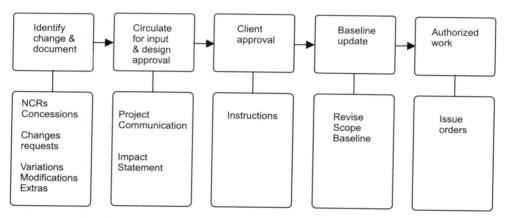

Figure 7.2: Configuration Control Flow Chart

Scope Changes: The control system should allow for scope changes to be motivated by anyone working on the project. Consider the following ways:

Non Conformance Report (NCR)	A non conformance report is usually initiated by quality control when they inspect a product which is outside the required condition and tolerance. The non-conformance would either be corrected and fall away or motivate a concession. For example, a door may be 100 mm (+/- 10 mm) out of position yet still functional.
Concession	A concession requests the client to accept an item which has been built and is functional, but outside the specification. If approved this would be shown as a scope change for this project only, it would be shown on the as-built drawings, but not on the baseline drawings. For example, the client is asked to accept the above mentioned door which, although it is out of position, is still functioning.
Change Request	Change requests, modifications and variations request the client to approve a change to the scope baseline.
Verbal	Any verbal comments or instructions should be backed up in writing with a project communication document, as verbal agreements are open to dispute.

As the project office is the centre of the control system (and document control system) this is the logical place to keep a register (library) of all the approved signed changes and their status. These documents may be required later to support invoices for additional work.

Change Request: A change request form is used to describe the scope change, list associated drawings and documents, together with the reason for the change (see figure 7.3).

CHANGE REQUEST

NUMBER :	DATE RAISED :
INITIATED BY :	

CHANGE REQUESTED (related drawings / work packages):

REASON FOR CHANGE :

APPROVAL:

NAME	POSITION	APPROVAL	DATE

Figure: 7.3. Change Request

Project Communication: The project communication document allows any stakeholder working on the project, to make a formal statement. This could be a question, identifying a problem or making a suggestion. Once the document has entered the system the configuration management system will ensure that it is acknowledged and actioned. This essentially puts the ball in the project office and client's court and forces them to give clear written instructions.

PROJECT COMMUNICATION

NUMBER: DATE RAISED:
INITIATED BY:
DESCRIPTION (related drawings / work packages):

COMMENTS / INSTRUCTIONS:

WE ACKNOWLEDGE YOUR ENQUIRY / INSTRUCTION:

VERBAL FROM: TO:
WRITTEN FROM: TO:
DATE:

PLEASE ADVISE HOW WE ARE TO PROCEED:

1. START IMMEDIATELY AND QUOTE WITHIN 7 DAYS
2. START IMMEDIATELY ON UNIT RATES
3. DO NOT START, QUOTE WITHIN 7 DAYS
4. OTHER

REQUEST FROM: INSTRUCTION FROM:

CONTRACTOR   CLIENT
PROJECT MANAGER   PROJECT MANAGER

Figure: 7.4 Project Communication

Impact Statement: The impact statement quantifies the implications of making the proposed change. The impact statement generally follows the client's response from the project communication, but in reality it is usually issued at the same time. An information pack is compiled by the project office to collect input, information, comments and approval from the responsible parties.

IMPACT STATEMENT	
Project:	
Complied By:	Date:
Department	**Comments**
Design Team	Prepare information pack
Technical	Can we make it, what is the impact on the build-method?
Procurement	Can we buy it?
Production	What is the resources impact?
Planning	What is the time impact?
Cost	What is the budget impact?
Quality	What is the quality impact?
Legal	What is the contractual impact?
Risk	What are the risks?
Project Manager	Comments / Approval
Client	Comments / Approval

Table 7.4: Impact Statement

All the above documents should be numbered consecutively, with a summary sheet showing the present status and clearly identifying the impact on the stakeholders.

Flow Sheet: The project manager uses a flow sheet to control the movement of the change requests and impact statements. The flow sheet determines the sequence of circulation, it logs the documents in and out of departments and collects comments, calculations and information, but most importantly it notes the acceptance or rejection of the proposed change (see figure 7.5).

IMPACT STATEMENT FLOW SHEET			
IMPACT NUMBER:			
DESCRIPTION:			
POSITION	DATE IN	DATE OUT	COMMENTS
PROJECT MANAGER			
DRAWING OFFICE			
PROJECT ENGINEER			
PROCUREMENT MANAGER			
PRODUCTION MANAGER			
PROJECT PLANNER			
PROJECT ACCOUNTANT			
QA MANAGER			
COMPANY LAWYER			

Figure 7.5: Flow Sheet

There are two possible methods of controlling the movement of the document:

    a) Hub and spoke (see figure 7.6)

    b) Consecutive (see figure 7.7)

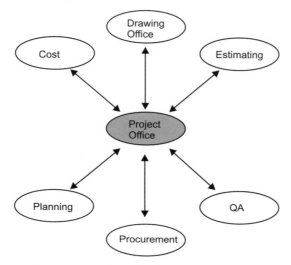

Figure: 7.6 Flow Sheet - Hub and Spoke

Although the hub and spoke arrangement doubles the movement of the documents, it does enable the project office to know exactly where the documents are at any time so the change request status can be communicated. With the consecutive method the lines of communication may be shorter, but if the documents do not reappear timeously, it will require a time consuming witch hunt to find them. Whichever system is used it must be able to update and communicate the status of any change requests.

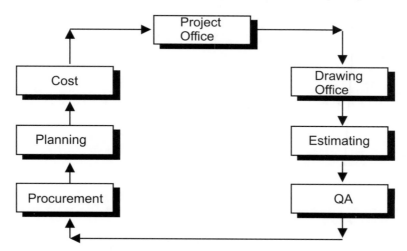

Figure: 7.7 Flow Sheet - Consecutive

Authorisation: The scope change authorisation formally authorises the project manager, team member or contractor to carry out the work. It should be based on the impact statement findings which will have determined the feasibility and acceptability of the change.

Scope Change Authorisation

Number:		DATE RAISED :	

Scope Change (related drawings / work packages):

Impact Statement (Reference):

APPROVAL:

NAME	POSITION	APPROVAL	DATE
	Project Manager		
	Client		

Figure: 7.8: Scope Change Authorisation - shows the formal approval to carry out the work

With the implementation of the scope change into the production system, this completes the configuration management control cycle.

6. Project Closeout

It is important to not only learn from the mistakes and successes of previous projects, but also learn progressively during the present project. The project closeout can be subdivide into three sections:

- Compile historical data from previous projects to assist new venture creation, feasibility study and estimating on future projects.
- Compile historical data from previous projects and the current project to predict trends and problem areas on the current project.
- Generate a closeout report which evaluates the performance of the current project against the project objectives and make recommendations for future projects.

Historical Data: The search for historical data from previous projects will clearly show the benefit of effective closeout reports, filing, library and storage. Learning from previous experiences is the most basic form of development and it is essentially free. There are, however, limitations with historical data, the correlation between projects may be tenuous. Consider the following:

- The scope of work between projects is unlikely to be exactly the same.
- The cost data will be influenced by inflation.
- The build-methods will change with the product and location.
- The management and leadership styles may be different.

Look closely to see what went right and what went wrong together with any recommendations, because the same mistakes have an uncanny habit of happening again, particularly if the cause has not been addressed.

Project Closeout Report: A closeout report can be generated at the end of each month, end of each project phase, the end of your contract or the end of the project itself. It is advisable to compile the report before the project participants disperse. For best results a structured report format is recommended - consider the following steps:

- Generate a comprehensive questionnaire and circulate it to project participants.
- Analyse responses and debrief the key managers.
- Compile draft closeout report for comments. This can also be used as an agenda for a formal closeout meeting.
- Hold a formal closeout meeting attended by all participants.
- Compile a final closeout report, circulate and file in the project office library.

An evaluation differs from a status report in that it considers the entire project lifecycle – management systems are evaluated, achievement of objectives are noted, budget comparisons are made, outstanding issues identified, together with the issues that contribute to the success or failure of the project. The emphasis is on feedback with an open forum (possibly anonymous).

Questionnaire: The main benefit of the questionnaire approach is to structure the responses. It must be made quite clear that this exercise is not a search for the guilty but an attempt to quantify what actually happened on the project. The net should be cast reasonably wide to include a broad range of opinions. The list of participants should certainly include the following:

- Client
- Project manager and project team
- Functional managers and other corporate participants
- Suppliers and subcontractors
- Stakeholders

The questionnaire would typically be structured to include the following questions:

Position	Identify your position in the project organisation structure and comment on the interface and cooperation with other disciplines.
Delegation	Comment on the delegation of responsibility and authority.
Scope of Work	Briefly outline your assigned scope of work.
Planning	Comment on planning schedules, budgets, quality and manpower performance. Where possible quantify performance with project data.
Performance	Give a candid assessment of your performance, analysing what went right and what went wrong. Comment on any non conformance reports (NCR) with reasons for any deviations and the level of re-work. If any audits were conducted comment on their findings.
Communication	Comment on the lines of communication, the issuing of instructions and information, the holding of meetings, the availability of information (filing and storage), procedures and reporting.
Technical Changes	Evaluate technical design changes, as-built drawings and operator manuals.
Scope Changes	Comment on any scope changes and concessions. Evaluate how smoothly the configuration system worked, were the changes approved and implemented timeously.
New Technology	Discuss the use of new technology, computerisation and automation.
Problems	Discuss any unexpected problems, how they impacted the project and their solutions.
Procurement	Comment on the performance of procurement suppliers and sub-contractors.
Manpower	Comment on manpower performance, their training and any industrial related problems.
Estimate	Evaluate the accuracy of the estimate and list any recommended changes to the company's tariffs.
Contract	Evaluate the contract document.
Future	General recommendations for future projects.

This type of questionnaire provides the project manager with an excellent tool for accurate and meaningful feedback. People generally do not like answering questionnaires, you may get more feedback through a debriefing meeting or telephone conversation using the questionnaire as the agenda.

Recommendations for Future Projects: Learning from achievements, mistakes and improving productivity are basic economic requirements and the fuel for sustained commercial competitiveness. These recommendations can provide an invaluable source of direction for future projects. The closeout report should highlight any recommendations simply and clearly, because many years from now this may be the only section which is read.

Besides assisting with the estimating recommendations from the previous closeout reports should also be tabled at the handover meetings. During the project, take a leaf out of a sports team's book – they watch videos of their games to critique their performance so they can continually improve their game plan.

Validating the project estimate is essential. Over estimating will generate good profits, but in a competitive market this will reduce the chance of winning further tenders; while underpricing will simply reduce company profits. Wherever possible the analysis should indicate perceived trends. These may be in technology, build-methods or management systems. The final statement should comment on the overall success of the project and suggest if the company is wise to tender on these types of projects again.

Storage: At the end of the project the files, photographs, all correspondence and particularly the closeout report should not be dumped and lost in the archives, but be readily available for inspection (company library). This is the data base for future estimating and is an auditable item.

Exercise:

1. Discuss the benefits of using scope management techniques in a project environment.
2. Discuss the scope change control process your company uses to manage their projects.
3. Discuss how you would conduct a closeout report on your projects.

8

Work Breakdown Structure

The purpose of the work breakdown structure (WBS) is to subdivide the scope of work into a number of manageable work packages, a list of jobs, or a checklist that makes it easier to estimate, easier to plan and easier to assign the work to a responsible person or department for completion. The breakdown structure should also strive to group similar work together to improve productivity and the efficient use of resources.

The WBS not only helps to fully define the scope of work, but it also forms the backbone of the planning and control system. It should be stressed at this point **– the WBS is the backbone of your project.** Without an effective backbone your project has no structure to plan and control all the parameters of time, cost, quality, procurement, and resources.

The WBS is an excellent tool for quantifying the scope of work as a list of work packages and it is an essential tool for ensuring the estimate or quotation includes the complete scope of work, because what is not included on a fixed price contract is taken straight off your profit margin. The main components of the WBS which will be discussed in this chapter are:

- Structure
- Methods of subdivision
- Numbering or coding system

1. Purpose of the WBS

The purpose of the WBS is to subdivide the scope of work into a number of manageable work packages. This may sound like a straight forward task, but this is the task many people new to project management have difficulty applying. Figure 8.1 shows the need for a WBS to provide a structure, through the cloud, to subdivide the total project into the work packages and checklists.

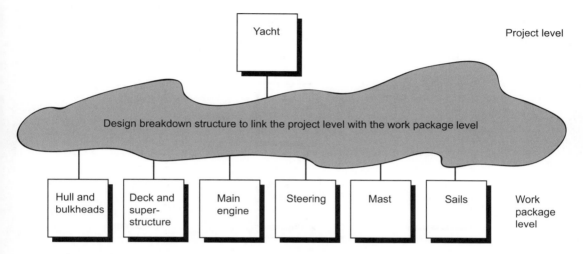

Figure 8.1: WBS – shows a need for the WBS to provide a structure to link the project to the work packages and checklist level

Work Package: Projects can be subdivided into a number of work packages which can be defined under the following headings;

Specifications	Duration
Quality requirements	Procurement
Estimate (manhours)	Resources / responsibility
Budgets	Equipment / materials

Activities: The work packages can be further subdivided into a list of activities. The activities are a list of jobs which are required to be done to complete the work package. Where the project manager would develop the WBS to the work package level, the supervisor responsible for the work package would develop it into a list of activities. This effectively pushes responsibility down the organization structure and empowers the supervisors.

Checklists: Checklists provide an effective management tool to confirm you have a list of all the items of work and materials. Why try to remember everything in your head when **checklists never forget?** Checklists are an excellent planning and control tool – even NASA uses them!

2. WBS Structure

There are two basic methods of presenting the WBS:

- Graphically in boxes
- Text indents (spreadsheet).

The WBS is a hierarchical structure which is best presented by a **graphical** subdivision of the scope of work into boxes. This logical subdivision of all the work elements is easy to understand and assimilate helping the project participants to quantify their responsibility and gain their commitment and support. Figure 8.2 shows a vertical subdivision, while figure 8.3 shows the same subdivision horizontally.

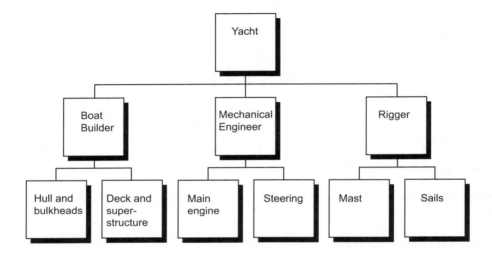

Figure 8.2: WBS – Yacht Building Project – shows a vertical subdivision by discipline and then by product

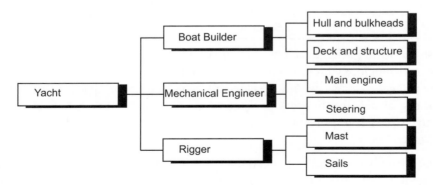

Figure 8.3: WBS – Horizontal Presentation – shows a horizontal subdivision of the yacht building project

Although boxes are an excellent means of presentation they are a cumbersome document to develop and edit on the computer. Boxes lend themselves more to graphic software than project planning software. Another method of presentation is to show the scope of work as text indents, where each level is tabbed to represent its level in the hierarchy. If you are using planning software this is how it develops lists of activities.

1.0.0 Yacht Building Project

- **1.1.0 Boat Builder**
  - 1.1.1 Hull and Bulkheads
  - 1.1.2 Deck and Superstructure
- **1.2.0 Mechanical Engineer**
  - 1.2.1 Main Engine
  - 1.2.2 Steering
- **1.3.0 Rigger**
  - 1.3.1 Mast
  - 1.3.2 Sails

Figure 8.4: WBS – Indent Presentation – shows text indents

The text indents can be taken a step further using a spreadsheet. The spreadsheet WBS presentation is the most practical and widely used document to build-up a complete list of work packages, jobs or checklist. Once this structure is established it is straight forward to add columns for the other parameters, such as, budgets, manhours, material, equipment and responsibility. The more detailed the list the greater the accuracy of the estimate and the greater level of planning and control.

IntroPM 8 - WBS - Yacht Building Project.xls

WBS		Budget / Work Package	Budget / Department	Budget / Project	Manhours	Materials	Equipment	Responsibility
1.0.0	Yacht Building Project			$				
1.1.0	Boat Builder		$					
1.1.1	Hull and Bulkheads	$						
1.1.2	Deck and Superstructure	$						
1.2.0	Mechanical Engineer		$					
1.2.1	Main Engine	$						
1.2.2	Steering	$						
1.3.0	Rigger		$					
1.3.1	Mast	$						
1.3.2	Sails	$						

Figure 8.5: WBS – Spreadsheet Presentation – shows how a range of the project's parameters (budget, manhours, materials, equipment and responsibility) can be linked to the WBS work packages

3. Methods of Subdivision

There are many methods of using the WBS to subdivide the scope of work - your imagination is the only limiting factor. Although the spreadsheet WBS is the most practical format of listing the work packages and managing your projects, for ease of understanding, this chapter will develop a number of graphical breakdown structures.

Designing the WBS requires a delicate balance to address the needs of the various departments and the needs of the project. There is not necessarily a right or wrong WBS structure, because what may be an excellent fit for one department may be an awkward burden for another. And further, as the project progresses other WBS subdivisions may become more appropriate.

The only way to determine which is the best WBS for you is to experiment with a few different subdivisions. With practice and experience you will develop a number of workable templates which can be used on all your projects.

Product Breakdown Structure: This represents a hierarchical view of the physical assemblies, sub-assemblies, components and parts needed to manufacture the product. Consider the subdivision of a car (see figure 8.6):

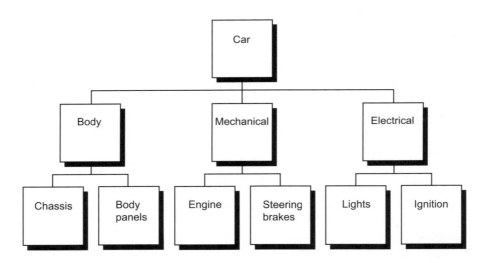

Figure 8.6: Product Breakdown Structure – shows the subdivision of a car (product) into the different components of the product

Organisation Breakdown Structure: The organization breakdown structure represents the hierarchy of the company managing the project. A discipline split is a logical subdivision into the departments or project team who are performing the work. Further subdivisions could include outside contractors and suppliers of the equipment and the materials.

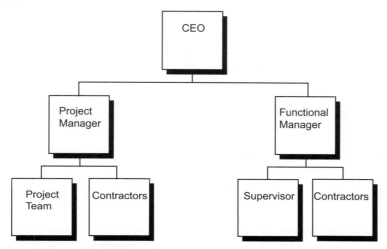

Figure 8.7: Organisation Breakdown Structure

Contract Breakdown Structure: The contract breakdown structure lends itself to the management-by-projects approach where the project is managed through the project office and all the work is outsourced to contractors.

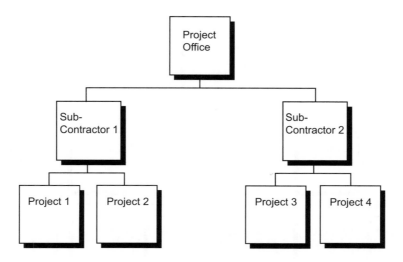

Figure 8.8: Contract Breakdown Structure - shows a management-by-projects approach

Location Breakdown Structure: The location breakdown structure subdivides the work by its location. This would be appropriate for a project that has work packages at different locations. Consider implementing a new banking product. The bank would have to install similar equipment at all its branches, together with the training of staff.

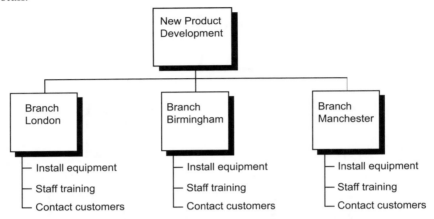

Figure 8.9: Location Breakdown Structure – shows the implementation of a new banking product

System Breakdown Structure: The system breakdown structure subdivides the work into the different systems within the product. A systems breakdown will probably cut across other breakdown structures, but would be useful for operating, commissioning, fault finding and problem-solving. Quality circles are a good example of how a production line (system) can be linked to improve production performance.

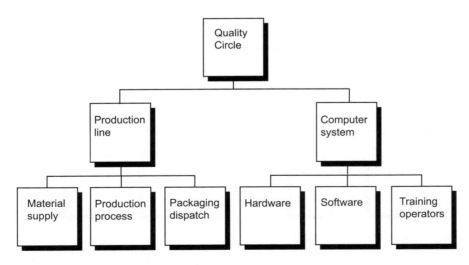

Figure 8.10: Systems Breakdown Structure

4. Activity List

The WBS can be used to subdivide the scope of work into a list of activities. In the discussion so far the scope of work has been subdivided into work packages for the purposes of assigning responsibility and a budget. This section will show that the work packages can be subdivided further into a list of activities for the CPM calculation and Gantt chart presentation.

Although the work packages may not be logically linked, the CPM and Gantt chart activities have to be logically linked to perform the time calculations. This adds another dimension and complexity to the WBS subdivision.

The house extension project below shows how a decorating work package can be subdivided into a number of activities. These activities will become the input for the CPM development of this example (see *CPM* chapter).

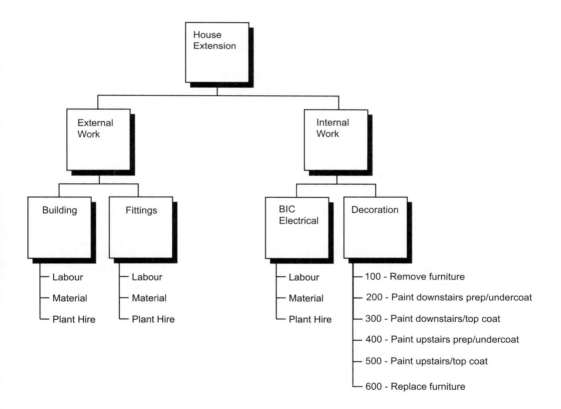

Figure 8.11: Activity List – shows how the WBS work packages can be further subdivided into a list of activities for the CPM calculation and Gantt chart presentation

5. Checklists

Checklists – love them or hate them – they do provide an effective management tool to confirm you have a complete list of all the items of work and materials. Checklists can be used as a prompt reminding you to consider a number of points, or as a step-by-step procedure to follow.

Checklists are also a form of expert system which can be developed from previous experience, knowledge and closeout reports. As checklists never forget this enables you to capture other people's advice and your own experience.

Operator Manuals: Operator manuals often use a checklist to start up and operate complicated equipment. See our book on *Bluewater Checklists* which outlines a number of checklists for bluewater cruising.

Shopping List: The shopping list is a popular type of checklist which most of us use. Consider the following shopping list which is subdivided into food types.

Veg	Fruit	Cereal	Jams/Spreads
Potatoes	Apples	Porridge	Marmalade
Onions	Oranges	Weatabix	Jam
Broccoli	Kiwi fruit	All-Bran	Honey
Carrots	Bananas		Marmite
Tomatoes	Avocado		
Cucumber	Ginger		
Mushrooms	Lemon		
Leeks	Lime		
Pepper			
Garlic			
Pumpkin			
Dairy	**Dried**	**Drinks**	**Cleaning**
Milk / long life	Peas	Tea - Breakfast	Washing powder
Milk powder	Beans	Tea – Early Grey	Washing up liquid
Milk / condensed	Mushrooms	Tea – Mint	Bleach
Butter	Sundried toms	Coffee	Dish cloths
Yoghurt		Chocolate	Scouring pads
Cheddar		Cocoa	Scouring cream
Goat cheese		Ginger	
Blue cheese		Lemon	
Parmesan		Wine	
Dried	**Oils / Vinegars**	**Packets**	**Cooking**

Figure 8.12: Shopping Checklist – shows a structured shopping checklist subdivided by food type

6. WBS Templates

Although 'product' and 'department' are popular criteria for subdivision, managers sometimes find difficulty thinking of suitable methods to subdivide their projects. In practice companies tend to standardize their WBS using a standard WBS template for their projects. Instead of starting each project with a blank sheet of paper, consider using a WBS from a previous project as a template. A standard WBS template ensures consistency and completeness as it also becomes a planning checklist with all the components that your particular type of projects would contain. Having a structured checklist also reduces the risk of omitting obvious items of work.

Even if the complete WBS template cannot be used, there may be portions of the template which are similar and can be copied across. Using proven structures will greatly speed up the planning process and help to structure your thinking. The figure below outlines a WBS where the first level is subdivided by location, the second level by department and the third level by expense type. This format could be used as a standard WBS template for the company. The only changes per project would be to the description rather than the structure.

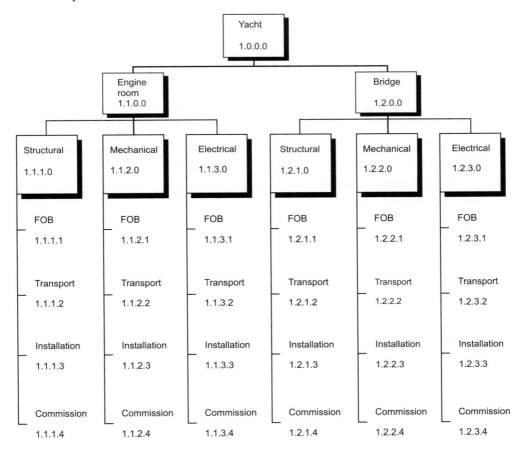

Figure 8.13: WBS Template - shows a template which can be used on a range of projects

7. The Numbering System

One of the beneficial features of the WBS is its ability to uniquely identify by a number or code all the elements of work in a numerical and chronological manner. With a unique number, all the work packages can be linked to the project's schedule, purchase orders, resources, accounts, together with the corporate accounts and the client's accounts.

The numbering system can be alphabetic, numeric, or alphanumeric (letters and numbers), in most of the examples here the numbering systems will be numeric. Consider the following example:

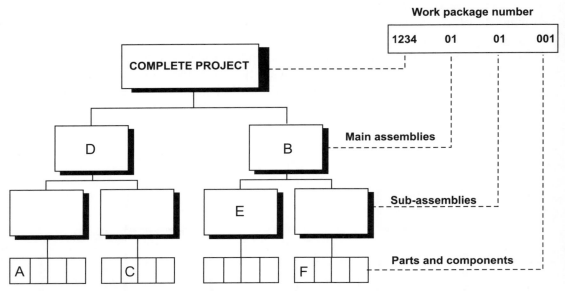

Figure 8.14: WBS Numbering System – shows how each work package can be uniquely identified - see example below

Numbering Exercise:

Referring to figure 8.14, if A, B and C are the following work package numbers, what are D, F and F?

A = 1234 01 01 001

B = 1234 02 00 000

C = 1234 01 02 002

D =

E =

F =

(Solutions see appendix 1)

8. Cost Breakdown Structure (Estimating)

If your company wins contracts by competitive bidding it is important to have a system for generating accurate quotations quickly. The WBS offers a top-down subdivision of the work, while estimating at the work package level, offers a bottom-up roll-up of project costs. The **accuracy** of the estimate will increase progressively as the work package's level of detail increases.

For example, a house extension project may be quoted on a surface area rate, but managed at the work package level. If the house extension is 200 m^2, @ $1000 per sq m, then the quote will therefore be $200,000.

When the contract is awarded the budget is prepared at the work package level using unit rates – will the two figures meet in the middle?

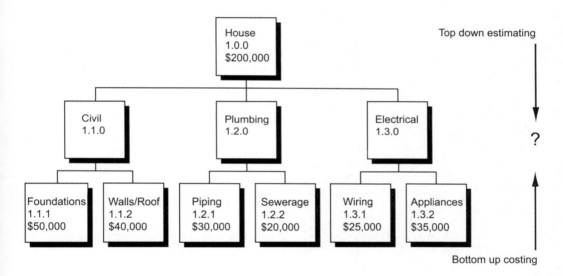

Figure 8.15: Top-Down Estimating / Bottom-Up Costing - shows the problem when a company quotes on a top-down estimate, but manages at the work package level

Exercises:

1. Discuss the reasons for subdividing projects into work packages.
2. Discuss the types of breakdown structures found in a project environment.
3. Produce a WBS template which can be used in a range of your company's projects.
4. Carryout the WBS numbering exercise from section 7 (see Appendix 1 for solutions).

9

Estimating Techniques

Learning Outcomes

After reading this chapter, you should be able to;

Identify the different types of project costs

Calculate labour costs for your project

Calculate unit rates for your project

Prepare a project budget

Project estimating uses a portfolio of special project management techniques to predict what will happen in the future. All the components of the baseline plan are underpinned by an estimate of what will happen. The accuracy of the planning and control is, therefore, directly dependent on the accuracy of the estimate. Project estimating also underpins problem-solving, decision-making and risk management.

It is logical that this chapter on project estimating follows the *WBS* chapter, because the *WBS* quantifies the scope of work and produces a list of work packages, checklists and activities which are easier to estimate (bottom-up).

If your company tenders for work then accurate estimating is even more essential because you are essentially committing your company contractually, based on the accuracy of the estimate.

The accuracy of the estimate is often based on a number of factors; your experience from previous projects, the amount of information available and the amount of time available to produce the estimate. However, in the commercial world, contractors usually have little time to quote, therefore, it is essential to develop a number of estimating techniques which will enable you to produce estimates quickly and accurately.

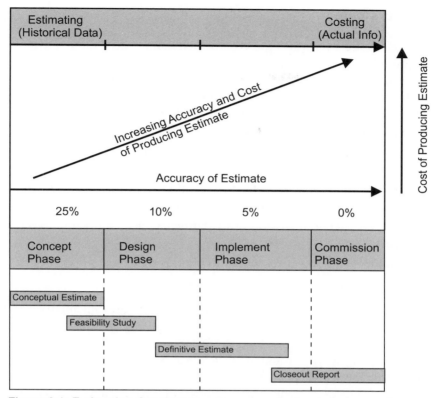

Figure 9.1: Estimating Continuum – shows how the level of accuracy is related to the level of effort and the cost to produce the estimate

1. Direct Costs

For ease of estimating project costs can be subdivided into a number of different categories. Direct costs, as the term implies, are costs which can be clearly identified and assigned to a job. The project management philosophy is to assign as much work as possible to direct costs as direct costs can be individually budgeted and controlled far more effectively and accurately than indirect costs. Consider the following;

- Direct management costs refer to the project manager, project team members and other people working on the project
- Direct labour costs refer to the 'doers' working on an activity
- Direct material costs refer to the material used to complete an activity
- Direct equipment costs refer to the cost of machinery and equipment used to complete an activity
- Direct bought-in expenses refer to the cost of services used directly to complete an activity.

The distinctive nature of direct costs is that the total expense can be charged to a job or project, this is the basis of the management-by-projects approach.

2. Indirect Costs

Indirect costs are overhead type costs which cannot be directly attributed to any particular job or project, but are required to keep the company functioning. Indirect costs are usually financed by an overhead recovery charge which is generally included (or added to) in the labour rate. For example, if your overhead recovery charge is 20% and your labour rate is $50, then the charge out rate will be $50 plus 20% = $60 per hour. Consider the following:

- Indirect management costs refer to head office staff (eg. Personnel, accounts, marketing)
- Indirect labour costs refer to reception staff, maintenance engineers and security guards required to keep the company running
- Indirect material costs refer to stationary, cleaning materials, maintenance parts, etc.
- Indirect equipment costs refer to photocopies and computers, etc.
- Indirect costs also include training and insurance, etc.

Indirect costs are notoriously difficult to manage as they are difficult to estimate (other than from historical costs) and difficult to pin down. They are usually financed through an overhead recovery charge added to the labour rate and if not properly managed they will eat away at your profits. The acid test is to check if it is cheaper to buy an internal company service from an outside contractor. If it is cheaper to outsource say cleaning to an outside company this means the internal indirect cost is either too high or inefficient.

3. Fixed and Variable Costs

Fixed and variable costs relate to how the costs change with the number of products made or services provided. For example, a hotel has fixed costs of rent, labour and certain overheads which are independent to the number of people staying at the hotel. But with each guest certain variable costs will increase - there will be an increase in materials (food), equipment (electricity), transport (to and from airport), and these costs relate directly to the number of people staying at the hotel. In the off season this is a good bargaining point to encourage the hotel to reduce their rates (specials), because anything above the variable costs is a contribution to their fixed costs.

4. Labour Costs

Labour costs are a key component of most jobs. If a labour rate can be added to the estimated number of hours to perform a task, this will simplify the estimating process. Labour costs are generally expressed as so much per hour, or a fixed cost based on an estimated number of hours.

This section will explain how to determine the labour charge-out rate for your company. The labour costs considered here are for the workforce and are, therefore, a direct cost. Although the salaries of your workforce can be clearly identified, there are also a number of other associated costs which form part of the labour rate. The labour rate is calculated by aggregating the various costs and dividing them by the number of hours worked. This process is explained in the following worked example. Here the costs have been subdivided into four main headings:

A. employee's salary	$4000 per month
B. employee's associated labour costs	see below
C. employee's contribution to overheads	25% of salary = $1000
D. employee's contribution to company profit.	25% of salary = $1000

		Costs per month	Days lost per month
B1	Medical insurance	$200	
B2	Sickness benefits		1
B3	Annual holiday		2
B4	Training course	$50	1
B5	Protective clothing	$50	
B6	Car allowance	$400	
B7	Housing allowance	$100	
B8	Subsistence allowance	$100	
B9	Pension	$200	
B10	Tool allowance	$100	
B11	Standing time		1
B12	Inclement weather		1
	Total	$1200	6 days

Table 9.1: Labour Rate

$$\text{Labour rate} = \frac{\text{Total monthly costs (A + B + C + D)}}{\text{Total number of normal working hours per month}}$$

Where the average working month is 21 days, the average days lost per month are 5 days, and eight hours are worked per day.

$$\text{Labour rate} = \frac{4000+1200+1000+1000}{(21 - 6) \times 8} = \$60 \text{ / hour}$$

Some of the above items may be difficult to quantify without access to statistical analysis, for example, days lost due to sickness and standing time, or waiting time. They should, however, be recognised as potential costs and a figure assigned if only as a contribution to an unknown amount. The end product of this analysis should be a labour rate per hour.

As a rule of thumb, the labour rate can be calculated approximately from the worker's wages (which are known). The expenses can be factored into thirds as below:

- 1/3 labour wages (package)
- 1/3 contribution to overheads
- 1/3 company profit.

An even easier way is to see what other companies are charging! You will have to do this anyway to ensure your rates are competitive.

5. Procurement Costs

This section will outline how to determine the cost to procure all the bought-in goods and outsourced services. The simplest method is to add a percentage to the buying price to cover all the procurement costs as an indirect costs. Consider the following table:

Department	Scope of Work	Cost
Design Office	Develop bill of materials (BOM), specifications	$ 1800
Buying Office	Source suppliers, tender cycle, place order	$ 500
Quality Department	Pre-qualify suppliers, receiving inspection	$ 500
Warehouse	Material handing, inventory and stock control	$ 1500
Accounts	Pay invoice	$ 500
Total Costs		$ 4,800

Table 9.2: Procurement Costs

$$\text{Procurement percentage} = \frac{\text{Procurement costs}}{\text{Total cost of materials}} \times 100$$

For example, if the total cost of all the procured items is $50,000 and the cost of running the procurement office is $4,800 as per table 9.2, then the percentage will be as below:

$$\frac{\$4,800}{\$50,000} \times 100 = 9.6\% \text{ (call it 10\%)}$$

Check to ensure none of the above costs are being covered by another budget. For example, the inspection and pre-qualifying of suppliers could fall under the QA budget, in which case, they should not be included here (double accounting). The procurement costs would generally be developed at the company level and apply to all the company's projects.

6. Unit Rates

Although projects tend to be a unique undertaking by definition, the scope of work is usually similar to previous jobs and your company's field of expertise. It is, therefore, expedient to use unit rates for common items of work based on your company's performance on previous projects. This technique estimates a job's cost from an empirically developed tariff of unit rates. For example, consider the following parameters in the table below:

Type of Rate	Type of Work	Unit Rate
Per linear metre	Piping, wiring, welding, textiles	$
Per square metre	Decorating, painting, house building	$
Per cubic metre	Concrete, water supply	$
Per tonne	Ship building, cargo freight	$
Per HP or KW	Power, electrical supply, install a generator	$
Per mile or KM	Transport	$
Per day	Plant hire, car hire	$
Per hour	Labour	$
Per minute	Fashion garment construction	$
Per Mb	Internet download	$

Table 9.3: Unit Rates – shows the relationship between the type of work and the unit rate you can use

Unit rates are probably the most commonly used estimating technique and will form the basis of most estimates because they are easy to measure, easy to budget for and easy to control. Even fixed priced contracts usually contain a unit price clause for charging out additional work.

The automotive industry has moved to unit rates. If you take your car in for a repair or maintenance, the garage should be able to give you a quote based on a national tariff of charges which have been complied by the motor industry in association with labour unions and employers.

7. Estimating Format (top-down / bottom-up)

The final estimate (quotation) is a compilation of figures (costs and expenses) from various sources (see figure 9.4). The left hand column quantifies the scope of work, which can be subdivided into WBS work packages, jobs and checklist. The WBS helps to ensure all the items of work are included in the list.

WBS (work package)	Description	Budget
1000		$
2000		$
3000		$
Project Management fee	Project Management fee (5%)	5%
Sub-Total		$
Profit	10%	10%
Total		$

Table 9.4: Estimating Format – shows the budget per work package

Each job can be further subdivided into labour, material, equipment and transport. By setting up the estimate on a spreadsheet, the amounts can be added horizontally and vertically to give the total cost per work package (job), the total cost for all the labour, material, equipment and transport, and the total cost of the new venture.

WBS	Labour	Material	Machinery	Transport	Total
1000	$5,000	$4,000	$2,000	$1,000	$12,000
2000	$6,000	$3,000	$1,000	$500	$10,500
3000	$9,000	$1,000	$2,000	$500	$12,500
Sub-Total	$20,000	$8,000	$5,000	$2,000	$35,000
Project Office costs (5%)	$1,000	$400	$250	$100	$1,750
Contingencies (10%)	$2,000	$800	$500	$200	$3,500
Total	$23,000	$9,200	$5,750	$2,300	$40,250

Table 9.5: Estimating Format – shows the WBS budgets subdivided into labour, material, machinery and transport

Contingencies: All project work is subjected to risk and uncertainty. It should be a company decision to decide how risk should be accommodated in the estimate. One option is to include it in each WBS work package, another option is to include it as a total figure for the whole project.

Estimating Data Base: A final important word on estimating – your experiences on your current venture can provide valuable estimating information for your future ventures (see project closeout report). Therefore, it is essential to keep an accurate project log book (journal). Project managers who do not analyse the performance of their previous projects are condemned to repeat their history of poor estimates and cost overruns.

Exercises:

1. Using a similar labour rate template as outlined in this chapter, calculate the labour rate for your project.

2. Show how unit rates can be used on your projects.

3. Using the WBS technique developed in the previous chapter, show how top-down and bottom-up estimating apply to your type of projects. The example in the WBS chapter referred to a house building project where it is common to refer to building costs as $x/m2 at the top level, and unit rates $x/m at the lower level.

10

Project Risk Management

Project management and project risk management both strive to achieve the project's objects – but in different ways. Where project management strives to maximise the chances of success, project risk management strives to minimise the chances of failure.

The purpose of this chapter is to provide an outline of project risk and opportunity, and a methodology for reducing risk to an acceptable level while keeping your entrepreneurial spirit alive, and to take advantage of marketable opportunities.

This chapter follows the estimating chapter because the two topics are intimately linked. An estimate is a prediction of the future, and all predictions by definition have inherent risks and uncertainties. The accuracy of the estimate is therefore directly related to the level of risk.

Company success is achieved by pursuing opportunities to gain a competitive advantage. Projects and new ventures are typically setup to take advantage of these opportunities - to make something new, change an existing facility, or respond to market needs. Consequently, risk is an intrinsic part of project management. With increasing market competition, increasing technology and an increasing rate of change, risk management is gaining significance and importance.

1. Risk Management Model

DEFINITION

The PMBOK defines project risk management as; *'....the processes concerned with identifying, analysing and responding to uncertainty* [throughout the project lifecycle]. *It includes maximising the probability and consequences of positive events and minimising the probability and consequences of adverse events to the project objectives'.*

DEFINITION

The APM bok defines project risk as; *'...factors that may cause failure to meet the project's objectives....'* Or limit the achievement of your objectives as defined at the outset of the project.

A project risk may be defined as any event that prevents or limits the achievement of your objectives as defined at the outset of the project. These objectives may be revised and changed as the project progresses through the project lifecycle. The generally accepted risk management model subdivides the risk management process into the following headings (see figure 10.1):

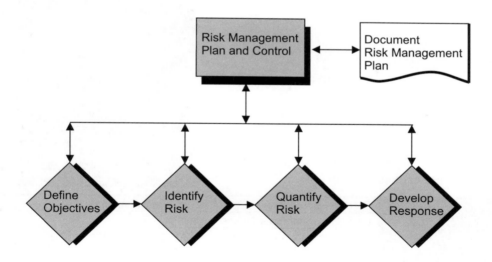

Figure 10.1: Risk Management Model – shows the main components of risk management

Risk management model components:

Define Objectives	The project's objectives define the goals and objectives the project sets out to achieve. A WBS can be used to define objectives at the work package level.
Identify Risk	Identify areas of risk, uncertainty and constraints which may impact on your project and limit or prevent you achieving your objectives.
Quantify Risk	Evaluate the risks and prioritize the level of risk and uncertainty and quantify their frequency of occurrence and impact on the objectives.
Develop Response	Define how you are going to respond to the identified risks - the response could be a combination of; eliminate, mitigate, deflect or accept.
Risk Management Plan	The APM bok defines the risk management plan as; *'....a formal approach to the process as opposed to an intuitive approach....'* The risk management plan documents how you propose to identify and respond to risk on your project.
Risk Control	The risk control function implements the risk management plan. This may involve in-house training and communication to the other stakeholders. As the risks and the work environment are continually changing, it is essential to constantly monitor and review the level of risk and the project manager's ability to respond effectively.

Photo: A fashion designer creates her latest collection (Northumbria University)

For example, on a fashion project the following risk management headings may include:

Define Objectives	Produce a new range of garments for the winter season.
Identify Risk	Late delivery of material and trimmings.
Quantify Risk	New garments must be delivered to the shops by mid February (northern hemisphere) for the spring/summer season. Late delivery will result in missed sales, even the rejection of the complete range.
Develop Response	Monitor progress, and be prepared to use locally available material and trimmings, air freight material and trimmings if coming from overseas, fast track the production.
Risk Management Plan	Document how you propose to identify and respond to the delivery risk and keep stakeholders informed.
Risk Control	Monitor procurement schedule and establish contingencies.

2. Define Objectives

A risk may be defined as any event or situation that prevents you achieving the project's goals and objectives. It is, therefore, necessary at the outset to define these goals and objectives in some detail. This is best achieved through a work breakdown structure.

Project:			
Complied By:			Date:
WBS	Description	Exclusion	Objectives
1.1	Paint structure	Paint owner supply	Paint to manufacturer's requirements (usually shown on side of paint tin)
1.2	Cook dinner	Washing up	Follow Gordon Ramsey's recipe
1.3	Promote new product	Posters	Generate 10% increase in business

Table 10.1: Objectives by WBS – shows objectives at the work package level

3. Risk Identification

Having defined the project's objectives, the next step is to identify the risks and uncertainties that could prevent you achieving these stated objectives. Risk identification is probably the hardest skill to achieve. Yet, risk identification is one of the most important parts of the risk management process, because, if you cannot identify a risk it will be excluded from further analysis and, therefore, you will probably not respond to it.

The process of risk identification should not be a one time event, but rather a continuous process, its frequency depending on the level of risk on the project and the schedule of the progress meetings.

Using your list of objectives as your starting point, add another column for risk.

Project:			
Complied By:			Date:
WBS	Description	Objectives	Risk
1.1	Paint structure	Paint to manufacturer's requirements (usually shown on side of paint tin)	Paint does not cure
1.2	Cook dinner	Follow Gordon Ramsey's recipe	Food not prepared on time
1.3	Promote new product	Generate 10% increase in business	Competitors product takes market share

Table 10.2: Risk Identification - shows the link between the WBS, objectives and risk

Why Projects Fail: Historically, one of the main reasons for developing project management techniques was to address the high rate of project failure. Listed below are some of the problem areas identified from previous closeout reports.

Topic	Problem
Client	The client was dealing with too many managers – the solution is to deal with only one key person – the project manager.
Feasibility Study	Products were built before being tested, build-method was not thought through - the solution is to design and test before implementation.
Scope	Unclear scope of work, unclear objectives, mixed and confusing tasks, specifications and approvals.
WBS	WBS not developed sufficiently to produce a complete list of manageable work packages and checklists. Project had no structure to control the scope of work.
Cost	Budgets not defined which led to uncontrollable expenditure.
Time	Poor time estimating and schedules not defined which led to insufficient time allowed to complete the work.
Procurement	Long lead items were ordered late which meant the items arrived late and delayed the associated activities.
Resources	Insufficient resources at peak loads caused resource overloads which delayed the planned completion.
Quality	Quality not defined led to unsatisfactory work, disputes and rework.
Leadership	No single project leader, instead, a number of functional leaders working independently.
OBS	Work was passed from one functional department to another – no one co-ordinating the work.
Team Work	No team leader led to interpersonal conflict.
Communication	Unclear lines of communication, documents not controlled which resulted in workers using old revisions.
Instructions	Verbal instructions (not backed up in writing) which led to misunderstandings.
Progress	Poor monitoring and tracking of progress which led to lack of progress and the product finished late.
Stakeholders	Disagreement among stakeholders regarding the expectations for the project which led to dissatisfaction and unsatisfactory end results.
Operators	Lack of user involvement which led to a product which was difficult to operate.

Table 10.3: Why Projects Fail – shows risks identified from previous project's closeout reports

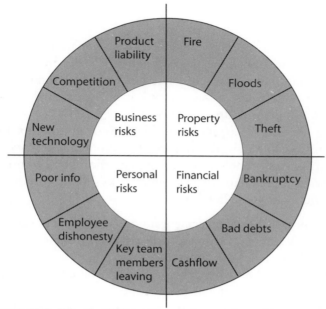

Figure 10.2: Wheel of Misfortune - source adapted from Longenecker.
Besides project risks there are a whole range of other risks to consider

Questionnaires, interviews and brainstorming are all ways to generate ideas and feedback from your colleagues, stakeholders, clients, engineers, suppliers, legal eagles and governing agencies. Checklists, breakdown structures and flow charts (CPM) are all ways to group and subdivide information for collation and presentation.

Risk identification should be a systematic process to ensure nothing significant is over looked. Techniques for identifying risk include:

- analysing historical records (closeout reports) (see the *Scope Management* chapter)
- structured questionnaires
- structured interviews
- brainstorming
- structured checklists (see the *WBS* chapter)
- flow charts (build-method, walk-through)
- judgment based on knowledge and experience
- system analysis
- scenario analysis (what-if).

The success of these techniques depends on how the risk management team have been selected and brought together. A balanced team which incorporates; experience, knowledge, judgment, internal members and external consultants, stands the best chance of success.

Experience: The university of life gives us the experience to help identify areas of risk, particularly the problems and situations experienced or observed in the past. Greater awareness and appreciation is followed by knowledge and judgment.

4. Risk Quantification

Having identified a range of risks, the next step is to quantify the probability of the risk occurring and the likely impact or consequence to the project, or the amount at stake. Risk quantification is primarily concerned with determining what areas of risk warrant a response and where resources are limited - a risk priority will identify the areas of risk that should be addressed first.

Quantifying risks sounds great on paper, but it is often very difficult in practice to put an exact number to a risk. To overcome this problem start by ranking the risks (high / medium / low risk), and see if that highlights the high risk work packages. With finite resources it is essential to establish which risks should be addressed first so you can prioritize and focus your efforts.

Perception: The project risk management model is based on the assumption that we are able to accurately identify and quantify the risks and are able to adequately respond to the risks - and here-in lies the problem.

When we identify and quantify a risk it is usually based on our perception of the risk - and this can vary from person to person, and further can vary within each person from time to time. This is because our perception of risk changes with our experience and knowledge of the situation. It is further influenced by the amount of information and the accuracy of the information we have on the situation, and by the time we have to consider all the trade-offs and make the decision.

If you are performing a job for the first time, for example, manoeuvring a yacht into a marina berth, you are, naturally, going to air on the cautious side. Whereas, someone who is doing the job everyday would consider it routine. The person's experience and knowledge of the job, as in this example, will obviously influence their perception of the risk.

Photo: "All hands on deck" - the dockmaster/expert manoeuvres a yacht in a busy marina - his perception of the manoeuvre is one of low risk, while the yacht owner's perception is one of high risk!

This attitude to risk can be shown on the risk perception scale (figure 10.3). If the real inherent risk is in the middle of the scale, then someone who is risk adverse might perceive the risk as being far greater than the actual risk. While an overconfident, risk positive person might underestimate the actual risk. So with these two extreme perceptions of the same risk, their individual responses are likely to be very different.

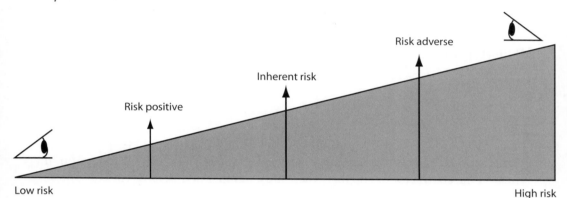

Figure 10.3: Perception Scale – shows how risk perception influences the response

5. Risk Response

Having identified, quantified and prioritized the risks, you now need to develop a risk response plan which defines ways to address adverse risk and enhance opportunities before they occur. There are a range of responses which should be developed in advance during the planning phase:

- Eliminate risk
- Mitigate risk (reduce)
- Deflect risk
- Accept risk

These are not mutually exclusive - your response may use a combination of them all. A natural sequence would be to first try and eliminate the risk completely - failing that, at least mitigate it. And, for the remaining risks, the options are to try and deflect and / or accept the risk with a contingency. Responses cost money, so a cost-benefit analysis should be performed as it may be more cost effective to accept a risk rather than taking expensive steps to eliminate it.

Eliminating Risk: Looks into ways of avoiding the risk completely by either removing the cause or taking an alternative course of action. This should initially be considered during the concept and design phases, where the level of influence is high and the cost to change is low (see the *Project Lifecycle* chapter).

Mitigating Risk: To mitigate a risk means reducing the risk's probability and impact. This could be achieved by using proven technology and standards to ensure the product will work. Developing prototypes, simulating and model testing are three methods which share the notion of using a representation to investigate selected aspects of requirements in order to be more certain of the outcome or suitability. A prototype is a working mock-up of areas under investigation in order to test its acceptance, and a model is a miniature representation of physical relationships (often used in car and ship design).

Deflecting Risk: Deflecting a risk transfers the risk in part or whole to another party. This can be achieved through:

- Contracting
- Retention
- Performance bonds
- Insurance.

Contracting: Project contracts are a means of deflecting risk, usually away from the client to the contractor or supplier. There are a number of different types of contracts used - consider the following;

- Fixed price contract
- Cost plus contract
- Unit rates contract
- Turnkey contract
- BOOT contract

These are developed in *Project Management - Planning and Control Techniques* (Burke)

Retention: Retention is when the client retains a percentage of the contractor's income against the contractor failing to complete their contractual obligations. The retention is usually 10% of the monthly payments until it reaches 5% of the contract value and then held until the end of the warranty period.

Bonds: Instead of retention, contractors often offer their clients a performance bond through a large organisation (usually a bank). The bond could be held against lack of performance or poor quality of work. If the contractor fails to perform, the client is compensated by the bond company, who in turn will take agreed assets from the contractor to cover the bond. Some contractors prefer this arrangement to retention, as they are paid their progress claims in full, thus improving their cashflow.

Insurance: A third party (usually an insurance company) accepts insurable risks in exchange for the payment of a premium. The premium is now the quantified impact of this risk on the project. Insurance could cover:

- Direct property damage
- Indirect consequential loss (business interruption)
- Legal liability
- Personnel liability.

Acceptance: Here you accept the consequence of a risk occurring, also called self-insurance. However, you may develop a contingency plan to protect your business from the risk event happening. A contingency plan defines actions you will take ahead of time - if 'A' happens we will do 'B'. For example, when planning a delivery, if there is an accident on route 'A' you can use route 'B' instead. Also, just in case your backed-up files at the office get damaged, you can keep a separate set of files offsite. The contingency plan could be established for:

- Minor internal design changes
- Underestimating BOM (Build, Operate, Make), procurement and resources
- Lack of experience (history, knowledge, judgment)
- Unexpected procurement price changes
- Correcting some erroneous assumptions
- Scope - insufficient detail resulting in changes
- Construction, implementing and commissioning problems that lead to schedule delays
- Unforeseen regulations.

A summary table should be developed to gather together all the identified risks and show how you intend to respond (see table 10.4 below).

Project:				
Compiled By:				
WBS	Description	Objectives	Risk	Response
100	Project documents	Safe keeping	Fire	Back-up and store off site
200	Production	Meet schedule	No resources	Approach list of contractors
300	Sales	Meet sales plan	Competition	Reduce prices

Table 10.4: Risk Response – shows the response to identified risks

Risk Management Plan: The risk management plan, documents the output from the previous sections;

- State objectives
- Identify risks
- Quantify risks
- Respond to risks

The risk management plan assigns responsibility for implementation of the plan. The next section on risk control implements the risk management plan to create a working document.

6. Risk Control

The risk control function implements the risk management plan and makes it happen – surprisingly this part of risk management is often neglected by the project team! The risk management plan needs to be communicated to all the project participants and, where necessary, followed up with appropriate training and practice runs. The training should not only ensure that the risk management plan is understood but also develop a company wide risk management culture and attitude.

The risk management plan should be monitored and updated on a regular basis to incorporate changes in the project.

WBS	Objectives	Risk	Respond	Control
100	Data file protection	Risk losing the data files	Back-up data files	Check the data files have been backed-up daily
200				
300				

Table 10.5: Risk Control – shows how the risks will be controlled

"....as I was saying, I've got a good book on risk management......oh**!!?...."

Exercise:

1. Discuss the consequences of not using a project management approach to managing projects.

2. Explain how you identify and quantify project risks that could prevent you from achieving your objectives.

3. Discuss the range of response options you have to reduce project risk.

11

Critical Path Method

Learning Outcomes

After reading this chapter, you should be able to;

Draw a network diagram

Calculate CPM start and finish dates

Identify the critical path

If a project is simple and straight forward, then a Gantt chart with periodic updating should be sufficient to plan and control your project. But as projects become more complex with a large number of participants and inter-dependencies, then you need to move to a more structured network diagram presentation and CPM calculation to identify the critical path.

Critical Path Method (CPM) is considered by many as one of the corner stones of project management scheduling (outlining what and when). The CPM will enable the project manager to juggle with an increasing number of variables. The CPM offers a structured approach to present the sequence of the activities in a network diagram and tabular format.

The reason the CPM's iconic features are so important is because it identifies and presents the logical relationship between the project's activities, and further identifies the critical activities that determine the duration of the project. These critical activities are so named because if any of these critical activities are delayed it will extend the end date of the project, and further, if any of these critical activities are reduced it will shorten the duration of the project. It is these critical activities which give this technique its name – the **critical path.**

This chapter will outline the techniques and practical applications of CPM, taking you step-by-step through the planning stages from developing the network diagram through to establishing the critical path.

The work breakdown structure (WBS), which was discussed in a previous chapter, provides a structured breakdown of the work or jobs into a number of manageable work packages. These work packages can be further subdivided into a list of activities. The next process is to establish a logical relationship between these activities using a network diagram.

1. Network Diagram

The network diagram may be defined as a graphical presentation of the project's activities showing the planned sequence of work. To draw the network diagram and perform the CPM calculation you need the following items of information:

- List of activities (developed from the WBS)
- Activity duration
- Calendar or work pattern
- Start date
- Logic relationships between the activities

The network diagram, also called precedence diagram method (PDM), is a development of the activity-on-node (AON) technique.

2. Definition of an Activity

An activity may be defined as any task, job or operation that must be performed to complete the work package or project. A WBS work package can be subdivided into one or more activities (also called tasks, work and job). In the network diagram an activity is always presented in a box with an identity number and description. The activity should be given a description to ensure the project team members understand the work content - this can be expanded later in a job card.

The characteristics of an activity include the following:

Number	An activity must have a unique activity code or number (A, or 010, or ABC100). The code may be alpha, numeric or alphanumeric.
Description	An activity must have a description. The description should be as informative and clear as possible.
Logic	There will be logical relationships between the activities, either in series or parallel.
Duration	All activities have a time duration for completing the task, even if it is zero.
Calendar	All activities have a calendar or work pattern to indicate when the work can be scheduled, even if it is seven days a week (continuous working).
Target Date	The activity can have target start and target finish dates assigned. Certainly a start date for the first activity is required.
Procurement	An activity may require materials and services to be procured. By linking these materials to an activity their delivery date can be established to produce a procurement schedule.
Resources	An activity may require resources. By linking these resources to an activity they can be scheduled to produce a resource histogram.
Costs	An activity may incur costs. By linking these costs to an activity they can be scheduled to produce a cashflow statement.
S Curve	When resources and costs are linked to the activities they can be integrated to generate a manpower S curve and the expenditure S curve respectively. These are required for the earned value calculation.

Table 11.1: Activity Description - shows a number of activity characteristics

3. Logical Relationships

The network diagram shows the sequence of the activities. There are two basic relationships:

- Activities in **series**
- Activities in **parallel**.

Activities in Series: When the activities are in series they are carried out one after the other. When the network diagram is first developed this will probably be the most common type of logical relationship. An example of activities performed in series on a decoration project would be the surface preparation (activity 100), followed by painting the undercoat (200), followed by painting the top coat (300). You read the network diagram as you would a page of writing, from left to right (see figure 11.1).

Figure 11.1: Activities in Series – shows activities happening consecutively

Activities in Parallel: When activities are in parallel the activities can be performed at the same time, which is a more efficient use of time than activities in series. An example on a decoration project would be the painting of the bedroom (activity 2000) and the painting of the dinning room (activity 3000) simultaneously after the surface preparation (activity 1000), and followed by the replacement of the furniture (activity 4000) (see figure 11.2).

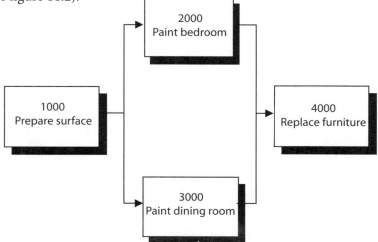

Figure 11.2: Activities in Parallel – shows activities happening at the same time

4. How to Draw the Logical Relationships

The terms logical relationship, constraint, dependency and link are all used interchangeably to represent the lines drawn between the activity boxes. The preferred presentation shows the constraint lines drawn from left to right, starting from the right side of one activity box into the left side of the following box. However, many software packages have the lines drawn from the top and bottom of the boxes. Initially an arrow at the end of the constraint may help you to follow the direction of work flow.

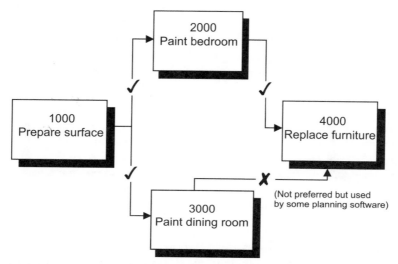

Figure 11.3: How to Draw Activity Constraints – shows the preferred presentation

Activity Box: The activity box key indicates where to position the values in the activity box. This layout varies with the software package, but the format in figure 11.4 will be used throughout this book.

EARLY START		EARLY FINISH
FLOAT	ACTIVITY NUMBER DESCRIPTION	DURATION
LATE START		LATE FINISH

Figure 11.4: Activity Box - shows the position of the values in the box

5. Activity Duration

We need three more items of information before we can proceed with the CPM time analysis:

- Activity duration
- Activity calendar or work pattern
- Activity logic.

An activity's duration will run from the start to the finish of the activity. An activity's duration is linked to resources - increasing the resources will obviously shorten the duration. At this point certain assumptions will have to be made and adjusted later. Time units can be expressed as hours, days, weeks, months, or shifts depending on the length of the activities and the project. For simplicity, the time units used in this book will be days (unless otherwise stated).

6. Definition of an Event

An event may be defined as an activity with zero duration – it is a point in time. An event, also called a **keydate** or a **milestone** represents a happening on a particular day. This could be when the order is placed, the start of the project, or the day the materials are received.

Many project managers prefer to manage their projects by setting milestones. This effectively pushes the planning and control down a level and empowers the team members. For example, the project manager may issue the instruction that an activity must be finished by Friday 10th June. The team members must now do their planning at their level, working back to achieve that completion date.

The whole project itself may be leading up to an event. For example, a wedding, a concert, a sporting fixture – in these cases the project is to prepare for the event. (Events are discussed in the *Gantt Charts* chapter).

7. Calendar / Work Pattern

Calendar or **work pattern** are common terms used by the planning software to describe an activity's working profile, in other words, on what days of the week the resources or activity will be working. As a first step we will assume the activity is working seven days a week - this is usually termed **continuous** working.

8. Activity Logic

The activity logic presents the sequence of the activities. For ease of reading, the logic information is often compiled in a tabular format, with each record (or line) defining a logical relationship. Planning software usually expresses the activity logic by stating the preceding activity. From the information in the 'preceding activity' column you can draw the network diagram (or vice versa).

Painting Example: This section will continue with the house extension example. Taking the list of activities developed in the WBS chapter (figure 8.11) as the scope of work, begin by drawing activity 100 (the start activity) to the left hand side of the page, then add the other activities as per the preceding activity column. In the activity boxes include the activity number and duration as per the position outlined in the key.

Activity	Description	Duration	Preceding Activity
100	Remove furniture	2	Start
200	Paint downstairs, prep / undercoat	3	100
300	Paint downstairs, top coat	3	200
400	Paint upstairs prep / undercoat	2	100
500	Paint upstairs, top coat	2	400
600	Replace furniture	2	300, 500

Table 11.2: Activity Table – shows activity description, duration and logic

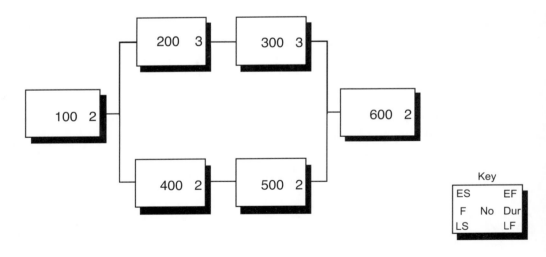

Figure 11.5: Network Diagram - shows the activities' logic presented graphically

9. Critical Path Method Steps

We are now ready to perform the CPM time analysis to establish the start and finish dates for all the activities. Before we do, let us first recap on the CPM steps we have outlined:

- Draw the logic network diagram
- Assign durations to all the activities
- Impose a work calendar.

In addition to the logic table, an activity table would include the following headings:

Start Date	We need to give the project a start date (this can always be changed later). The CPM analysis needs a start date from which to schedule the work. If no date is given the planning software would use the current date as the default option. By setting the start date the first iteration will give the planner a feel for the end date of the project using the given logic, activity duration and calendar. If a target completion date is given, the above parameters (logic, duration, calendar and start date), can be adjusted accordingly.
Early Start	The early start date is the earliest date by which an activity can start assuming all the preceding activities are completed as planned.
Early Finish	The early finish date is the earliest date by which an activity can be completed assuming all the preceding activities are completed as planned.
Late Start	The late start date is the latest date an activity can start to meet the planned completion date.
Late Finish	The late finish date is the latest date an activity can finish to meet the planned completion date.
Target Start	The date work is planned to start.
Target Finish	The date work is planned to finish.

Table 11.3: Activity Table

Target Start and Target Finish: In addition to the calculated dates there may be a number of imposed dates, influenced by the delivery of materials, access to work areas, availability of sub-contractors, or other milestones.

10. Forward Pass

We use the term forward pass to define the process of calculating the early start date (ES) and early finish date (EF) for all the activities. For convenience the early start date of the first activity in all the examples will be Monday the first day of the month (i.e. 1st May).

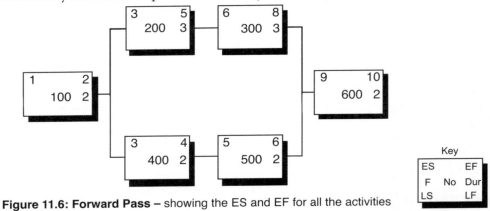

Figure 11.6: Forward Pass – showing the ES and EF for all the activities

For the painting project beginning with activity (100), add the early start date (ES) of 1 (Monday). The early finish date of an activity is calculated by adding the activity duration to the early start date, using the following formula.

$$EF = ES + Duration - 1$$
$$EF\ (100) = 1 + 2 - 1 \quad = 2\ (Tuesday)$$

In the equation the minus one is required to keep the mathematics correct. The Gantt chart in figure 11.7 will clarify this requirement. Shown as a Gantt chart it can be clearly seen that a two day activity that starts on day 1 (Monday) will finish on day 2 (Tuesday). To calculate the early start date (ES) of activity 200 use the following formula.

$$ES\ (200) = EF\ (100) + 1$$
$$= 2 + 1 \quad = 3\ (Wednesday)$$

Activity (200) can only start the day after Activity (100) has finished. Continue through the project calculating ES and EF. When there are two or more activities preceding an activity, for example, 300 and 500 precede 600, then select the activity with the latest EF to calculate the ES of the following activity.

Figure 11.7:
Early Start
Gantt Chart

Activity Number	Mon 1	Tue 2	Wed 3	Thu 4	Fri 5	Sat 6	Sun 7	Mon 8	Tue 9	Wed 10
100	▬▬									
200			▬▬▬▬							
300						▬▬▬				
400			▬▬							
500					▬▬					
600									▬▬	

11. Backward Pass

Now that we have completed the forward pass the next step is to perform a backward pass to calculate the late start date (LS) and late finish date (LF) of each activity. The late finish date for the last activity may be assigned, if not, use the early finish date of the last activity (see figure 11.8).

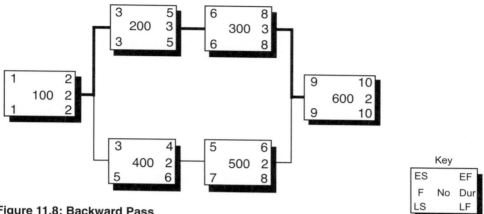

Figure 11.8: Backward Pass

Key

ES		EF
F	No	Dur
LS		LF

$$LF\ (600) = EF(\ 600) = 10\ (Wednesday)$$

To calculate the late start date (LS) of activity 600 use the following formula:

$$LS\ (600) = LF\ (600) - Duration\ (600) + 1$$
$$= 10 - 2 + 1 = 9\ (Tuesday)$$

Note the plus one in the formula to keep the mathematics correct. This can be clearly seen on the LS Gantt Chart (figure 11.9)

$$LF\ (500) = LS\ (500) - 1$$
$$= 9 - 1 = 8\ (Monday)$$
$$LS\ (400) = LF\ (400) - Duration\ (400) + 1$$
$$= 8 - 2 + 1 = 7\ (Thursday)$$

Continue through the project calculating the LS and LF. When there are more than one activity leading into an activity, as 200 and 400 lead into 100, then select the lowest LS to calculate the LF of the previous activity.

Figure 11.9: Late Start Gantt Chart

Activity Number	Mon 1	Tue 2	Wed 3	Thu 4	Fri 5	Sat 6	Sun 7	Mon 8	Tue 9	Wed 10
100	▬	▬								
200			▬	▬	▬					
300							▬	▬		
400				▬	▬					
500								▬		
600									▬	

12. Activity Float

Activity float, also called slack, is a measure of flexibility, or inherent surplus time in an activity's scheduling. This indicates how many working days the activity can be delayed or extended before it will impact on the next activity and extend the completion date of the project or any target finish dates (milestones). Float is calculated as:

Float = Late Start - Early Start

From the painting project:

Float (100) = LS (100) - ES(100)

= 1 - 1

= 0

Float (200) = LS (200) – ES (200)

= 3 – 3 = 0

Float (400) = LS (400) – LS (400)

= 5 – 3 - 2

Continue calculating the float for each activity and add the value to the activity box as per the key. Note activities (100, 200, 300 and 600) all have zero float, this means they are on the **critical path.** If any of these activities are delayed it will delay the whole project. Meanwhile the other activities (400 and 500) have 2 days float, so these activities could be delayed 2 days before impacting on the end date of the project. The data from the CPM float network diagram (figure 11.10) can be presented in a Gantt chart (figure 11.11) which shows the early start, late start and float information.

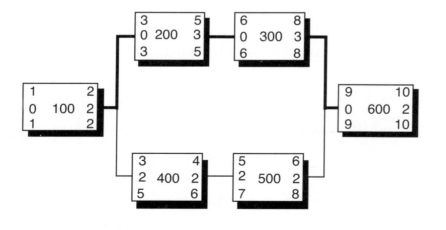

Figure 11.10: CPM Float

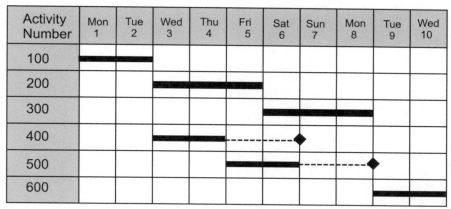

Figure 11.11: Network Diagram Showing Float – the activities with zero float are joined up to show the critical path

This completes the *CPM* chapter, the following chapter will discuss *Gantt Charts* as a methodology for communicating schedule information.

Exercises:

1. Discuss the purpose and benefits of the CPM calculation in a project environment.

2. Calculate the following network diagram (see appendix 1 for solution)

Activity	Duration	Logic
100	1	Start
200	2	100
300	4	100
400	3	200
500	2	300
600	2	400, 500

Table 11.4: Activity Table - Exercise 2

3. Calculate the following network diagram (see appendix 1 for solution)

Activity	Duration	Logic
100	2	Start
200	6	100
300	2	100
400	2	300
500	3	200, 400

Table 11.5: Activity Table - Exercise 3

12

Gantt Charts

Learning Outcomes

After reading this chapter, you should be able to;

Produce a Gantt chart for your project

Produce a milestone chart for your project

Produce a hammock activity for your project

The Gantt chart is one of the most popular and widely used planning and control documents for communicating schedule information. It was originally designed before the first World War by an American, Henry Gantt, who used it as a visual aid for planning and controlling his shipbuilding projects. In recognition, planning barcharts often bear his name – and are called Gantt charts.

The Gantt chart is widely used on projects because it provides an effective presentation which is not only easy to understand and assimilate, but also conveys scheduling information and instructions accurately and precisely.

The Gantt chart can either be developed on its own for a simple project, or linked to the critical path method (see the *CPM* chapter) to present the schedule of a complex network diagram. Either way the scheduled Gantt chart must be developed as a timeline for other techniques which include; procurement schedule, resource histogram and the cashflow statement.

The project manager and team leader are responsible for producing the Gantt chart as a planning and control, and instruction document. It is essential that the team members understand the Gantt chart's content and purpose. The team members can also use the Gantt chart to record their progress and give short term planning with a rolling horizon Gantt chart.

1. How to Draw a Gantt Chart

The Gantt chart (figure 12.1) lists the scope of work as WBS work packages or activities in the left hand column [1}, against a time scale along the top of the page [2]. The scheduling of each activity is represented by a horizontal line or bar, from the activity's start date [3] to finish date [4]. The length of the activity line is proportional to its estimated duration. Consider the following list of activity data from a garage building project (table 12.1):

Activity Number	Activity Description	Duration	Start Date	Finish Date
1000	Lay Garage Foundations	4 Days	1 May	4 May
2000	Build Garage Walls	5 Days	5 May	9 May
3000	Fit Garage Roof	4 Days	10 May	13 May
4000	Install Garage Doors	2 Days	14 May	15 May

Table 12.1: Activity Data – shows a garage building project

The calendar time scale is usually presented in days or weeks, but hours, months and years are also possible. The examples here will use days (see figure 12.1).

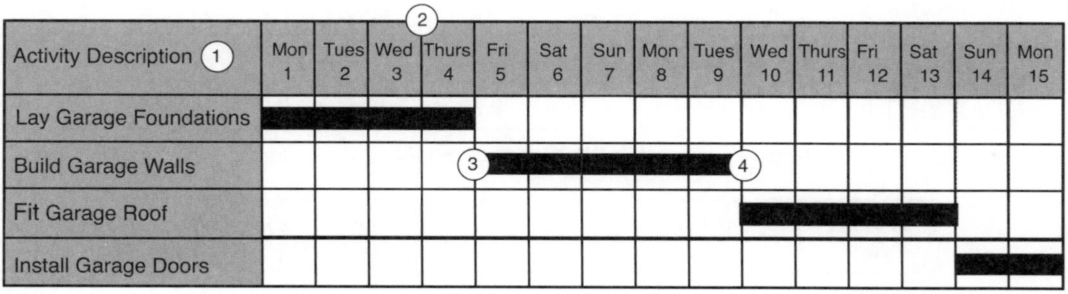

Activity Description (1)	Mon 1	Tues 2	Wed 3	Thurs 4	Fri 5	Sat 6	Sun 7	Mon 8	Tues 9	Wed 10	Thurs 11	Fri 12	Sat 13	Sun 14	Mon 15
Lay Garage Foundations	██	██	██	██											
Build Garage Walls					██ (3)	██	██	██	██ (4)						
Fit Garage Roof										██	██	██	██		
Install Garage Doors														██	██

Figure 12.1: Simple Gantt Chart – shows a garage building project

Although the Gantt chart looks like a simple document, it does contain a wealth of information. For example, the list of activities and sequence (logic) will have been defined and gathered from the technical experts and the project manager's own field of expertise. The durations start and finish dates of the activities imply knowledge or assumption of procurement delivery dates, resource loading, resource availability, funds availability and cashflow.

2. Tabular Reports

Tabular reports provide an important link between the CPM time analysis and the Gantt chart. On complex projects it is essential to develop the WBS and CPM before the Gantt chart, as the CPM is the best document to establish the logical sequence of work. Table 12.2 is the output from the CPM example (figure 11.10) in the *CPM* chapter, with its corresponding Gantt chart (see figure 12.3). Tabular reports provide an excellent structure to store and present project information.

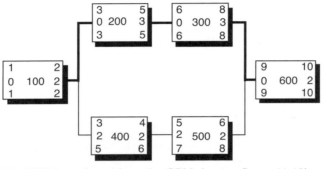

Figure 12.2: CPM (transferred from the *CPM* chapter, figure 11.10)

Activity Number	Duration	Early Start	Early Finish	Late Start	Late Finish	Float	Responsibility
100	2	1 May	2 May	1 May	2 May	0	Glynn
200	3	3 May	5 May	3 May	5 May	0	Warren
300	3	6 May	8 May	6 May	8 May	0	Jan
400	2	3 May	4 May	5 May	6 May	2	Jim
500	2	5 May	6 May	7 May	8 May	2	Tony
600	2	9 May	10 May	9 May	10 May	0	Trish

Table 12.2: Tabular Report - shows the CPM values in figure 12.2 transferred into a tabular report

Activity Number	Mon 1	Tue 2	Wed 3	Thu 4	Fri 5	Sat 6	Sun 7	Mon 8	Tue 9	Wed 10
100	███	███								
200			███	███	███					
300						███	███	███		
400			███	███						
500					███	███				
600									███	███

Figure 12.3: Gantt Chart - shows the CPM and tabular report transferred into a Gantt chart

3. Activity Float

The Gantt chart presentation can also show the activity float (figures 12.4 and 12.5). The accepted presentation is to show the float at the end of the activity from early finish (EF) to late finish (LF), and denote it as a dotted line with a symbol at the end (usually a diamond or an upturned triangle).

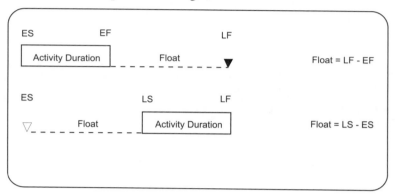

Figure 12.4: Activity Float – shows how the float can be presented before or after the activity

By implication it may be assumed that any activity without float is on the critical path. However, in practice planners are reluctant to show float as it is only human nature for people to delay work to their late finish making all the activities critical. It is better to try and make everyone start at the early start date (ES) and keep the float as a contingency.

Activity Number	Mon 1	Tue 2	Wed 3	Thu 4	Fri 5	Sat 6	Sun 7	Mon 8	Tue 9	Wed 10
100	▬	▬								
200			▬	▬	▬					
300						▬	▬			
400			▬	▬	-	-	◆			
500					▬	▬	-	-	◆	
600									▬	▬

Figure 12.5: Gantt Chart - shows the float after the activity

4. Hammocks

A hammock or summary activity is used to gather together a number of sub-activities into one master activity. This is a useful technique for layering or rolling-up the planning presentation. The hammock activities need to be documented at a suitable level of detail to support the included planning activities. Consider the garage building project from the beginning of this chapter. Table 12.3 and figure 12.6 shows how the first activity 1000 (lay the garage foundation) can be subdivided into three tasks; mark out the foundations, dig the foundations and throw the concrete.

Activity Number	Activity Description	Duration	Start Date	Finish date
1000	Lay Garage Foundation	4 days	1 May	4 May
1001	Mark out garage foundation	1 day	1 May	1 May
1002	Dig foundation	2 days	2 May	3 May
1003	Throw concrete	1 day	4 May	4 May
2000	Build garage walls	5 days	5 May	9 May
3000	Fit garage roof	4 days	10 May	13 May
4000	Install garage doors	2 days	14 May	15 May

Table 12.3: Hammock Activities – shows the included sub-activities

With hammock activities the Gantt chart can now be presented at the appropriate level of detail - less detail for the senior managers who just want the overall picture of the project, but more detail for the people at the coalface carrying out the work. This ability to vary the level of detail is a fundamental feature of project planning and control.

Activity Description	Mon 1	Tues 2	Wed 3	Thurs 4	Fri 5	Sat 6	Sun 7	Mon 8	Tues 9	Wed 10	Thurs 11	Fri 12	Sat 13	Sun 14	Mon 15
Lay Garage Foundations	████	████	████	████											
Mark out garage	▭														
Dig foundation		▭	▭												
Throw concrete				▭											
Build Garage Walls						████	████	████	████	████					
Fit Garage Roof										████	████	████	████		
Install Garage Doors														████	████

Figure 12.6: Hammock Gantt Chart – shows the hammock bar drawn from the start of the earliest activity to the end of the latest included activity

5. Events, Keydates and Milestones

The principle difference between an activity and an event is that an event has zero duration - it is a point in time. An event, also called keydate or milestone represents a happening on a particular day, this could be when the order is placed, the plans are approved, goods are received or even the start and finish dates of an activity. Consider the following characteristics:

No Duration	An event has no duration, it is a point in time. In Microsoft Project, for example an event is an activity with zero duration and would appear on the screen as a diamond symbol.
Start or Finish	An event may be the start or finish of an activity, WBS work package, project phase or the project itself.
Checkpoint	An event focuses the project on a checkpoint, a major accomplishment, a deliverable result, a stage payment or an approval to proceed.
Interface	An event could be the interface between trades or contractors as one hands over to another.
Data Capture	Data capture will be more accurate if the scope of work is subdivided into milestones.

An example of an event would be the award of contract (see table 12.4).

Event Number	1000
Description	Quality Hold Point
Budget	Nil
Duration	0 Days
Resources	Nil

Table 12.4: Event Characteristics (award of contract)

Managing events, or management-by-events gives a clear focus on when work must be completed and hence a clear measure of progress. Using plenty of milestones pushes the planning down to an appropriate level and empowers the team members. Consider changing figure 12.3 with the start and finish of each activity as an event shown in figure 12.7. This would empower the supervisor to manage their resources to meet these keydates.

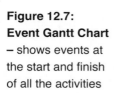

Figure 12.7:
Event Gantt Chart
– shows events at the start and finish of all the activities

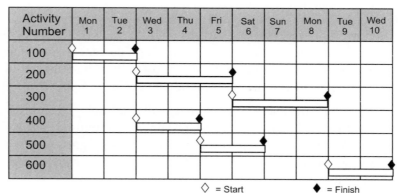

The milestone schedule offers another type of planning presentation which can be used on its own or in conjunction with a scheduled Gantt chart.

6. Revised Gantt Chart

The Gantt chart was originally designed as a planning and control tool where the actual progress was marked up against the original plan. This progress bar can be drawn above, inside or underneath the original bar. This way the project manager can see at a glance how each activity is progressing and where control may be required to guide the project to completion.

Baseline Plan: For effective control the project's baseline plan must be frozen - accepting only approved changes. Without a baseline plan it would be difficult to calculate progress variances and control would be lost.

Data Capture: To draw the revised Gantt chart the planner needs to capture progress information. This can be achieved by setting-up a progress reporting sheet - consider the following (table 12.5):

Project:		Report Date:					
Complied By:							
WBS	**Activity Number**	**Description**	**Start Date**	**Finish Date**	**Percentage Complete**	**Remaining Duration**	
	1000		1 May		50%	2 Days	
	2000				0%		
	3000		1 May		75%	1 day	
	4000				0%		
	5000		1 May		25%	3 days	
	6000				0%		

Table 12.5: Data Capture Template

The progress report should start with the reporting date or timenow. The progress should be reported against a WBS number or an activity number. The start and finish dates are important milestones which clearly state if the activity has started and if the activity has finished.

To draw the revised Gantt chart the planner needs to know the remaining duration as the Gantt chart scale is a time scale not a percentage complete scale. Percentage complete and remaining duration are often used interchangeably, but this can be misleading or inaccurate - consider the following example.

When you report that a 12 day activity will take another 6 days to complete, you have implicitly stated that the material, resources and funds are available to complete the work. However, if you report the same activity's progress is 50% complete, you have confirmed what has been done, but say nothing about when you intend to complete the activity.

If an activity has a long duration it may be more convenient to initially report percentage complete and assume the remaining duration, but as the activity nears completion the project manager will have a more accurate feel for the remaining duration as opposed to the percentage complete. For example, if painting a house is one activity, then as you progress through the house it may be easier to say each room is 5% of the work, but as you near the last few rooms you should be able to accurately state how many days it will take to finish.

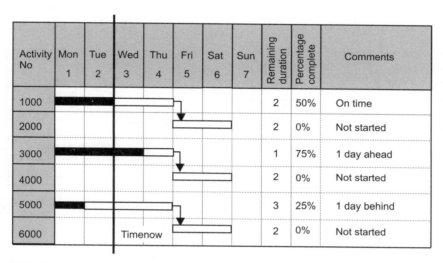

Activity No	Mon 1	Tue 2	Wed 3	Thu 4	Fri 5	Sat 6	Sun 7	Remaining duration	Percentage complete	Comments
1000								2	50%	On time
2000								2	0%	Not started
3000								1	75%	1 day ahead
4000								2	0%	Not started
5000								3	25%	1 day behind
6000			Timenow					2	0%	Not started

Figure 12.8: Revised Gantt Chart - shows the progress drawn relative to timenow. The revised Gantt chart is easy to mark-up by hand and clearly indicates progress against the original baseline plan, and therefore where control is required. If the progress over the successive weeks is marked up on the same document progress trends can also be established.

If you are intending to apply control to bring the project back on track the knock-on impact to the end date of the project is of little interest, however if any keydates are delayed this could disrupt the project. The disruption on the keydates in the short term can be identified by using a three week rolling horizon Gantt chart (see the next section, figure 12.9).

As the work progresses there may be changes to the project's activity logic. These should be reported so the CPM's network diagram can be updated.

7. Rolling Horizon Gantt Chart

The rolling horizon Gantt chart, or rolling wave Gantt chart is a simplified version of the Gantt chart which focuses on the activities that are working and only a short period ahead. This short period maybe two or three weeks ahead for the activities being worked on, and four weeks ahead for pre-planning (making sure all the drawings, procedures, job cards, equipment, materials etc. are going to be in place). This type of Gantt chart lends itself to a manual presentation as the scope of work is limited to just the activities that are working.

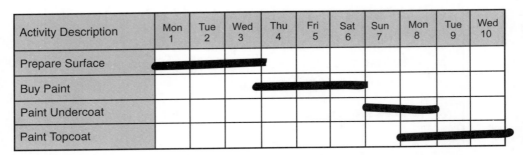

Activity Description	Mon 1	Tue 2	Wed 3	Thu 4	Fri 5	Sat 6	Sun 7	Mon 8	Tue 9	Wed 10
Prepare Surface	■	■	■	■						
Buy Paint			■	■	■	■				
Paint Undercoat							■	■		
Paint Topcoat								■	■	■

Figure 12.9: Rolling Horizon Gantt Chart – shows how a Gantt chart can be marked up by hand for the next two or three weeks

The rolling horizon Gantt chart can also be marked-up on the original Gantt chart - this will give a clear indication of progress. The main purpose is to focus on what can be done, rather than what was planned in the original Gantt chart.

The rolling horizon Gantt charts are generally best produced by the team leader or site manager who is at the work face. The project manager or planner should then incorporate the information into a master schedule to check the keydates will still be met. If they have changed this needs to be communicated to the interested parties.

This type of Gantt chart should be very accurate as it is based on the latest data and drawn up by the team member who is working close to the action. It is quick to draw and only includes relevant information on the activities that are in progress.

Exercises:

1. Discuss the benefits of using Gantt charts to plan and control your projects.

2. Go back to Chapter 11, exercise 2 and transpose the network diagram into a Gantt chart (see Appendix 1 for the solution).

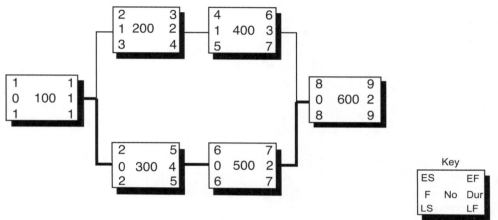

Figure 11.12: Critical Path Method, exercise 2

3. Go back to Chapter 11, exercise 3 and transpose the network diagram into a Gantt chart (see Appendix 1 for the solution).

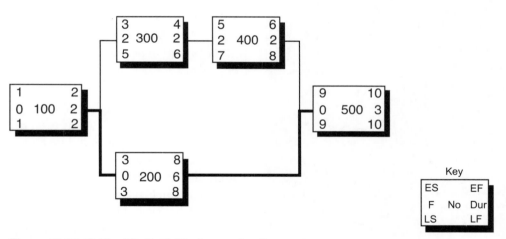

Figure 11.13: Critical Path Method, exercise 3

4. Discuss the benefits of using milestone planning and give examples based on your experience in a project environment.

5. Discuss the benefits of using Hammock activities and give examples based on your experience in a project environment.

13

Procurement Schedule

Learning Outcomes

After reading this chapter, you should be able to;

Set up a project procurement management system
Identify long lead items
Develop a procurement schedule
Understand how to expedite procurement items

Procurement management deals with the acquiring of goods and services required to perform and complete the project's scope of work. This could be drawings, materials, equipment or professional services from a number of suppliers, or company departments outside of the project team.

> **DEFINITION**
>
> The PMBOK defines procurement management as; '... *the processes required to acquire goods and services* ...'

> **DEFINITION**
>
> The APM bok defines procurement as; '... *the process of acquiring new services or products.*'

The procurement schedule should be considered after the CPM and Gantt chart have been established, but before the resource histogram and cashflow statement. It is important to identify the items which have a long lead time (particularly those items on the critical path), and identify any special handling and storage requirements. The procuring of long lead items may delay the start of its associated activities. These need to be identified and managed by either:

- Accelerating the procurement cycle, or
- Adjusting the schedule Gantt chart.

1. Procurement Cycle

The procurement process can be effectively presented as a cycle outlining a series of steps. In practice, there may be some iteration between certain steps and indeed the steps may be carried out in a different order.

The procurement planning will be viewed from the buyer in the project office's perspective. Procurement planning is the process of identifying what products and services are best procured outside the project organisation.

Scope of Work: The scope of work is the starting point as it identifies the complete list of jobs (from the WBS) with their associated material, components and equipment requirements.

Executive Strategy: The executive strategy takes the scope of work and decides what will be best procured from outside the company and what will be best made inside the company with the company's own resources. This is the **buy-or-make** decision (see table 13.1) which is a key component of the execution strategy. Procurement items to consider are:

- What to procure?
- How much to procure?
- When is it required?
- When to procure?
- How to procure (type of contract)?

These decisions may require input from experts and outside suppliers to assess market conditions and the company's expertise and resource loading.

Buy the Components	When your company resources lack the expertise and machinery, or when your resources are overloaded, or when an outside sub-contractor makes you an offer you cannot refuse.
Make the Components	When your company resources, expertise and machinery are available and under utilised, and the costs are less than using outside sub-contractors.

Table 13.1: 'Buy-or-Make' Decision

Procurement List: The procurement list is developed from the project's scope of work. On a small project this could be an expansion of the WBS. Against each work package or activity the material list should give all the product details; manufacturer, model number, specification, type, colour, rating, level of inspection, etc.

WBS	Description Specification	Materials Components	Services
100			
200			
300			

Table 13.2: Procurement List – shows the relationship between the procurement topics and the WBS

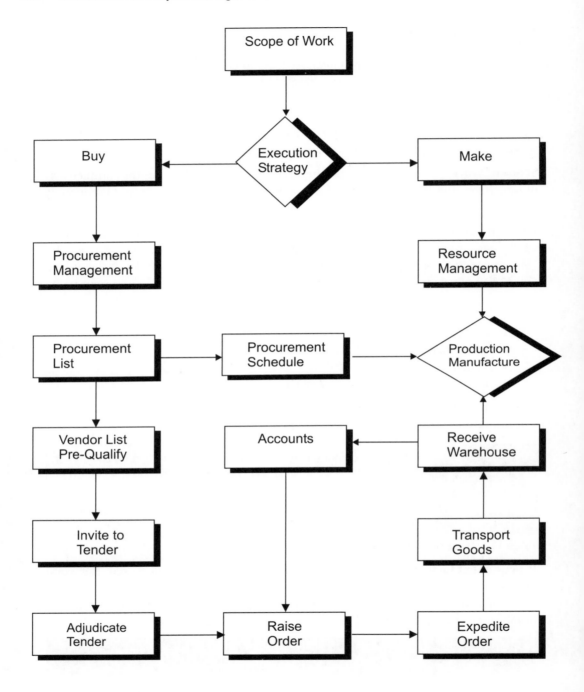

Figure 13.1: Procurement Cycle – shows the relationship between the procurement topics

Procurement Schedule: The procurement schedule is developed after the CPM and Gantt charts have been established as a logical sequence of work, but before the resource histograms and cashflow statements have been considered. Procurement is considered before resources and cashflow because long lead items are usually the least flexible.

By working back from the activities early start dates, subtracting the purchase order lead time and the just-in-time (JIT) margin, this will give the order by date.

WBS	Description	Purchase Order	Early Start	Lead Time	JIT	Order Date
100						
200						
300						

Table 13.3: Purchase Order Schedule – shows the date items need to be ordered so that they arrive on time

Supplier and Vendor List: All potential suppliers need to be identified and pre-qualified according to the project quality plan. You need to be satisfied that the supplier has the production and quality management systems to deliver the product to the required specification, quality standards and schedule. The reputation and financial stability of the company should also be considered. For example, check the quality of the products the company has previously made.

Invite to Tender: When you invite a supplier to give you a quote you need to compile a bid package (enquiry document) for the suppliers to quote against. As the initial enquiry document is the basis for the contract it should be progressively adjusted and marked up as more information becomes available.

Tender Adjudication: Scrutinise the quotations (tenders) and compile a technical and commercial bid tabulation (spreadsheet) of the quotations to ensure you are comparing 'apples with apples'. Consider suppliers suggestions and negotiate to achieve the best price and conditions, while striving for a win-win arrangement. This process should take advantage of market conditions.

Raise the Order: Using your company's standard terms and conditions of contract (which may have been written for you by a lawyer) raise the purchase order. The purchase order should be a stand alone document, superseding all previous documents and correspondence, and must be formally accepted by the supplier. Where possible pass on any contractual requirements from your client with back-to-back agreements with your suppliers. For example, you do not want to be held liable for, a 'schedule penalty' which you cannot pass on to your supplier who may have been the cause of the delay in the first place. For this reason, it is risky to finalise your contracts with your sub-contractors before signing a contract with your client.

Expedite: The expediting function follows-up on the order to ensure and encourage the suppliers to meet their contractual requirements (particularly quality and time). Expediting makes the order happen (see section later in this chapter).

Transport: The transport function considers the different methods of transport for materials and your product. Where possible the product's quality should be checked and confirmed before leaving the factory - this particularly applies to items being imported or exported.

Receiving: The receiving function checks the goods into your company. This involves checking the goods against the delivery note, checking the delivery note against the order and checking the quality of the products against the required condition.

Warehousing: The Warehouse function stores the delivered items for safe keeping and retrieval. Check if warehousing requires any special handling equipment and storage facilities. For example, the goods may be on a pallet and require a forklift truck, or the goods may be perishable and require refrigeration.

Accounts: The accounts department's function is to check the budget, purchase order, invoice and delivery note for variances before making payment.

Project:					
	Project Name:				
WBS	Description	Budget	Purchase Order	Actual Cost	Variance
1000	Buy Computer	$10,000	PO 1001	$8500	$1500
2000	Buy Materials	$5000	PO 2001	$5500	($500)
3000	Website Design	$3000	PO 3001	$3000	$0

Table 13.4: Purchase Order Control Sheet – shows the list of items to be procured linked to the WBS. The actual costs are compared to the budget and any variance is reported to the responsible persons

2. Procurement Schedule

The procurement schedule integrates the procurement list (items to buy), the project schedule (Gantt chart), the procurement lead time (delivery time) and the warehousing just-in-time (JIT) stock control. Consider the following house extension example where figure 13.2 (Gantt chart) shows when the work is planned. And table 13.5 shows when the material is required (where JIT is one day).

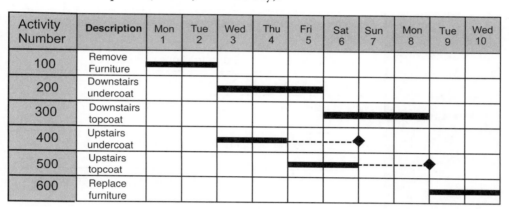

Activity Number	Description	Mon 1	Tue 2	Wed 3	Thu 4	Fri 5	Sat 6	Sun 7	Mon 8	Tue 9	Wed 10
100	Remove Furniture	■									
200	Downstairs undercoat			■							
300	Downstairs topcoat							■			
400	Upstairs undercoat			■		◆					
500	Upstairs topcoat					■			◆		
600	Replace furniture									■	

Figure 13.2: Gantt Chart - House Extension (copied from figure 11.12)

WBS	Description	Material	Required Date (ES – JIT)	Delivery Date	Variance
100	Remove furniture				
200	Downstairs undercoat	Paint 1	2 May (Tuesday)	2 May	0
300	Downstairs top coat	Paint 2	5 May (Friday)	6 May	-1
400	Upstairs undercoat	Paint 3	2 May (Tuesday)	3 May	-1
500	Upstairs top coat	Paint 4	4 May (Thursday)	4 May	0
600	Replace furniture				

Table 13.5: Procurement Lead Time – shows the difference between the delivery date and the required date

From the variance column table 13.5 the deliveries of paint for activities 300 and 400 are both going to be 1 day late. From the schedule Gantt chart (figure 13.2) you can see activity 300 is on the critical path, so if you cannot organize a faster delivery this will extend the duration of the project. On the other hand, activity 400 has 2 days of float, the activity can accommodate a later delivery.

If late delivery items cannot be accelerated, then the schedule will have to be adjusted, because you cannot perform the work without the materials. The procurement schedule will now be the input for resource planning and the cashflow statement.

3. Expediting

The progress expeditor (progress chaser) follows-up on all the purchase orders and instructions to the suppliers. On a large project the expeditor is an important team member, who becomes the project manager's eyes and ears. On a small project the expeditor and project manager may well be the same person. Consider the following expediting checklist:

Received	Ask the contractor if the purchase order and instructions have been received?
Understood	Are the purchase order and instructions understood?
Job Number	What is your job number?
Project Manager	Who is your project manager or foreman?
Planned	Has the job been planned into your production system? (Show me)
Drawings	Do you have all the construction drawings, specifications and planning information? (Show me)
Materials	Has the supplier ordered the materials and components they require? Have they been received and inspected? (Show me)
Instructions	Have the instructions been given to the foreman to carry out the work?
Resources	Are there suitably qualified resources available? (Name them and show qualifications)
Progress	Is the work progressing as planned?
Problems	Are there any problems? Are there any claims?
Delivery	Will you meet the contracted delivery date?

By asking all these questions the expeditor becomes an invaluable source of progress information giving early warning of any supply problems so that the project manager has time to respond.

Exercise:

1. Discuss how you would set up a project procurement system in a project environment.
2. Discuss how you would identify long lead items. Give examples of how long lead items have been addressed on your projects.
3. Discuss how you would expedite project procurement in a project environment.

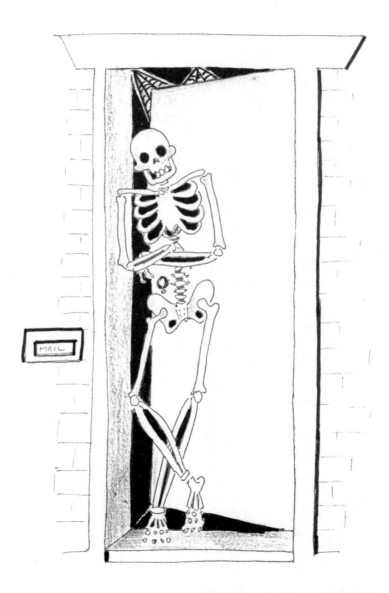

"...Sorry for the late delivery. I hope it won't make your project late!..."

14

Resource Planning

Learning Outcomes

After reading this chapter, you should be able to;

Understand the resource duration trade-off

Draw the resource histogram

Level resources for resource-limited projects

A resource may be defined as the machine or person who will perform the scope of work. Resource planning is therefore forecasting the number of resources required to perform the scope of work within the time plan. The resource constraint should be considered after the CPM, the Gantt chart and the procurement schedule have been developed, but before the cashflow statement.

In the previous chapters, the *Critical Path Method*, *Gantt Charts* and *Procurement Schedule*, an unlimited supply of resources was assumed to be available to meet the time estimates. In reality, this is obviously not the case, so here the text will outline methods and techniques for integrating resource planning with time planning.

1. Resource Estimating

The resource estimate is linked directly to the scope of work (SOW) and the bill of materials (BOM). The scope of work may be expressed as so many square metres of wall to paint, or so many products to make. From this description the estimator can convert the scope of work into manhours per unit "X".

The next step is to consider the direct trade-off between the resource requirement and the activity's duration. Consider the following: if the scope of work is to prepare and paint 20,000 m2 of wall surface and the estimator knows from past experience that the work can be done at a rate of 10 m2 per hour and the men work 8 hour shifts, then the equation is:

$$\frac{(20,000 \text{ m2})}{10 \text{ man-hrs per m2} \times 8 \text{ hrs per day}} = 250 \text{ man days}$$

The resource / duration trade-off would then be as follows:

Mandays	Resources Available	Duration (days)
250	10 men	25
250	11 men	22.7
250	12 men	20.8
250	13 men	19.2
250	14 men	17.9

Table 14.1: Resource Duration Trade-Off – shows the number of days to complete the work with the men available

By varying the resource availability, the duration of the activity will change. At the outset the estimator will probably assume a certain availability to give an acceptable time duration. During the detailed planning and development phase the estimator needs to check the calculations and firm up on the figures.

2. Resource Histogram

The resource histogram is a popular planning tool because it gives a good visual presentation which is easy to understand and easy to communicate. The prerequisites are:

- Early start Gantt chart (after considering the procurement requirements which ensures the materials and equipment are available to do the work)
- Resource forecast (estimate) per activity.

By using the early start Gantt chart it is assumed that the planner wishes to start all activities as soon as possible and keep the activity float for flexibility. Once the resource requirements have been added to the early start Gantt chart, the daily requirements are summed by moving forward through the Gantt chart one day at a time to give the total resource required per day.

The total daily resource requirements are then plotted vertically to give the iconic resource histogram. It is important to note that separate resource histograms are required for each resource type (painter, computer operator etc). Consider the painting example (table 14.2) and the resource histogram, figure 14.1:

Activity No	Description	Start Date	Finish Date	Resource Per Day
100	Remove furniture	1	2	4, 4
200	Paint downstairs, prep / undercoat	3	5	3, 1, 1
300	Paint downstairs, top coat	6	8	3, 1, 1
400	Paint upstairs, prep / undercoat	3	4	3, 1
500	Paint upstairs, top coat	5	6	3, 1
600	Replace furniture	9	10	4, 4

Table 14.2: Resource Table – shows the number of resources required per day

How to the draw the resource histogram:

Step 1	Draw the Gantt chart (see figure 12.5).
Step 2	Transfer the resource per day from the table 14.2 to the Gantt chart figure 14.1.
Step 3	Add the resource per day vertically to give a total daily requirement.
Step 4	Plot the resource histogram (see figure 14.1).

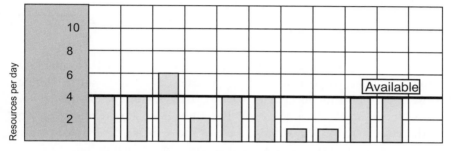

Activity Number	Mon 1	Tue 2	Wed 3	Thu 4	Fri 5	Sat 6	Sun 7	Mon 8	Tue 9	Wed 10	Thu 11
100	4	4									
200			3	1	1						
300						3	1	1			
400			3	1							
500					3	1					
600									4	4	
Total	4	4	6	2	4	4	1	1	4	4	

Figure 14.1: Gantt Chart and Resource Histogram – shows the resource forecast each day and the number of resources available

Resource Loading: The resource forecast is now compared with the resources available. The ideal situation is when the resource requirement equals the resources available. Unfortunately, in the real world this seldom happens because it is not always possible to adjust supply with demand, so you either have to reschedule or adjust the number of resources.

A resource overload is when the resource forecast requirement exceeds the available resources (for example, 10 men required but only 8 men available), while a resource underload is when resource forecast is lower than the available resource (for example, 10 men required, but 12 men available). A resource overload will lead to some activities being delayed, while a resource underload will under utilise the company's resources, which could have a detrimental impact on the company's profitability.

In figure 14.1 the resource histogram shows the total resource required per day and compares it with the resources available (four in this case). On Wednesday 3rd May there is an overload (six needed but only four available). But on Thursday 4th May two resources are required and on Sunday and Monday only one resource is required. This situation is crying out for the activities to be moved to smooth the resource loading.

3. Resource Smoothing

Resource smoothing is the process of moving activities and adjusting the availability of resources to improve the resource histogram profile. The project manager has a number of resource smoothing options - consider the following:

Resource Smoothing	Assign resources to critical activities first, because if you delay a critical activity this will delay the whole project.
Time-Limited Resource Scheduling	If the end date of the project is fixed the resources must be increased to address any overloads.
Resource-Limited Resource Scheduling	If the maximum number of resources are fixed the end date may need to be extended to address any overload.
Increase Resources	To address an overload.
Reduce Resources	To address an underload (under utilized).

Table 14.3: Resource Smoothing Options

Consider the painting example in figure 14.1, if there are only 4 resources available the resource histogram will be overloaded on 3 May (Wednesday). This resource overload can be addressed by simply moving activity 400 by two days. However, as the network diagram shows (see figure 14.2), activity 400 has a finish-to-start relationship with activity 500, therefore activity 500 will also have to move forward by two days. The resulting Gantt chart and smoothed resource histogram are shown in figure 14.3.

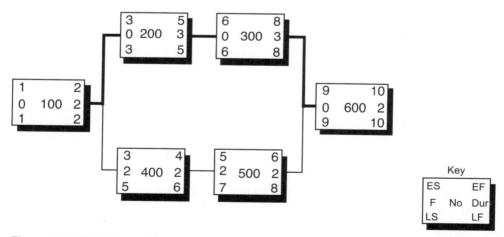

Figure 14.2: CPM (copied from figure 11.10)

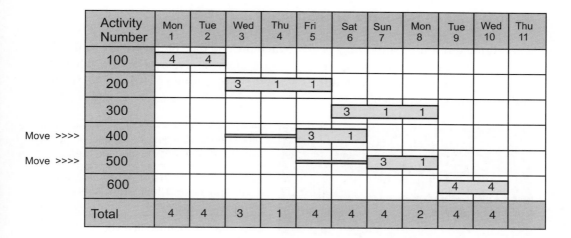

Activity Number	Mon 1	Tue 2	Wed 3	Thu 4	Fri 5	Sat 6	Sun 7	Mon 8	Tue 9	Wed 10	Thu 11
100	4	4									
200			3	1	1						
300						3	1	1			
400					3	1					
500							3	1			
600									4	4	
Total	4	4	3	1	4	4	4	2	4	4	

Move >>>> (row 400)
Move >>>> (row 500)

Figure 14.3: Smoothed Gantt Chart and Resource Histogram – shows the smoothed resource histogram after moving activities 400 and 500 within their float

4. Time-Limited Resource Scheduling

Time-limited resource smoothing is used when the end date of the project cannot be exceeded (for example, an event). In which case, any resource overloads will have to be addressed by increasing the resources when they are required (see figure 14.4). This situation could occur when:

The project has heavy time penalties.	Time penalties are designed to encourage contractors to meet the planned dates.
The project is part of another project with critical access dates.	For example, carpet fitters for an event only have a few hours to fit the carpets.
Building a chalet for summer tourists.	If the chalet is opened late you will lose income.
Making a product for an event.	If your product arrives the day after an event the order will be cancelled.

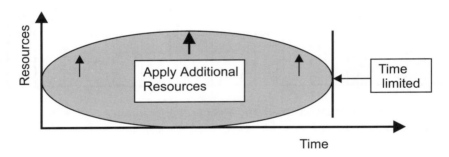

Figure 14.4: Time-Limited Resource Scheduling

Once the end date of the project and milestones have been contractually agreed, time-limited scheduling will become a powerful tool to assist the planner to achieve these commitments.

5. Resource-Limited Resource Scheduling

Resource-limited resource scheduling is when there is a resource limit which cannot be exceeded. If there are any resource overloads then some planned activities will have to be delayed. If this process delays any critical activities, then the end date of the project will be extended. This situation could occur in any of the following situations:

A confined space will limit the number of people able to work there.	An engineer repairing a PC.
Where there are limited facilities.	The number of workers on a ship may be limited to the number of bunks available.
Where there are equipment limitations.	For example, the number of computers, machines, drawing boards, lifts or scaffolding for the work.
Health & safety requirements may limit the number of workers in a certain area.	Restrict working overhead.
Restricted access might limit the movement of materials and equipment.	Busy downtown office blocks have limited parking and restricted road access.

The frustration of the real world, of course, is that your employer will always expect you to achieve the contractual end date even though the resources are not available (see figure 14.5).

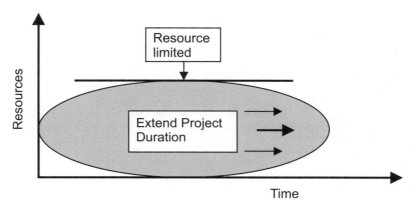

Figure 14.5: Resource-Limited Resource Scheduling

6. How to Increase Resources

When the resources are overloaded there are a number of options to increase the resources available:

Working Overtime	This will increase the number of work hours available without having to employ more staff.
Working Shifts	This will increase the utilisation of machines, equipment and also increase the number of manhours worked in confined spaces.
Increase Productivity	Education and training should improve productivity.
Automation	Install equipment to make your products with less resources.
Learning Curve	If the project involves a certain amount of repetitive work, the project manager could expect to see the number of manhours reducing on subsequent units.
Sub-Contractors	Using sub-contractors will increase the workforce in the short term. The benefit being that there are no long term commitments, but the labour costs will be higher.
Scope of Work	If it is not possible to increase resource availability, consider reducing the scope of work to meet a fixed end date.

7. Reduce Resources

When there is not enough work during slack periods and the resources are under loaded or under utilised there are a number of options for reducing the available resources:

Move Resources	Move unemployed resources to other activities, particularly critical activities.
R&D	Move unemployed resources to R&D jobs, or fill-in jobs such as building a spec product.
Hire Out	Hire out resources internally or externally.
Pre-Manufacture	Pre-manufacture components before they are needed.
Maintenance	Maintain equipment.
Train	Train your workforce to gain new skills.
Leave	Send the under utilised workforce on leave.

The profit of a company in the long term may well depend directly on the efficient utilisation of its resources.

8. Resource Planning and Control

The initial CPM analysis was performed without considering the resource constraint. Now that the resource analysis is complete, certain activities may have been moved during the resource smoothing, the baseline plan will therefore need to be re-scheduled.

The resource calculations outlined above indicate the optimum resource utilisation to meet project objectives, but they do not address the human element. The project manager must bridge the gap, in terms of communicating explanation and persuasion, between what should be done mathematically and what can be done practically. It is generally accepted that a workforce will tend to be more adaptable and committed when given the opportunity to participate in the planning process.

Exercise:

1. Discuss the resource / duration trade-off and relate the trade-off to your projects.

2. Draw the resource histogram for your project and comment on the type of resource which is most likely to be over / under loaded.

3. As project manager you have a number of options on how to address resource overloads. Discuss the options you use on your projects.

15

Project Accounts

Learning Outcomes

After reading this chapter, you should be able to;

Produce a cashflow statement

Understand the cashflow timing and cash distribution

Draw an expense S curve

The financial success of a project depends not only on the project making a profit, but also on being able to finance the project's expenses through the project lifecycle. Statistics clearly indicate that more companies go into liquidation because of cashflow problems than for any other reason. It is, therefore, essential for the project manager to closely monitor the project's cashflow.

DEFINITION

The PMBOK defines cost management as: '... *the processes required to ensure that the project is completed within the approved budget.*'

DEFINITION

The APM bok defines project accounts as: '... *estimating the proper cost that should be reasonably expected to be incurred against a clear baseline, understanding how and why actual costs occur, and ensuring that the necessary response is taken promptly to ensure actual costs come under budget.*'

Project accounting should not be confused with financial accounting or management accounting which are used during the operational phase. From the definitions, however, you will see there is some common ground.

Financial Accounting: Financial accounts keeps a record of all the financial transactions, payments in and payments out, together with a list of creditors and debtors. This information gives the financial status of a company using the generally accepted accounting principles. The three main reports are; the balance sheet, the income statement and the cashflow statement.

Management Accounting: Management accounting also called cost accounting, uses the above financial information particularly from the profit and loss account to analyse company performance. This analysis will assist management decision-making with respect to estimating, planning, budgeting, implementation and control.

Project Accounting: Project accounting uses a combination of both financial accounting and management accounting techniques together with a number of special project management tools and techniques (WBS, CPM, cost-to-complete, crashing and earned value) to integrate the project accounts with the other project parameters.

1. Cashflow Statement

The cashflow statement is a document which models the flow of money in and out of the project's account. The time frame is usually monthly, to coincide with the normal business accounting cycle. The cashflow statement is based on the same information used in a typical bank statement, except that here the income (cash inflow) and expenditure (cash outflow) are grouped together and totalled.

During a project the contractor's income would come from the monthly progress payments, and the expenses would be wages, materials, overheads, interest and bought-in services. While the client's (entrepreneur's) income would come from the operation of the facility after the project has been completed and the expenses would be the invoices from the contractors and suppliers to make the facility or product. The client will, therefore, have to fund the project from savings, income or borrowings.

Cashflow Example 1: As a first step consider how the project costs are incurred and how they would look in a cashflow statement which does not consider the timing of the costs (cashflow exercise 2 will consider the timing of the costs).

This is a simple example of a four month project which considers the incurred income and costs from the contractor's position. The client pays four payments of $5000. The contractor incurs costs for the hire of equipment, labour and materials. Use the following steps as a guideline to solve the exercise.

Step 1	Set up the cashflow statement headings as per table 15.1. Use monthly headings (fields or columns) to cover the duration of the project - six months in this case.
Step 2	The brought forward (B / F) for February is zero.
Step 3	The inflow of cash from February to May is $5,000 per month.
Step 4	There are three items of expenditure from February to May; Hire of equipment - $1,500 per month Labour - $2,000 per month Materials - $500 per month.
Step 5	Starting with February, the total funds available are $5,000. The total expenses are $4,000. Closing balance is therefore, $1,000
Step 6	The closing balance for February of $1,000 becomes the brought forward for March.
Step 7	Repeat the calculations to May.

	January	February	March	April	May	June
Brought Forward		$0	$1,000	$2,000	$3,000	
Income		$5,000	$5,000	$5,000	$5,000	
Total $ Available		**$5,000**	**$6,000**	**$7,000**	**$8,000**	
Expenses						
Equipment		$1,500	$1,500	$1,500	$1,500	
Labour		$2,000	$2,000	$2,000	$2,000	
Materials		$500	$500	$500	$500	
Total Expenses		**$4,000**	**$4,000**	**$4,000**	**$4,000**	
Closing Balance		$1,000	$2,000	$3,000	$4,000	

Table 15.1: Cashflow Statement, example 1 (incurred costs) – shows the incurred costs between February and May

2. Cashflow Timing

The previous section considered when the costs were incurred, this section will consider when the cash actually flows in or out of the project's accounts.

The cashflow statement, as the name suggests, is a measure of the cash in and cash out of the project's account. The catch is that the cashflow is usually not the same as the sales figures or expenses for the month because of the timing of the incomes and payments. Listed below are some typical examples of cashflow timings:

Part payment	Part payment with placement of order - this is often used to cover the manufacture's cost of materials and ensure the purchaser's commitment, particularly on imported goods.
Stage payment	Stage payments or progress payments for items which may take many months to complete.
Purchase	Payment on purchase - this is normal practice with retailers.
Monthly	Monthly payments for labour, rent, telephone and other office expenses.
Credit	30 or 60 days credit; normal terms for bought-in items.

It may help the learning process to look at the data presented the other way round.

Labour	Labour costs are usually paid in the month they are used.
Material	Material costs can vary from an up-front payment, cash on delivery (COD), to 1 to 3 months credit.
Services	Bought-in services and plant hire costs can be paid within 1 to 3 months after delivery.
Income	Income from the client can vary from up-front payment, stage payments or progress payment one month after invoice.

These figures are usually compiled monthly on a creditors and debtors schedule. It is the project accountant's responsibility to chase up late payments

Non Cashflow Items: Company assets should not appear on a cashflow statement as they do not represent a movement of cash. Although appreciation and depreciation may represent a flow of value, physically, it does not represent an inflow or outflow of cash. This also applies to the revaluation of property and the value of the company's shares.

3. Cost Distribution

The cashflow statement is an integral part of the critical path method (CPM) - it combines the WBS, the estimate, the project schedule, the procurement schedule and the resource histogram. At this point we need to make some assumptions about the distribution and profile of the cost and cashflow with respect to the schedule of the activities. For ease of calculation it is usually assumed to be linear unless otherwise stated (see figure 15.1).

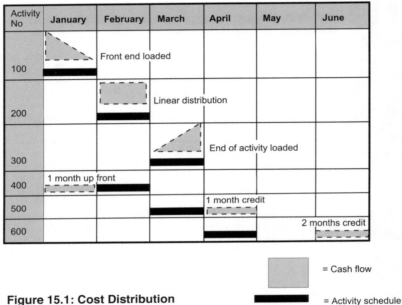

Figure 15.1: Cost Distribution

□ = Cash flow

■ = Activity schedule

Labour costs are generally uniform over the duration of the activity, whereas, the cost of materials and other bought-in items may need to be qualified. As stated in the previous section, the costs can vary from up-front payments to 1, 2 or 3 months later depending on the supplier.

Projects with many activities will tend to smooth out any distortions caused by non-linear cashflows. However, if there are activities with disproportionately large material or equipment payments these can be separated out to form new activities with appropriate durations to match the expense profile.

Cashflow Example 2: The second cashflow example will apply the timing of the cashflow to example 1. In this project the client pays their invoices after 30 days. The equipment hire company requires their payments to be made 30 days in advance. The labour is paid in the month they work, and the material supplier gives 30 days credit.

Step 1	Set up the cashflow statement headings as per table 15.2. Use monthly headings (fields or columns) to cover the duration of the project.
Step 2	The brought forward (B / F) for January is zero.
Step 3	The client pays invoices after 30 days, therefore, the $5,000 per month income is from March to June.
Step 4	There are three items of expenditure incurred from February to May; Hire of equipment - $1,500 per month Labour - $2,000 per month Materials - $500 per month.
Step 5	The equipment hire is 30 days in advance, therefore, insert the payments of $1,500 per month from January to April.
Step 6	The labour is paid in the month of work, therefore, insert the payments of $2,000 per month from February to May.
Step 7	The material supplier gives 30 days credit, therefore, insert the payments of $500 per month from March to June.
Step 8	Starting at January. There is zero brought forward and no income, but there is an expense of $1,500, which gives a closing balance of ($1,500) and, therefore, an opening balance for February of ($1,500).
Step 9	In February there is no income so there is ($1,500) available and the expenses are $3,500 which gives a closing balance of ($5,000). This calculation is continued through to June.

	January	February	March	April	May	June
Brought Forward	$0	($1,500)	($5,000)	($4,000)	($3,000)	($500)
Income	$0	$0	$5,000	$5,000	$5,000	$5,000
Total Available	$0	($1,500)	$0	$1,000	$2,000	$4,500
Expenses						
Equipment	$1,500	$1,500	$1,500	$1,500		
Labour		$2,000	$2,000	$2,000	$2,000	
Materials			$500	$500	$500	$500
Total Expenses	$1,500	$3,500	$4,000	$4,000	$2,500	$500
Closing Balance	($1,500)	($5,000)	($4,000)	($3,000)	($500)	$4,000

Table 15.2: Cashflow Statement, example 2

Both cashflow example 1 and 2 end in June with $4,000, but when the cashflow is considered all the months end with a negative balance until June. This means finance would need to be organised in advance.

4. How to Draw an Expense S Curve

Another method for modelling the cashflow is to use S curve analysis which provides the link between the budget and the timeline. Experience has shown that a project's accumulated costs tend to follow the S curve shape. To draw the S curve use the following procedure on the Gantt chart (figure 15.2).

Step 1	Draw an early start Gantt chart for the project (see figure 15.2).
Step 2	Assign expenses evenly over the duration of the activity. Therefore, activity 100, for example, is $100 over two days giving $50 per day.
Step 3	Add the cost values vertically to get daily totals. On 1st May the total is $50 as there is only one activity (100) working, but on 5th May the total is $200 because there are four activities (200, 300, 400, 500) working.
Step 4	Accumulate the values by calculating the total to date. For example, add 1st May total [$50] to 2nd May total [$50] giving [$100]. Then move to the next day [$50 + $100] giving $150 .... and so on.
Step 5	Plot accumulated figures on a graph of cost against time (figure 15.3). This will produce the distinctive S curve.

Activity	$	1	2	3	4	5	6	7	8	9	10
100	$100	50	50								
200	$150			50	50	50					
300	$100					50	50				
400	$100					50	50				
500	$150					50	50	50			
600	$100							50	50		
700	$100							50	50		
800	$100								50	50	
900	$50									50	
1000	$50										50
Daily		50	50	50	50	200	150	150	150	100	50
Accumulated		50	100	150	200	400	550	700	850	950	1000

Figure 15.2: Gantt Chart – shows how the expenditure can be presented as a S curve

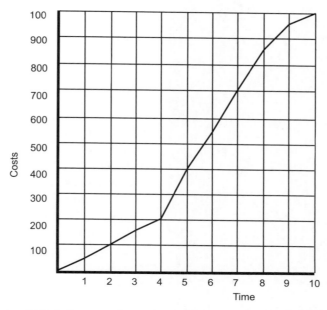

Figure 15.3: S Curve – shows the S curve of accumulated expenses

Exercise:

1. Continuing with cashflow example 2 (figure 15.2) produce the cashflow statement using the information below (see appendix 1 for solution).

Brought Forward	January $500
Income	$8,000 per month from February to June
Equipment	$2,000 per month from January to April
Labour	$4,000 per month from February to June
Materials	$1,000 per month from February to June

Table 15.3: Cashflow, exercise 1

16

Project Control

Learning Outcomes

After reading this chapter, you should be able to;

Identify a range of planning and control documents

Explain how to capture progress data to measure progress

Execute processes and standards to support project change control

Apply project control

The development of a project plan or baseline plan completes the planning phase of the planning and control cycle. The next phase is project execution and control using the baseline plan as the means to achieving the project objectives and an outline of the required condition. Needless to say planning is a pointless exercise unless the execution of the plans are tracked and controlled through accurate reporting on performance.

A structured approach to planning and control is recommended by experienced practitioners because, through a well disciplined project management system, all parties will know:

- What is expected of them
- Their required performance
- The reports they must generate.

The baseline plan may be seen as a number of documents which indicate the path the project should follow. Consider the comparison with the course a yacht steers - by taking bearings the navigator can plot the yacht's position. If the yacht has gone off course they can apply steering control to bring the yacht back on course.

Similarly, the project's baseline plan is the course to steer, with the tracking and monitoring functions ascertain the project's position with respect to scope, time, procurement, resources and costs. If the project is off course, then control in the form of corrective action must be applied.

1. Control Cycle

This chapter will focus on monitoring, tracking and applying the control functions of the control cycle. The expediting function has already been discussed in the *Procurement Schedule* chapter.

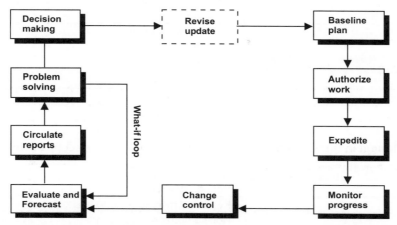

Figure 16.1: Project Control Cycle – shows the key components of the control cycle

2. Scope of Control

The project manager and the project management office (PMO) are responsible for managing the planning and control documents.

Scope Management: The scope of work defines what the project is producing or delivering. The control of the scope of work is also called configuration management.

Planning Documents:	Project charter, project brief, project proposal
	Work Breakdown Structure
	Activity list / bill of materials (BOM)
	Drawing register
	Specification register
	Parts list
	Contract
Control Documents:	Project communications
	Impact statements
	Variations and Modifications
	Change requests
	Concessions
	Closeout report

Technical Support: Technical support from the design office extends from interpreting the client's brief to addressing day to day problems within statutory regulations and good practice.

Planning Documents:	Client's brief
	Statutory regulations
	Specifications
	Design calculations
	Build-method
Control Documents:	Configuration control
	Impact statements
	Commissioning
	As-built drawings

Time Management: Outlines the sequence and timing of the scope of work.

Planning Documents:	Network diagram/CPM
	Scheduled Gantt chart
	Keydate / milestone schedule
	Rolling horizon Gantt chart
Control Documents:	Progress report (actual vs planned)
	Revised Gantt chart
	Earned value
	Trend documents

Procurement Management: The procurement function identifies all the bought-in items. These must be procured to specification, time schedule and budget.

Planning Documents:	BOM, Parts list
	Procurement schedule
	Material requirement planning (MRP)
	Procurement budget
Control Documents:	Purchase order
	Expediting status report
	Revised procurement schedule and budget

Resource Management: Resource management integrates the resource estimate with time management to produce the resource forecast. This is usually related to manpower requirements.

Planning Documents:	Resource forecast
	Resource availability
	Resource levelled manpower histogram
Control Documents:	Time sheets
	Revised manpower histogram

Cost Management: Cost management allocates budgets and cashflows to the work packages.

Planning Documents:	Cost breakdown structure
	Activity budgets
	Department budgets
	Cashflow statement
Control Documents:	Expenditure reports (actual vs planned)
	Committed costs and cost-to-complete
	Revised budgets

Change Control: As the project progresses the scope of work is revised and controlled through the following documents.

Change Control:	Project communications
	Impact statements
	Non Conformance Reports (NCR)
	Change Requests and Concessions
	Drawing revisions
	Modifications and Variation Orders (VO)
	Specification and Configuration revisions.

Quality Management: Outlines how the company will assure the product will achieve the required condition.

Planning Documents:	Project quality plan (ISO 9000)
	Quality control plan
	Parts lists, specifications and standards
Control Documents:	Inspection reports
	Non conformance reports (NCR's)
	Concessions
	Data books and operation manuals
	Commissioning

Communication Management: The communication function is to disseminate information and instructions to the responsible parties.

Planning Documents:	Lines of communication
	List of controlled documents and Distribution list
	Schedule of meetings and agendas
Control Documents:	Transmittals
	Minutes of meetings

Human Resource Management: This sets the framework for the human factors.

Planning Documents:	Project organisation structure
	Responsibility matrix
	Job descriptions and work procedures
Control Documents:	Time sheets
	Performance evaluations

3. Data Capture

Data capture is part of the progress reporting cycle where information is regularly reported back to the project manager on the project's progress and status. The data capture function may be assumed to be at the start of the information cycle and so the accuracy of the subsequent calculations are based directly on the accuracy of the data capture. It is, therefore, extremely important for the data capture to be at an appropriate level of accuracy. Consider the following points:

Responsibility	The person responsible for the quality of the data capture needs to be clearly identified by the project manager. One method of improving data capture is to make the department that uses the information responsible for updating it. This should encourage the users to ensure that the data input is accurate.
Critical Activities	A higher level of accuracy is required on critical activities because any delays on these activities will extend the project's duration.
Simple Report Format	Negotiate the design of your reports with the people who will use them. Try to make the reports simple and easy to use, this will help to ensure accuracy and commitment.
Written	The use of written communication should be encouraged because it addresses the human failing of misinterpretation and forgetfulness.
One Page Reporting	Managers should have a propensity for one page reporting, giving quality not quantity. People are more likely to read a one page document than a 50 page report.
Timing	If information is received after the decision has been made, the value of the information is reduced to being a historical closeout report.
Accuracy	The accuracy of the data capture will directly impact the accuracy of any reports generated. Data capture with an accuracy of +/- 20% will give subsequent reports an accuracy of +/- 20%. As a guide, the accuracy of the report should be the same or better than the profit margin of the project and in line with the level of risk and level of control required.

If these points are used as a guideline for data capture the quality and accuracy of the information should match the appropriate level of control.

Data Capture Example: Consider a website design office which may have a project to design 50 websites (table 16.1). By setting-up a suitable data capture template the project manager will be able to quantify the design office team's performance to date and get a feel for *"how they are doing"*.

Data Capture Template (table 16.1): The website design numbers are listed in the left hand column. The scope of work is subdivided into three headings (design, construct, and test sites) and weighted. As each website may require different hours to complete this is accommodated in the planned hours column. The progress is reported as a percentage of each section, so if on website number 10 the design is 100% complete, this means they have earned 100% of 20%, which equals 20% of the allocated hours (80 hrs). And if the construction of the website is 50% complete, this means they have earned 50% of a 60% weighting, which equals 30% of 80 hrs.

Website Number	Design 20%	Construct 60%	Test Sites 20%	Percentage complete	Planned hours	Earned hours	Actual hours
10	100% 20%	50% 30%	0%	(progress) 50% (actual)	80	40	40
20	100% 20%	90% 54%	0%	74%	40	30	40
30	100% 20%	50% 30%		50%	60	30	35
40	40% 8%			8%	50	4	5
50					60	0	0
Total				36%	290 hrs	104 hrs	120 hrs

Table 16.1 Data Capture Template – shows the portfolio of websites is 36% complete

Analysis: The data capture template lends itself to spreadsheet calculations. This project is 36% complete, this should be compared with the planned progress to see if the rate of work is sufficient to complete the project on time. To measure productivity compare the earned hours with the actual hours. Overall in this case the actual hours (120) are more than the earned hours (104). This means more hours are required to complete the work than originally estimated. Action is required to either increase productivity or update the estimating data base.

Data Capture Format: Table 16.2 shows a typical data capture template for a maintenance type project. The job number refers to the items of work and the percentages refer to a typical maintenance routine. Where possible you should develop these type of data capture templates and tailor them to your work.

DATA CAPTURE						
WBS	Removal	Inspection	Repair	Install	Test	Percentage Complete
	10%	5%	70%	10%	5%	
Job 1						
Job 2						

Table 16.2: Typical Data Capture Template

Size of Activity: As the size of the work packages, activity and subsections are reduced so the accuracy of the data capture will increase, but so will the effort to capture the data - you will need to strike a balance. As a guide, relate the subsections to the reporting period so that a subsection is completed within each reporting period. Therefore, for weekly reporting the subsection should not be greater than 30/40 hours per person.

Barchart Data Capture: The schedule Gantt chart itself can be a useful format for data capture. Request the foreman or supervisor to mark-up their progress on the schedule Gantt chart. The Gantt chart will now contain the planned work (last week), progress to date and planned work for next week (rolling horizon). This information should be accurate as the foreman is at the operational end of the project. The report is also quick and easy for them to complete in a format they are familiar with. This exercise is similar to the rolling horizon Gantt chart.

4. How to Apply Project Control

There are many ways of applying project control, this section has gathered together a number of pointers as a general guide:

Awareness	An effective way to achieve commitment is to make the person aware of the cost of any delay to the project.
Discuss	Any changes to the plan should be discussed with the foreman first: • to see if the changes are possible • to get the foreman's input for the planning • to gain the foreman's commitment.
Too Busy	An excuse often used for not feeding progress back to the planner is *"we don't have the time"* or *"we are too busy doing the work"*. This may be true, but the project manager needs to know are they working in the right direction, and are more resources needed?
Co-Ordinate	It is important to coordinate and communicate information between departments to avoid a duplication of effort, and to allow for cross checking. Cross checking is a useful method for identifying discrepancies and future problems.
Priorities	It is the project manager's responsibility to establish priorities and differentiate between what is urgent and what is important. If you allow the workforce to set their own priorities they may leave low paying jobs and jobs they dislike until last. This could adversely impact the scheduling of the project.
Respond Early	Respond early to any variation before small problems become major disasters.
Deviations	Encourage the team members to inform you of deviations and exceptions.
Estimate	As the schedule is only an estimate, you must expect activities not to be exactly as per the schedule - introduce a degree of flexibility.
Baseline Plan	Although plans should be revised to reflect the current progress, it is important not to forget the original baseline plan to guide the project to completion.

Exercise:

1. Discuss what planning and control documents you use in a project environment.

2. Discuss how you measure percentage complete and remaining duration.

3. Discuss how you apply project control to bring your project back on track.

17

Earned Value

Learning Outcomes

After reading this chapter, you should be able to;

Draw the earned value curve

Compile the earned value table

Determine the progress from the SV and CV variances

Earned value is a powerful planning and control technique which integrates costs and time, or manhours and time to give a true measurement of progress in comparable units.

Although the earned value technique was initially set up to track the progress of cost and time, in practice it is usually more appropriate to track progress measured as earned manhours and time. In fact, any parameter that flows through the project can be used; tonnes of steel, cubic meters of concrete, metres of pipe, or pages of a document.

Earned value measurements compare actual work expended against work performed (earned), to give a measure of efficiency. And also compares work performed (earned) against the planned work, to give a measure of schedule performance.

1. Earned Value Terminology

Earned value more than any other planning and control technique covered in this book is shrouded in esoteric terminology. The key to mastering earned value is to understand the terms. It may be argued that if you wish to enter the field of project management, then you must speak the language of project management.

Budget at Completion	BAC	
Planned Value	PV	BCWS
Percentage Complete	PC	%
Earned Value	EV = PC * BAC	BCWP
Actual Value	AV	ACWP
Estimate at Completion	EAC = (AV / EV) * BAC	
Scheduled Variance	SV = EV - PV	
Cost Variance	CV = EV - AV	

Table 17.1: Table of Earned Value Terms and Abbreviations

Budget at Completion (BAC): Is the original cost estimate or quotation, indicating the funds required to complete the work. For example in figure 17.1 the BAC is $1000. At the project management level the BAC does not include profit. The reason for this will become clear later when the actual costs are compared with the planned costs. The BAC becomes a generic term when manhours or another parameter are used.

Planned Value (PV): Also called budgeted cost for work scheduled (BCWS) is the integration of cost and time or more commonly manhours and time to give the characteristic S curve which forms the baseline plan (see the *Project Accounts* chapter which explains how to draw an S curve).

Percentage Complete (PC): The PC is a measure of the activities performance and progress up to timenow and is required for the earned value calculation. For this example the PC is 40% at timenow. Timenow is the date up to which the progress is measured.

Earned Value (EV): Also called budgeted cost for work performed (BCWP) is a measure of achievement or value of the work done to timenow. The EV is calculated by the equation:

$$EV = \text{PC (earned progress at timenow)} \times BAC$$
$$= 40\% \times \$1000$$
$$= \$400$$

Actual Value (AV): Also called actual cost for work performed (ACWP) is the amount payable for the work done to timenow. It is the real cost incurred executing the work to achieve the reported progress. For this example at timenow EV is $600.

Estimate at Completion (EAC): The EAC is a revised budget for the activity, work package or project, based on current productivity. The EAC is calculated by extrapolating the performance trend from timenow to the end of the project. This value assumes that the productivity to-date will continue at the same rate to the end of the project. The productivity is defined by the ratio of actual costs (AV) to earned value (EV). If the actual costs (AV) are less than the earned value (EV), then the EAC will be less than the BAC and vice versa.

$$EAC = \frac{AV}{EV} \times BAC$$

But $$EV = PC \times BAC$$

Therefore $$EAC = \frac{AV}{PC \times \cancel{BAC}} \times \cancel{BAC}$$

$$EAC = \frac{AV}{PC}$$

For this example at timenow (see figure 17.1)

$$EAC = \frac{\$600}{40\%} \times 100$$

$$= \$1500$$

The budget variance is therefore BAC - EAC, $1000 - $1500 = -$500 or ($500). The project is forecast to be $500 over budget.

Schedule Variance (SV): The schedule variance calculation is a measure of the time deviation between the planned progress (PV) and the earned progress (EV). The interesting feature about this time variance is that it is measured in money units.

$$SV = EV - PV$$
$$= \$400 - \$500$$
$$= -\$100$$

The sign of the variance will indicate if the project is ahead or behind the planned progress

Negative variance: The project is behind the planned progress.

Positive variance: The project is ahead of planned progress.

Cost Variance (CV): The cost variance is a measure of the deviation between the earned value (EV) and the actual cost of doing the work (AV) (see figure 17.1).

$$CV = EV - AV$$
$$= \$400 - \$600$$
$$= -\$200$$

The sign of the variance will indicate if the costs are under or over the estimate.

Negative variance: The cost is higher than the original estimate (BAC).

Positive variance: The cost is lower than the original estimate (BAC).

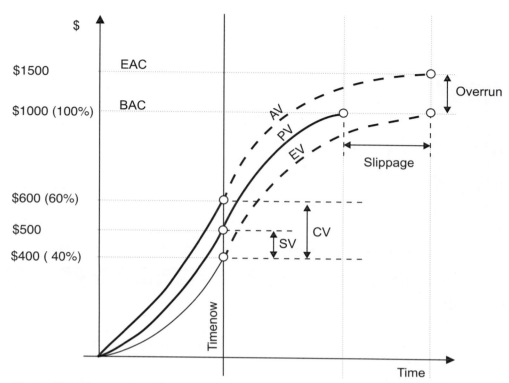

Figure 17.1: Earned Value Graph – shows the planned value, actual value and earned value curves, where the X axis represents the project's schedule and the Y axis represents the level of work or value

2. Earned Value Graph

The earned value graph (see figure 17.1) is produced using the following steps:

Step 1:	Draw the planned value (PV) curve (see how to draw an S curve in the *Project Accounts* chapter).
Step 2:	Draw the EV curve to timenow and extrapolate until the line intersects with BAC. This intersection will give a forecast completion date. This completion date, however, should not be looked at in isolation because it does not consider the network logic, critical path and timing of the activities.
Step 3:	Draw the actual value (AV) curve to timenow and extrapolate to the new end date of the project and EAC. Where EAC = (AV / EV) x BAC. This equation assumes progress to timenow will continue at the same rate to the end of the project.
Step 4:	Draw the SV and CV variances.
Step 5:	Determine how far the project is ahead or behind.

Table 17.2: Earned Value Graph - shows steps to draw the earned value graph

3. Earned Value Table

The earned value data can be presented in both a tabular format (table 17.4) and/or a line graph (figure 17.1). Consider the following steps to set up the earned value table 17.3:

Step 1:	Set up an earned value table (table 17.4) using the following abbreviated field headings (see table 17.1).
Step 2:	List the full scope of work in the WBS column.
Step 3:	Input BAC values for all work packages.
Step 4:	Calculate PV to timenow.
Step 5:	From the data capture sheet transfer the values for PC and AV.
Step 6:	Calculate EV = BAC x PC
Step 7:	Calculate SV, CV and EAC
Step 8:	Sum the following columns: BAC, PV, EV, AV and EAC.
Step 9:	Calculate the total PC, SV and CV.

Table 17.3: Earned Value Table – shows the steps to compile the earned value table

WBS	BAC	PV	PC	EV	AV	SV	CV	EAC
1000	$1000	$500	40%	$400	$600	-$100	-$200	$1500
2000								
Total								

Table 17.4: Earned Value Table - shows the values to timenow from figure 17.1

4. Project Control

Determining Percentage Complete: The weakest link in the earned value calculation is determining percentage complete (PC). If the activity has not started it is zero and if it is complete it is 100%, but all points in between are somewhat of a guess even if you use a structure. A quick way to estimate PC is to use the 50/50 rule, if the job has started give it 50% and when it is finished give it 100%. This rule can be distorted to 40/60, 30/70, 20/80 and 10/90. If the work packages or activities are kept small, or short (less than 50 hours), then this method will work well. Consider the following:

- The earned value analysis should not be used in isolation. An activity with a large schedule variance may have plenty of float and not be a problem, while an activity with a small schedule variance may be on the critical path and need prompt action to prevent project over-run.
- Estimate-at-completion (EAC) is based on the ratio of past performance, but if the original estimate is fundamentally flawed, or performance is significantly different to planned, then the rest of the project should be re-estimated.
- NASA manager: *"Earned value is only useful if the difference between planned and actual is 10% to 15%, if greater then use other methods."* [Rolling horizon barchart]

If the progress indicates that both SV and CV are negative and significant, then ordering a small contractor to increase their resources may actually put them into liquidation quicker! There is obviously a problem which needs to be investigated - is the contractor's estimate over optimistic or is the contractor's productivity under performing?

During the project the activities are usually at various stages of completion; some on target, some ahead of plan, some behind plan, some on budget, some overspent and some under spent. In this situation it is extremely difficult to quantify the project's overall status visually, and it may be argued that a subjective assessment on a complex project is bound to be inaccurate. This problem can be addressed by using the earned value model to roll-up all the activity data and report a bottom line for the project giving an overall position.

5. Client's View of Earned Value

So far the earned value technique has only been looked at from the sub-contractors' point of view. This section will consider the client's position.

Fixed Price	If the sub-contractors are working to a fixed price contract then EV and AC will always be the same.
Progress	The client can effectively use earned value to track the progress of their projects in terms of manhours or costs.
Over Claim	The client must check that sub-contractors do not over claim. If a sub-contractor has claimed 80% of the contract by value, but only completed 50% of the work, there is little financial pressure you can exert.

This section clearly shows that earned value can provide the client with a powerful planning and control tool.

6. Earned Value Reporting

The earned value output lends itself to effective reporting for the following reasons.

Overall Status	The overall status of the project can be seen at a glance on a graph and the tabular reports present more detailed information at the work package and activity levels.
Responsibility	When reporting to functional management the report should clearly indicate the activities that fall under their responsibility. This information can be separately reported if a responsibility field has been included in the data base.
MBE	The reports can use a management-by-exception (MBE) technique to identify problem areas. The MBE thresholds can be set using any of the following: a) Threshold variance SV and CV. b) Activity float = 0 days, identifies the critical path, or sets activity float < 5 days, to identify activities which could go critical in the next week.
Trends	Plot trends wherever possible to indicate the direction of the project.
Extrapolate	Extrapolating trends will give an indication of future events and a quick feedback on recent actions. Even if the variances are negative, but reducing, this will show a positive trend indicating that the project is coming back on course.

7. Earned Value Example

The earned value technique is best learned by walking through an example. Consider a simple project to decorate the four walls and ceiling of your office. The contractor estimates that it will take 2 mandays (16 hrs) per wall and ceiling to prepare and paint. The contractor plans to complete one wall per day, starting work on Monday and finishing on Friday. The materials are available and charged separately.

Activity	BAC	Mon	Tues	Wed	Thurs	Fri
100 – Ceiling	16 hrs	16 hrs				
200 - Wall 1	16 hrs		16 hrs			
300 - Wall 2	16 hrs			16 hrs		
400 - Wall 3	16 hrs				16 hrs	
500 - Wall 4	16 hrs					16 hrs
Daily Total	80 hrs	16 hrs	16 hrs	16 hrs	16 hrs	16 hrs
Running Total PV		16 hrs	32 hrs	48 hrs	64 hrs	80 hrs

Table 17.5: Painting Example Plan - shows the scope of work and schedule

Progress Report: Timenow 1 (end of Monday)

WBS Activity	Percentage Complete	AV Actual Hours
100 – Ceiling	100%	16 hours
200 – Wall 1		
300 – Wall 2		
400 – Wall 3		
500 – Wall 4		

Earned Value Table at timenow 1 (end of Monday)

WBS Activity	BAC Budget	PV Plan	PC	EV Earned	AV Actual	SV	CV	EAC
100	16 hrs	16 hrs	100%	16 hrs	16 hrs	0	0	16 hrs
200	16 hrs	0						16 hrs
300	16 hrs	0						16 hrs
400	16 hrs	0						16 hrs
500	16 hrs	0						16 hrs
Totals	80 hrs	16 hrs 20 %	20%	16 hrs	16 hrs	0 hrs	0 hrs	80 hrs

Table 17.6: Earned Value Table at Timenow 1 - shows the project is on time and within budget

Exercise 1:

Continue with this painting example and produce the earned value table similar to table 17.6 for timenow 2, and timenow 3 (see Appendix 1 for solutions).

Progress Report: Timenow 2 (end of Tuesday)

WBS Activity	Percentage Complete	AV Actual
100 – Ceiling	100%	16 hrs
200 - Wall 1	50%	20 hrs
300 - Wall 2		
400 - Wall 3		
500 - Wall 4		

Progress Report: Timenow 3 (end of Wednesday)

WBS Activity	Percentage Complete	AV Actual
100 – Ceiling	100%	16 hrs
200 - Wall 1	100%	24 hrs
300 - Wall 2	100%	8 hrs
400 - Wall 3	50%	4 hrs
500 - Wall 4		

18

Quality Management

Quality is a much misused and often misunderstood term. In everyday language quality implies superior characteristics and a better quality product. In project management, quality means achieving the required condition.

To achieve the required condition you have to establish a quality management system which involves the following:

- Establish what you need to achieve (scope and required condition)

- State how you are going to achieve it (build-method and quality control plan)

- Set up a quality system to make the product (quality assurance)

- Prove you have made the product to the required condition (quality control)

- Integrate all the components of the quality system (TQM).

DEFINITION
The PMBOK defines project quality management as; '... *the processes required to ensure that the project will satisfy the needs for which it was undertaken* [by addressing] *both the management of the project and the product of the project*'.

DEFINITION
The APM bok describes quality management as; '... *covering quality planning, quality control and quality assurance*.'

The project manager needs to consider both the quality management system to assure the team is capable of designing and building the product (see *Feasibility Study* chapter) and also the quality control system which tests and inspects the product to confirm the team has achieved the required condition. For example, when BMW produces a new car their design office will incorporate the latest technology and latest features, and the production line will make the car, which will then be inspected and tested to confirm it has been made to the required condition.

1. Quality Definitions

Be careful not to confuse quality with degree of excellence or grade, where grade is a category of rank given to products which have the same function but different quality requirements. For example, the Rolls Royce and the Mini cars are often quoted as being at opposite ends of the quality continuum, the Rolls Royce being built to a much higher quality than the Mini. However, if you wish to buy an economical small car that will do 50 + miles to the gallon and is easy to park, then the Mini is the quality car that 'conforms to the client's requirements'.

Quality Assurance: Is a systematic process of defining, planning, implementing and reviewing the management processes within a company in order to provide adequate confidence that the product will be consistently manufactured to the required condition. The body of knowledge defines quality assurance as; *'... the planned and systematic activities implemented within the quality system to provide confidence that the project will satisfy the relevant quality standards.'*

Quality Planning: Is the process of identifying the quality standards the project and product needs to comply with, to achieve the required condition and satisfy the terms of the contract.

Quality Control: Is the process companies go through to confirm that the product has reached the required condition as determined by the specifications and the contract.

Quality Control Plan: The quality control plan integrates the project's scope of work, with the schedule and with the quality control inspection and testing. This is achieved by listing against the sequence of work - the performance requirements and the inspection and testing requirements.

Quality Circles: Quality circles are a management concept the Americans set up for Toyota cars in Japan after the Second World War, to continuously improve their manufacturing process by bringing all the people in a production line together (used in its wider context) to identify and solve problems.

Quality Audit: The body of knowledge defines quality audit as; *'... a structured review of other quality management activities. The objective is to identify lessons learned that can improve performance.....'* [on this project and future company work]. An audit in the project management context should be seen as a search for more information to assist problem-solving and decision-making.

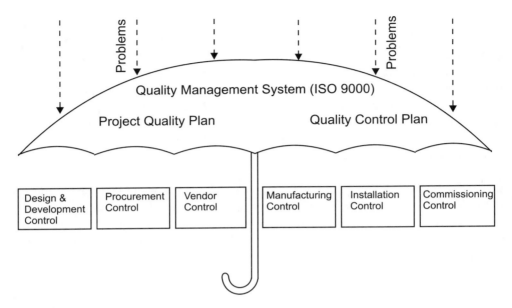

Figure 18.1: Quality Assurance Umbrella – shows how the quality management systems protects the project from an array of problems

Quality Training: Quality training is a company wide issue, from the COE to the receptionist. All employees should undertake quality training so that they understand and can contribute to the quality of the management system and the quality of the product.

Project Quality Plan: The project quality plan is a detailed document explaining how the company will assure that the product will be made to the client's requirements. The sub-headings from the ISO 9000 quality management system can be used to structure the document.

Total Quality Management (TQM): TQM considers the wider aspects of quality by integrating all of the quality management features. Total quality has a people and outcome focus. It first identifies what the client really wants and how it can best be achieved. TQM keeps an emphasis on continuous improvement and also aims to keep the customer satisfied. For quality to be effective it needs to be introduced to all members and all aspects of the company's operation. TQM advances the rational that just as each organisation has unique products, so each company needs a unique quality management system.

2. Quality Control

Quality Control is the process companies go through to confirm that the product has reached the required condition as determined by the specifications and the contract. Quality control defines the method of inspection (testing), in-process inspection and final inspection to confirm the product has met the required condition. The body of knowledge defines quality control as; *'... monitoring specific project results to determine if they comply with relevant quality standards and identify ways to eliminate causes of unsatisfactory results.'*

The required condition should be laid down in the scope of work, specifications, contract which all roll-up to form the project quality plan. The method of testing should be outlined in the project quality plan – this could involve; checklists, inspections, reviews, verification and validation against standards and requirements. Analysis may include statistical analysis, and comparison of results against a baseline or specification.

When a non-conformance has been identified the resulting non-conformance report (NCR) is communicated to the nominated quality stakeholders. This may initiate a quality audit to gather more information before corrective action is authorised to eliminate the causes of unsatisfactory performance of the product. In some cases the corrective action may call for quality awareness training.

In the past, quality management focused on the inspection of the product after it was built. There was little involvement with the manufacturers. The emphasis was on *'catching'* defects before they were released – the management tended to be inward looking. Now there is a general acceptance that you cannot inspect quality into a product if the product was not made properly in the first place. The emphasis has shifted to the workers at the *'coalface'* assuring they have the support, equipment and training to make the job right the first time.

3. Quality Control Plan (QCP)

The purpose of the quality management system is to ensure the project delivers the product the client ordered or required. This should be quantified in the contract as the required condition. The project quality plan will then outline how the required condition can be achieved, inspected and documented.

The quality control plan links the quality requirements to the build-method and scheduled Gantt chart. The quality control plan offers you the facility to impose the predetermined work sequence that you want, rather than what the production department may determine as resource efficient. This can be imposed with a quality control plan which lists the sequence of work and the level of inspection and testing. The sequence of work is determined by the build-method and network diagram. The level of inspection is determined by the level of risk and the level of control required – this can be imposed as: surveillance, inspection, witness, testing or hold points. Consider the following painting project:

Quality Control Plan					
Project:			Complied By:		
WBS	Description	Required Condition (Specification)	Level of Inspection	NCR	Sign Off (Accepted by Client)
100	Surface preparation	SA 2.5 standard	Hold point Inspection		
200	Paint undercoat	Check thickness of paint. Check ambient temperature and humidity	Hold point inspection		
300	Paint topcoat	Check thickness of paint. Check ambient temperature and humidity	Hold point inspection		

Table 18.1: Quality Control Plan – shows the sequence of work, required condition and level of inspection

The painting project has three activities. Activity 100 is to prepare the surface by grit blasting to SA 2.5. The surface is then inspected with a gauge before it can be painted.

Activity 200 is to paint the undercoat. Before painting the temperature and humidity are checked. On completion the paint thickness is measured. This is a hold point which means the top coat cannot be painted before the undercoat has been approved.

The non conformance report (NCR) column enables the quality control to highlight a non conformance. For example, if the surface preparation failed the inspection, the quality inspector would raise an NCR and the grit blasting would have to be done again.

The QCP is an excellent document to plan and control the work, clearly stating the sequence of work and the required condition.

Exercise:

1. Discuss how you would establish the required condition for your project.

2. Discuss how you monitor and test work on your project.

3. When you find an item that does not conform, discuss how you organise for it to be fixed.

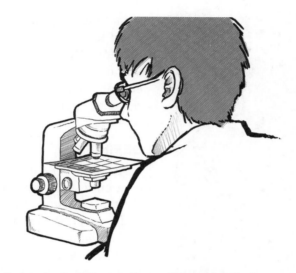

"...hey look at the quality on this project!!..."

19

Project Communications

Communication is one of those subjects that is hard to separate from what we do naturally everyday. So why does it warrant being a knowledge area? For a project to succeed there is a continuous need for effective communication to issue instructions, solve problems, make decisions, resolve conflicts, and keep everyone supplied with the information they need.

Learning Outcomes

After reading this chapter, you should be able to;

| Develop a project's lines of communication |
| Develop a filing system for the project |
| Identify, file and retrieve documents |
| Develop handover documents |
| Understand the document control function |

DEFINITION

The PMBOK defines project communication management as; '... *the process required to ensure timely and appropriate generation, collection, dissemination, storage and ultimately disposition* [disposal] *of project information. It provides the critical links among people, ideas and information that are necessary for success.*'

The project manager and the project office are in the key positions to develop and maintain all the communication links, both within the company and project team, and outside the company with the client, contractors, suppliers and other stakeholders. The project office is like the 'front door' to the project. It is estimated that project managers spend about 90% of their working time engaged in some form of communication, be it; meetings, writing memos, emailing, faxes, reading reports, or talking with team members, senior managers, customers, clients, sub-contractors, suppliers and other stakeholders.

The ability to communicate well, both verbally and in writing, is the foundation of effective leadership. Through communication team members share information and exchange ideas and influence attitudes, behaviours and understanding. Communication enables the project manager to develop interpersonal relationships; inspire team members, handle conflict, negotiate with stakeholders, chair meetings, and make presentations

It, therefore, makes sense to rank communication management along with the other knowledge areas because without effective communication project success will be self-limiting.

It is often stated that *"Information costs money"*, but conversely, *"lack of information could be even more expensive"*. The cost of communication failure may be quantified as; poor problem-solving and poor decision-making (both based on incomplete information), rework due to the shop-floor using old drawings, downtime due to managers not being advised of late delivery of material, and managers turning up for meetings which have been cancelled. A trade-off needs to be established between the cost of mistakes and the cost of supplying good information.

Projects are particularly prone to communication difficulties because of the unique nature of projects and the matrix organisation through which they are generally managed. There may be overlapping responsibilities, decentralised decision-making and complex interfaces all applying a strain on the communication system. However, if the communication system is well managed it could be the single most important factor determining product quality, efficiency, productivity and customer satisfaction.

The Internet and mobile phones have enhanced the communication mediums - a silent revolution is taking place as we move away from post (snail mail) and faxes. The mobile office and virtual office are now real possibilities for the project team. Consider the communication facilities available:

- Email (one-to-one, or one-to-many)
- Web sites
- B2B procurement
- Real time progress reports
- Video conferences
- Mobile email and internet connections
- Mobile communication nationally and internationally

1. Communication Theory

Communication is essentially the interpersonal process of sending and receiving messages. The key components of the communication process are shown in figure 19.1. They include the sender who encodes and sends (transmits) the message, and the receiver who decodes and interprets the message. The receiver then feeds back a response to the sender and closes the loop. The communication model focuses on each element of the process to identify what should happen and prevent misunderstanding.

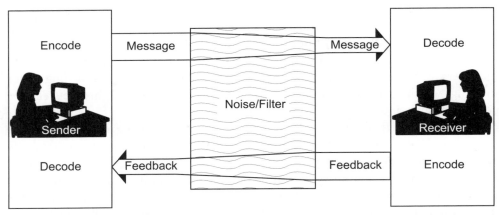

Figure 19.1: Communication Process - showing the communication cycle as a closed loop

Sender: The sender is the originator of the message and the starting point of the communication cycle. The sender will have a purpose to communicate. This may be to; request information, send information, ask a question, issue an instruction, encourage team building, marketing, networking or make a courtesy call.

Encoding: Encoding is the process of converting thoughts, feelings and ideas into 'code or cipher'. In its broader sense code and cipher are the words, numbers, phrases and jargon we use to express ourselves, which can, if we are not careful, sound like a foreign language.

Medium: The medium is the vehicle or channel to convey the message. Project communications can be transmitted in many forms; formal or informal, written or verbal, planned or ad-hoc. Consider the following:

Formal Written	Letters, faxes, email, memos, minutes, drawings, specifications and reports
Formal Verbal	Telephone, voice mail, meetings, video-conferencing
Informal Verbal	Casual discussion between friends
Non-Verbal	Body language

The choice of medium will influence the impact of the message, for example, another memo or email will not have the same impact as a face-to-face discussion.

The use of written communication should be encouraged on the project because it addresses misinterpretation and forgetfulness. All the important agreements and instructions should be confirmed in writing. You will be thankful for keeping a written trail of agreements if (when) problems develop later in the project. Written communications are acceptable for simple messages that are easy to convey and for those messages that require extensive dissemination to all stakeholders. However, verbal channels work best for complex messages that are difficult to convey, may need explanation, and where immediate feedback to the sender is valuable. Verbal communications are also more personal, and this helps to create a supportive and inspirational climate.

Non-Verbal Communication: As the phrases suggest; *'a picture is worth a thousand words'*, and *'actions speak louder than words'*, tells us that our non-verbal actions are an important part of our communication process. This could be:

- Body language
- Hand movements
- Facial expressions
- Eye contact
- Use of interpersonal space.

Eye contact and voice intonation can be used intentionally to enforce certain words or phases. Body language expresses your feelings even though you remain silent. It may also send confusing messages if you are saying one thing, but your body is saying something else. In a meeting a person under attack will unconsciously (instinctively) lean away, or sit back on their chair away from the antagonist. Some researchers claim that gestures can make up more than 50% of communication, a consideration as more and more of our communication moves to emails where non-verbal communications are completely lost.

Receiver: The receiver is the person or persons who receive the transmitted message. Their ability to receive will depend on their; hearing and listening skills, selective listening, eyesight and reading skills, visual activity, tactile sensitivity and extra sensory perception.

Decoding: Decoding is the process of converting the message back into a readable format.

Noise, Filters and Perceptions: These are all factors that interfere with the effectiveness of the communication process. Distortions occur during encoding and decoding; communication channels can be blocked by too many messages; and filters and perceptions may influence our interpretations and impressions.

Physical distractions can interfere with your communication, such as; telephone interruptions, drop-in-visitors, or lack of privacy in an open plan office. It is important to have a place where you can shield yourself from any noise - a place where you can conceptually think issues through (a cave).

Our backgrounds, culture, education and personalities introduce communication filters and perceptions - consider the following; language (lost in translation), social background, semantics, innuendos, intelligence, technical expertise, knowledge base, religion, politics, personal values, ethics, reputation, environment background and organisational position. Consider the OBS block when you tell your boss what he wants to hear for fear that he will shoot the messenger - this will effectively filter the information.

Other factors which will influence your response are: preconceived ideas, frames of reference, needs, interests, attitudes, emotional status, self-interests, assumptions about the sender, existing relationships with the sender and lack of responsive feedback from previous communications with the sender.

Feedback: It is good manners to not only acknowledge receipt of the communication, but also give the sender a time frame for a reply to any questions. It is important to feedback to the sender so that they can gauge how effectively the message was understood, and also for the receiver to confirm they have interpreted the message correctly. No effective communication has occurred until there is a common understanding.

2. Communication Plan

Communication planning pulls the project stakeholders together. The project manager and project office are at the heart of the project's information and control system. It is the project manager's responsibility to not only develop the project organisation structure, but also to develop the project's communication plan and lines of communication. The communication plan should outline the following:

Who	Lines of communication - sender and receiver - responsibility and authority, stakeholders
What	Scope of communication, content and format
How	Email, document, telephone, meeting, presentation
When	Schedule of meetings
Feedback	Confirms message received and understood - document control, transmittals
Filing	Filing, retrieval, storing, back-up, disaster recovery

Lines of Communication: A line of communication may be defined as a formal or informal link between two or more; people, departments, companies, suppliers, contractors or stakeholders. The lines of communication tend to follow the organisation chart, which not only outlines the project manager's (project office) position, but also implies responsibility, authority and who reports to whom. Further, the stakeholder analysis will identify all the other interested parties, both internal and external to the company (see figure 19.2).

Every effort should be made to include all the key people in the project's lines of communication. To leave out a key person will not only limit their knowledgeable contribution to the project, but may also result in them adopting a hostile and negative attitude to the project. If senior people are included in your circulation list this will add weight to the document's perceived importance.

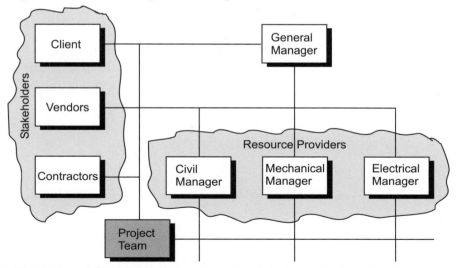

Figure 19.2: Lines of Communication – shows lines of communication with internal (resource providers) and external stakeholders (client, vendors and contractors)

Scope of Communication: What should be communicated??? This is a tricky issue - if you filter the information, you may be accused of being manipulative. However, if you give everyone all the information, they will be overloaded and are unlikely to read it. The objective should be to communicate sufficient information for the recipient to solve problems, make good decisions and feel involved and part of the project. Certain information should be controlled - contract, specifications, drawings, instructions and scope changes. The controlled list (people and content) should be developed by agreement. The art of good communication is to strike a balance with the value of information supplied against the cost and time it takes to collect, process and disseminate the information.

The scope of communication can be a field on the Responsibility Gantt Chart (see table 19.1) where responsibility is linked to the scope of work. If communication can be linked to a WBS work package, then it should be easier to identify the interested parties.

WBS	Description	Responsibility	Stakeholders to be Informed
1001	Production	Production Manager	Vendor supplying materials
1002	Quality	Quality Manager	Client's quality representative
1003	Transport	Transport Manager	Traffic Department for wide loads

Table 19.1: Scope of Communication – shows the link between the WBS, responsibility and the stakeholders

Format: The reporting **format** and **content** should be discussed with the participants. Where possible the client should be encouraged to accept the contractors standard forms (templates), which may have been developed over many projects. The information presented should be in an easy to understand format so that the recipient can quickly assimilate the situation and take appropriate action if required.

Timing: The frequency of reports and turnaround time for responses should be discussed and agreed at the handover meeting. An information sequence may be established. For example, the progress may be captured on a Friday, processed on a Monday and reported on a Tuesday at the progress meeting.

3. Project Information and Control System

The project's information and control system is the life blood of the communication plan, and the data for the project's planning and control cycle. This information flow applies to each line of communication, which can be considered as separate cycles within the total information and control system.

For the information flow to be effective, all parties must be aware that they are part of a linked system and that the quality of the information (like cogs in a wheel or links in a chain) will directly relate to the weakest link (who you may not be able to vote off!).

With the advances in computer aided data processing and reporting, the weak link in the information flow is probably located at the human interface with the data capture function where the project's status and progress are quantified (see *Project Control* chapter).

The project manager also needs to encourage communication between other parties - both formal and informal. Informal channels are often essential to ensure the smooth operation, particularly in a matrix situation where there can be considerable ambiguity, and formal channels are required to dot the 'i' and cross the 't'.

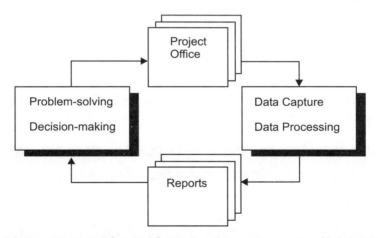

Figure 19.3: Information and Control System – shows a sequence of information flow

Effective communication is more than just people talking to each other and the transmission of facts. In the project context communications are mostly going to use structured reporting forms.

4. Project Reporting

Project data can be collected, processed and reported in many ways, this section will outline a few of the commonly used methods. The format (structure), frequency and circulation of reports needs to be established during the start up phase of the project. The reports should be designed to assist problem-solving and decision-making by the various levels of management so that they can ensure the project will meet its stated goals and objectives.

Status Reports: Status reports simply quantify the position of the project. This data capture function is the first link in the information and control system - all subsequent evaluations are based on this data. Status reports may be specific and focus on the key areas of the project, like time, cost and quality, or they may be general and include a much wider scope (see table 19.2).

Status Report		
Project:		
Complied By:		
Activity	**Description**	**Status**
100	Website	Concept approved
200	Marketing	Brochures approved
300	Procurement	Shipment arrived

Table 19.2: Status Report

Variance Reports: Variance reports quantify the difference between actual and planned, for example, the revised budget being compared with the original budget. The variance is simply the difference between the two values (see table 19.3).

Budget Variance Report				
Project:				
Complied By:				
Activity	**Original Budget**	**Revised Budget**	**Variance**	**Variance %**
100	$20,000	$22,000	($2,000)	(10%)
200	$25,000	$20,000	$5,000	20%
300				

Table 19.3: Budget Variance Report

When a variance is reported as the difference between two values it does not take the size of the parameter into consideration. This problem can be addressed by converting the variance into a percentage of the planned value. Now the variance is expressed as a percentage of the original base.

Trend Reports: The status report tells the manager where the project is, but not where the project is going. The trend report uses historical data and extrapolates this forward to give the manager a feel for the direction of the project. Figure 19.4 shows the earned value graph where both BCWP and ACWP are extrapolated to show their current trends.

Earned Value: The earned value report integrates the variable parameter of cost with time. This technique can also be used to integrate manhours and time. The integration of data enables the planner to model the various parameters more realistically (see figure 19.4 and the *Earned Value* chapter).

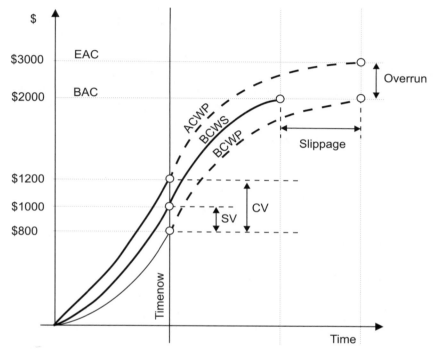

Figure 19.4: Earned Value - showing extrapolated trends

Exception Reports: Exception reports are designed to flag an occurrence or event, which is outside predetermined control limits. This threshold can be set by the project manager as a guideline for the planner to follow and filter out the important information. For example, the planner may be requested to report:

- All activities that have a float less than 5 days - this would highlight all the activities that could go critical in the next week.
- All the deliveries that are due in the next week - this would focus on deliveries that could disrupt the work and resource planning.
- All non-conformance reports (NCR) where the product has not attained the required condition as outlined by the specifications or contract - this would focus on the workforce that may need training, or equipment that may need upgrading.

Monthly Reports: On a long project, monthly reports give the project manager an excellent forum to quantify what is happening on the project and report it to senior management and key stakeholders. The monthly report should roll-up the weekly progress meetings and any other special meetings to give an overall picture of the project. The report should highlight any significant trends or variance, particularly those where the CEOs action is required. It should also identify all major events happening in the next month so that the client, CEO and other stakeholders can plan ahead.

Reporting Period: The agreed timing of the reports should link-in with a schedule of meetings and report roll-ups. This would generally be weekly, but should also include key milestones and be adjusted to accommodate risk and the level of control required

It is important to use structured reports as much as possible, as ad-hoc reports may not include the information the project manager needs; and people naturally tend to report the good news while they are economical with the bad news. However, if managers are asked to report against a structured format they will generally answer it honestly.

Reports should be quick, easy to prepare and read. The managers should not spend too much time reporting - about an hour per reporting period would be a reasonable amount. If it takes longer then the managers should rightly complain they are being distracted from productive work.

5. Document Control

If the project's information and control system is the life blood of the communication plan and the project's planning and control cycle, then the document control system outlines the mechanics of making them happen. The purpose of the document control system is to ensure that key documents are sent timeously to the key people and there is proof of the delivery.

It is the project office's responsibility to manage the document control system. This would be presented to the client as part of the company's document control policy. However, if there are special client requirements, these would be developed and presented in the project quality plan.

Project Filing System: The project office's filing system manages the movement of all the project information. A filing system can be defined as the collecting, sorting, cataloguing (naming and numbering), filing (storage, library), retrieval, issuing, and tracking of project related documents. For the project office to control the flow of information effectively they need to consider a hub and spoke arrangement, where all the information is channelled through (in and out) the project office. This way the project office can track and monitor all the communications and control changes and new versions (revs) (see hub and spoke diagram in *Scope Management* chapter).

Collecting: The lines of communicate should identify the what, where, when and how information is transmitted to and from the project office. See the *Project Control* chapter for discussion on data capture techniques.

Sorting and Cataloguing: The project's filing system should be structured and indexed (named and numbered) to reflect the needs of the project to enable ease of filing and retrieval. For example, it should link in with the WBS structure of the scope of work. An inventory of the project documentation should be prepared and maintained in accordance with the agreed filing system. Multiple versions of documents should be correctly filed and annotated in accordance with the agreed filing system.

The actual layout of the files may be set out by the client in the contract document but should certainly be confirmed at the handover meeting. This is one of the ways the client ensures the contractors are managing their filing correctly. This layout also gives a clear required condition for a document control audit.

Confidential Documents: The document control system must accommodate sensitive and confidential documents, ensuring their safe transmittal and safe custody.

Circulation: At the outset of the project you should agree and confirm the circulation list of controlled documents with the client. The circulation list would typically be identified by the project organisation structure, lines of communication (for client, contractors and supplier companies) and the responsibility matrix.

What Documents? : The documents to be controlled should be agreed with the client, but would typically include; contract, specifications, drawings, schedules, reports, certain correspondence and materials (traceability).

Controlled Copies: An audit trail of transmittals should demonstrate that the controlled documents (usually marked controlled copy) have been sent to the right people and there is a signature confirming date of receipt. It is important that the documentation system confirms that everyone is working to the latest revisions and that old revisions are removed from the system (or boldly stamped cancelled).

On large projects document control would be the responsibility of the configuration department or a document controller, however, on small projects this would be the responsibility of the project manager and the project team.

Transmittal Note: A transmittal note or delivery note is sent with every controlled document. The addressee must sign the transmittal note and return a copy to the project office to confirm the document has been received – as they would with a couriered document (see figure 19.5).

TRANSMITTAL NOTE	
NUMBER:	DATE ISSUED:
FROM:	TO:
	RECEIVED BY:
	DATE:
CONTENT:	

Figure 19.5: Transmittal Note (to confirm receipt of document)

It is the project office's responsibility to control the flow of these controlled documents. The project office must ensure that these controlled documents reach their destination timeously. A control sheet (of the controlled documents) is essential (see table 19.6). Each week the document controller should confirm receipt by telephone or email and ensure the signed transmittals are returned. A list of non-returned transmittals can be tabled at the next progress meeting to encourage compliance.

Transmittal Number	Date Issued	Document Type	Document Number	To / Destination	Date Transmittal Returned

Figure 19.6: Document Control Sheet – shows a transmittal summary

Maintained: All files and documentation are maintained by the project team to ensure they are current, up-to-date, neat and clean.

Information Back-Ups: The document control system should include an information back-up procedure. If information is channelled through a central computer system then the whole system can be saved daily (or even hourly) and a copy held off site. This would be central to the project's and company's disaster recovery system

Handover Documents: One of the areas that is often conveniently forgotten by the contractors is the handover of project documents when the project is complete. At the handover meeting the client, contractors and suppliers should agree on what the handover document's include, their content, format, timing and location.

The savvy project manager should identify the handover documents as a work activity early on in the project (handover meeting) so that they can be planned, monitored and controlled. These documents should be identified in the contract, but would typically include; as-built drawings, quality control inspections, equipment manuals, operator manuals and service manuals.

Exercise:

1. Discuss how you would develop a filing system exclusively for your project.
2. Discuss how you use templates to capture and communicate information.
3. Discuss how you determine the official lines of communication on your project.
4. Progress reports keeps the project office and the project manager informed on what is happening on the project. Discuss the report templates you use to monitor and control work on your project.
5. Document control ensures the right people receive the right documents and there is proof of transmittal. Discuss how you achieve this on your project.

20

Project Meetings

Learning Outcomes

After reading this chapter, you should be able to;

Explain the purpose, objective and scope of project meetings

Plan a project meeting

Arrange and support a project meeting

Run brainstorming workshops

Project meetings are a key part of the project communication process. Some managers prefer many small meetings, while other managers prefer the occasional big meeting with all the stakeholders attending. Some managers prefer informal ad hoc meetings, while other managers prefer formal structured meetings.

Discussing the project around the coffee machine may be good team building, but it is not an effective way to control the flow of information. To make the most of a meeting there needs to be structure. This chapter will discuss four different types of project meetings;

a) Preparing for a meeting (generic)

b) Handover meeting (to initiate a project phase or contract)

c) Progress meetings (to guide the project to a successful completion).

d) Brainstorming workshop (to generate ideas and solve problems).

Whichever type of meeting you use there are five basic reasons for holding a project meeting:

Information	Information sharing - exchange of data
Problem-Solving	Problem-solving, brainstorming, generating ideas, options and alternatives
Decision-Making	Decision-making, select a course of action, gain support and commitment from the team
Planning	Planning and execution – what, who, when, how, where and why
Progress	Evaluation, monitoring, measuring, reviewing and forecasting

Table 20.1: Reasons for Project Meetings - shows five basic reasons for holding a meeting

As the project manager is responsible for establishing the project communication plan, he is also responsible for setting up the schedule of project meetings. Project team members typically attend more meetings than their function colleagues. This is because projects tend to be multi-disciplined with a high degree of uncertainty and require more communication to keep everyone informed.

Although a high percentage of the communications and meetings will be informal and ad hoc, it is essential to have a formal structure (of communications and meetings) to confirm all the agreements and instructions, and keep all the stakeholders informed.

For project meetings to be effective they require good planning to ensure genuine participation from the entire team. Advance notice must be given outlining the purpose of the meeting, and an agenda should be established to enable the participants to prepare.

1. How to Prepare a Meeting (generic)

Whatever the purpose of the meeting, all meetings benefit from advance preparation and structure. This section will outline how to prepare for a typical project meeting – the following sections will focus on the 'Handover Meeting', the 'Progress Meeting' and the 'Brainstorming Workshop'.

Call Meeting	As the single point of responsibility the onus falls on the project manager to call project related meetings. These meetings may be one-off meetings or part of a schedule of regular meetings.
Purpose	The chair person needs to define the purpose of the meeting - they need to be clear about the precise objectives of the meeting. The project manager needs to ask the question, *"do I need to hold a meeting?"*
Chair Person	The project manager or chair person needs to identify themselves as all attending need to know who is in charge of the meeting.
Agenda	The agenda is a list of the topics to be discussed at the meeting. The agenda makes sure everyone knows exactly what is going to be discussed, why and what is wanted from the discussion. The agenda should be prepared as a logical sequence of items, with time allocated to each item on the basis of its importance - this gives the chair person a means of controlling the meeting to limit the discussion wandering on to other topics and becoming a talking shop. If you then run out of time, at least the important issues will have been covered.
Attendance	The purpose of the meeting will determine who should attend. You need to balance the size of the meeting with the purpose. As meetings grown in size the meetings tend to become increasingly unproductive. If everyone is expected to participate, try and keep the attendance to less than 10 people. The size of the meeting will influence the input from certain people. Some individuals do not like to speak in large groups, preferring to contribute in smaller groups, or to the project manager directly. They may well approach the project manager after the meeting with some valuable input.
Book Venue	The venue needs to be selected and booked. The facilities of the venue need to be organized – table, chairs, white board, OHP, powerpoint, DVD player, tea, coffee, water etc.
Circulate Background Information	Reading material relevant to the discussion needs to be circulated to each team member attending the meeting in advance. Each person should know what is expected from them so they can come prepared.
Time Limit	A formal meeting should have a time limit as meetings can be a great time waster. Allocate time to each item on the agenda to set the speed of the meeting, and try and end on time as team members may have other meetings to attend.

Start on Time	This sounds obvious, but if your meetings start late then team members will tend to arrive late for the following meetings you hold. Starting on time is also symbolic that the meeting is important. Schedule your meetings for 10 minutes after the hour, to give people time to get to your meeting from their previous meeting.
State the Purpose	The chair person should start the meeting by stating the explicit purpose and clarify what should be accomplished by the time the meeting is over.
Rules	The chair person should set out the rules, which may include; mobile phones off, and speaking through the chair.
Minutes	The chair person should assign a person to take the minutes.
Encourage Participation	A sign of a good meeting is lots of interactive discussion and cross-flow of ideas. If the project manager only wants to present information he should send an email or a memo. The project manager's challenge as chairperson is to encourage interactive discussion and encourage full participation. This is a balance between drawing out the silent and controlling the talkative. However, redirecting the discussion is usually more effective than trying to quieten the talkative. A few subtle techniques go a long way toward increasing participation. A good meeting is not a series of dialogues but a cross-flow of discussion and constructive debate. The chair should guide, mediate, stimulate and summarize. The chair should refrain from preaching or one-on-one dialogue, the point is to listen and facilitate discussion. Because junior members of the team are usually reluctant to disagree with senior members, it is best to encourage them to get their ideas on the table first. Give credit were credit is due - make sure the people who suggest ideas get the credit, because people often make someone else's ideas their own. Giving due credit encourages continued participation.
Summarise	Before moving onto the next item on the agenda summarise what points have been made and what action has been agreed. Confirm who is responsible for what, and what deadlines must be achieved. These points should be included in the minutes.

Table 20.2: Preparing a Meeting – shows a checklist for preparing a meeting

Minutes: Minutes of a meeting are a permanent certified record of what was said and agreed by the team members. Minutes should be taken for all meetings and produced as soon as possible after the meeting (preferably the next day) and communicated to the key people as per the communication plan and document control. The minutes should document discussions and agreements taken during the meeting, together with actions to be carried out before the next meeting. The minutes of one meeting usually form the agenda of the subsequent meeting.

If problems arise, such as, disputes and legal action, the minutes are often used as evidence of decisions made up to that point in the project. It is, therefore, important that the minutes are accurate and a true reflection of the meeting; this is why the first item of an agenda should be the approval of the previous meeting's minutes. The certified copy should then be filed in the project office's library as an historical reference and available for the closeout report.

Minutes		
Type of Meeting:	Progress Meeting	
Meeting Number:		Date:
Next Meeting:		
Complied By:		
Circulation:		
Attendance:		
Agenda:	Discussion	Action

Table 20.3: Minutes of Meeting Template – shows the main headings to structure the minutes

2. Handover Meeting

The purpose of the handover meeting is to formally commence the project, the project phase or subcontract. The attendance would normally include the client, senior management, the project team members and other concerned parties; contractors, suppliers and stakeholders. The purpose of the handover meeting is to set the scene for the project, what it has to achieve, how it will be achieved and establish how it will be managed. It is the client's prerogative to chair the meeting.

A little pre-planning will help get the meeting off to a good start. In the handover meeting you need to establish your leadership and outline your management style. This will serve as a model for future meetings and set the tone of professionalism, because if the meeting does not go well you will lose credibility. A typical agenda for the handover meeting may include:

Purpose of the Meeting	Confirm the purpose of the meeting and agree on the agenda, sign off any previous meetings and assign a person to take the minutes.
Project Charter	Confirm the identity of the project (name and number). Outline the purpose of the project and the scope of work.
Contract	Discuss contractual requirements, scope of work, specification, retention, bonds, penalties and warranties.
Scope of Work	Outline the subdivision of work, who is **responsible** for what and who has the **authority** to issue instructions. Outline the lines of communication. Outline how the **scope of work** will be documented; this may include; a drawing register, parts list, specification, brief, proposal, feasibility study etc.
Project OBS	Identify and introduce all the relevant project participants and stakeholders. Discuss the scope of work and contracts - who does what, people's responsibilities and authority.
Project Team	Discuss the importance of the **project team** and the need for team members and stakeholders to work together to achieve the project goals. Encourage the team members to participate, introduce themselves and discuss their areas of expertise.
Communication Plan	Discuss the lines of communication and the document control system. Discuss what documents will be controlled, who they will be sent to, and how they will be transmitted.
Build-Method	Discuss how the product will be made, walk through the sequence of events. Discuss the required condition and hold points.
Closeout Reports	Review relevant closeout reports from previous projects and discuss what can be learnt.
Baseline Plan	Discuss the baseline plan, particularly the project's schedule and milestones, the procurement schedule, the resource loadings, the budgets and cashflows.

Instructions	Explain the procedure for issuing instructions, the format and who has authorization (client and contractor). List the documents that will be used for issuing instructions, these could be: drawings, schedules, minutes, memos, letters, faxes and email.
Reporting	Discuss the project's reporting requirements, the content, format, frequency and circulation.
Meetings	Discuss the schedule of meetings, attendance, venue, agenda and minutes. At the start of the project there will be a juggling of time tables, meeting schedules and venues to suit the availability of the project's participants, and link in with the contractors reporting periods.
Configuration Management	Discuss how scope changes will be incorporated and communicated. Outline procedures for scope changes and identify the people with approved signing power.
Payments	Discuss how the progress will be measured and how payments will be made.
Client Supply	List of client supplied items.
Inclusions	List of inclusions and exclusions.
Commissioning	Discuss how the product will be run-up, tested, accepted or rejected. Discuss how the product will be handed over and the need for operator manuals and training.
Issue the Minutes	Issue the minutes timeously (preferably the following day) to those who were present and any other key stakeholders. It is important to make a formal record of all decisions made, actions discussed, tasks assigned and comments made during the meeting. Although the minutes should be brief and clearly indicate actions required, consider including some history for complicated items.
Follow-up	Although you may have achieved commitment at the meeting, it may require some follow-up to ensure the minutes will be actioned timeously and not turn into a rush before the next meeting.

Table 20.4: Handover Meeting – shows a checklist for running a handover meeting

It is important to get the handover meetings right to set the framework and tone for the project, and then follow-up with progress meetings to keep the momentum going and the project on track.

Although the handover or start-up meeting is outlined here as one discrete meeting, in practice this may be conducted over a series of meetings or informal get together (a drink or meal), and by using other communication mediums (telephone, fax, email, video-conference).

3. Project Progress Meetings

Progress meetings are generally held every week to monitor progress and guide the project to a successful completion. Progress meetings provide an effective forum for the project manager to co-ordinate, integrate and manage the project's participants. Meetings provide a dynamic environment where interaction and innovation will enhance the cross flow of ideas and help solve problems. The meetings should also provide the venue for consensus and decision-making. A typical progress meeting would contain the following:

Agenda	The agenda should be circulated before the meeting to the list of participants who are responsible for the topics outlined in the agenda. The agenda should list action points so the participants can prepare for the meeting.
Minutes	Approve the minutes of the previous meeting. Confirm who will take the minutes for this meeting.
Actions	Report on actions from previous meetings. An action item is a problem which is logged and assigned to a person to be resolved - and tracked until closeout. Confirm the activities to be performed to solve the problem, identify the owner of each activity. List dependencies of each activity and their owner. Estimate the duration of each activity, outline how the activities will be tracked - even track on a daily bases if appropriate, but never lose focus on completing the project.
Progress	Report progress by work packages - prioritise if necessary.
Configuration Management	Discuss scope changes and concessions - their implications and approval.
Document Control	List controlled documents transmitted and police signing of transmittals.
Claims	Discuss any claims since the last meeting.
Quality	Discuss NCRs and quality issues.
Payments	Approve invoices for payment.
Minutes	Issues the minutes of the meeting the next day.

Table 20.5: Project Progress Meeting – shows a checklist for running project progress meetings

4. Brainstorming Workshops

They say *"... two heads are better than one"* – so five or six heads interacting together in a brainstorming workshop could be better still to generate a stream of innovative ideas.

Sunday Times: *'Brainstorming was born on Madison Avenue in the 1950s. Brainstorming was long considered the preserve of those wild and crazy folk in advertising. In more recent years, however, it has spread into the mainstream and is now used by businesses of all kinds, not to mention everyone from civil servants to scientists and engineers, or, indeed, anyone with a problem to solve."*

Brainstorming workshops are a great technique for generating creative ideas. Generally performed in groups, it is a fun way to get lots of fresh ideas on the table and get everyone thinking and pulling together. The participants should be relatively at ease with one another, so that they are comfortable shouting out off-the-cuff zany ideas - this often generates the best results.

A typical brainstorming session would include the following:

Venue	Meet in a room which is conducive for the workshop, use white boards and flip charts to capture the ideas for all to read.
Team Size	Restrict the workshop to about 5 to 10 people, any less and you do not get the volume of ideas and cross fertilization – any more and people cannot get a word in edgeways.
Purpose	The chairperson should state the purpose of the session and define the problem. Where necessary give background to the problem and recent history of decisions.
Rules	The chairperson should outline how the brainstorming session will be run.
Suspend Criticism	All ideas, no matter how crazy they may seem, should be encouraged and recorded on a flip chart without comment or criticism from the group. The general goal of brainstorming is to collect as many ideas as possible, making quantity much more important than quality at this initial stage. If people's ideas are criticized they may clam up and not generate any more ideas. The ideas can be evaluated later.
Freewheel	Team members need to free-up their mind of inhibiting constraints. Get them to close their eyes and dream - working around the problem. Think laterally to generate extreme views - the wackier the ideas the better. Use word association to generate ideas.
Cross Fertilize	Encourage the team members to listen to other people's ideas, and try to piggy back and build on the suggestions to generate even more ideas (synergy). Cross fertilization enables you to combine and improve on ideas which can sometimes result in surprising twists and turns.
Reverse	Reverse brainstorm - *'In how many ways can this way fail'*.

Quantity	The more ideas the better – run the session at a fast pace - go for 50 ideas in 15 minutes. Work on the rationale that no idea is a bad idea.
Document	Use flipcharts and white boards to note the ideas, maybe grouping them if possible. Leave the ideas up for incubation. When the session is finished, copy the ideas onto paper and circulate.
Time	Restrict the session to about 30 minutes, any more and the ideas drop off, and people get bored.
Follow-up	After the session circulate the ideas to the team and ask them to consider the problem and send any further suggestions to Mr Minute.

Table 20.5: Brainstorming Workshop – shows a checklist for running a brainstorming workshop

Brainstorming Limitations: Brainstorming is one of the team idea generating techniques that has achieved general acceptance. But, it should be recognised that one of the limitations of brainstorming is that it is rarely preceded by prolonged detail study that preludes most creative endeavours. Preparation is a vital part of the creative process, such as, looking at closeout reports and re-defining the problem.

Exercises:

1. Discuss the purpose and reason for having project meetings.
2. Discuss how you would prepare and run a handover meeting.
3. Discuss how you would prepare and run a project progress meeting.

21

Project Organisation Structures

Learning Outcomes

After reading this chapter, you should be able to;

Understand the advantages and disadvantages of the functional organization structure managing multi-disciplined projects

Understand the advantages and disadvantages of matrix organization structures managing multi-disciplined projects

Explain the application of the organisation structures in project management

Explain the difference between matrix and functional organisation structures

Hierarchical organisation structures where decisions are taken at the top, executed at the bottom, and supervised in the middle, have proved to be too cumbersome for today's environment of rapid change.

Projects are performed by people and managed through people, so it is essential to develop an organisation structure which reflects the needs of the project (tasks), the needs of the project team and just as importantly the needs of the individual. To achieve this projects are managed through three types of structures;

- Functional organisation structures
- Matrix organisation structures
- Team structures (see *Project Teams* chapter)

DEFINITION

The PMBOK defines project human resource management as; '... *the process required to make the most of the people involved with the project.*'

DEFINITION

The APM bok says; '...*issues typically important in the structuring of a project include the degree of project / functional orientation, the extent of the project management (office) authority .... the allocation of resources ..... authorisation and reporting procedures and system*'.

1. Functional Organisation Structure

This **traditional** organisation structure is based on the subdivision of product lines or disciplines into separate departments, together with a vertical hierarchy. The figure outlines a typical structure with a number of functional departments reporting to the general manager. Also called **wedding-cake** corporate structure (see figure 21.1).

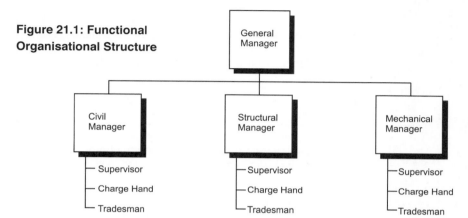

Figure 21.1: Functional Organisational Structure

The **advantages** of the functional organisation structure (particularly for managing projects within their own department) are:

Simple	They are simple.
Flexible	They can achieve a high degree of flexibility, because people in the department can be assigned to the project, then immediately re-assigned to other work. Switching back and forth between projects is easily achieved.
Home	Functional departments provide a home for technical expertise which offers technical support and continuing development.
Support	They provide good support as work is usually carried out in the department.
Career Path	The functional department provides the normal career path for advancement and promotion.
Estimate	Functional department's work is simpler to estimate and manage as the scope of work is usually restricted to its own field; and the functional data base should contain information from previous projects (closeout reports).
Communication	Lines of communication within the department are short and well established.
Reaction Time	There is quick reaction time to problems within the department.
Consistent	Some employees prefer working in a consistent work routine, rather than the challenge of diverse projects.
Responsibility	They offer clearly defined responsibility and authority for work within the department.

The **disadvantages** of the functional organisation structure (particularly when being used on multi-disciplined projects) are:

Responsibility	No single point of responsibility as the project's scope moves from one department to another, this can lead to co-ordinating chaos.
Communication	On multi-disciplined projects there are no formal lines of communication between the people within the different departments. Generally, the only formal line of communication is through the functional managers, which will lengthen the lines of communication and slow down the response time. With these long communication cycles, problem-solving and decision-making will be adversely impacted.
Conflict	Competition and conflict between functional departments may limit effective communication of important project information.
Priority	Departmental work may take priority over project work. If there is a resource overload the project's schedule may be pushed out. This could adversely impact the handover to the next department and delay the project's completion.
Client	For functional managers the project is not always the main focus of concern, particularly when the scope has moved to another department. The client may well feel like a football being passed from one department to another. Clients prefer to deal with one person - the project manager.
Stakeholders	The responsibility for external co-ordination with the client, suppliers and other stakeholders may become muddled because of overlap, underlap and inadequately defined responsibilities.
Co-ordinating	Without defining who is the project manager the client may end up co-ordinating the different functional departments themselves.
Myopic	The department may myopically focus only on their scope of work in preference to an holistic view of the project, and a departmental solution to a problem may not be the best solution for the project as a whole.
Motivation	The motivation for people assigned to the project can be weak if the work is not perceived to be mainstream.
Multi-Discipline	Multi-discipline projects call for horizontal forms of co-ordination, a characteristic that is foreign to vertically orientated functional hierarchy structures.

The functional organisation structure does offer excellent facilities within its own department, but where a multi-disciplined scope of work calls for interaction with other departments then the system may be found lacking. To address this problem the matrix organisation structure offers an interaction of both functional and project interests.

2. Matrix Organisation Structure

The topology of the matrix structure has the same format as a mathematical matrix, in this case the vertical lines represent the functional department's responsibility and authority, while the horizontal lines represent the project's responsibility and authority, thus giving the matrix structure its unique appearance and name.

The matrix structure is a temporary structure created to respond to the needs of the project where people from the functional departments are assigned to the project on a full-time or part-time basis. Consequently, the matrix structure is initially superimposed on the existing functional structure.

The matrix structure is considered by many practitioners to be the natural project organisation structure, as it formalises the informal links between departments. On multi-disciplined projects people need to communicate at the operational level to perform their tasks. Where the lines of responsibility intersect, this represents people to people contact, thus providing shorter formal lines of communication.

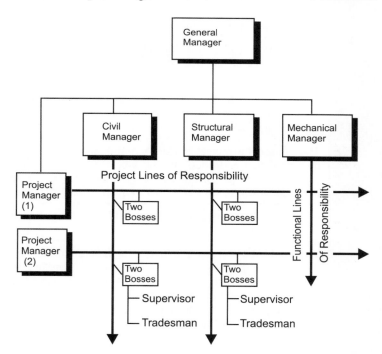

Figure 21.2: Matrix Organisation Structure – shows the project and functional lines of responsibility

A characteristic of project management is that it relies on a number of functional departments and contractors to produce the product, each appearing to act autonomously and yet requiring strong communication bonds with each other. The project manager needs to cut across organisational lines to co-ordinate and integrate specific resources located in different departments. To achieve this, the project manager must have appropriate tools, in particular an information system that not only accommodates interdisciplinary tasks but also has the cross-functional capability of retrieving data from the different departments. Consider some of the **advantages** inherent in the typical matrix organisation structure:

Responsibility	The project has a clear single point of responsibility - the project manager.
Resources	The project can draw on the entire resources of the company. When several projects are operating concurrently, the matrix structure allows a time-share of expertise which gives a higher degree of resource utilisation.
Equipment	By sharing the use of equipment, the capital costs can be shared between projects and functional departments.
Seconded	With seconded resources project termination is not necessarily a traumatic event (worrying about continuing employment), the resources can return to their original functional department.
Client	There is rapid response to client needs. The client communicates directly with the project manager.
Corporate Link	The corporate link will ensure consistency with company policies, strategies and procedures, yet give the flexibility to tailor these to the project's needs.
Job Descriptions	The matrix structure can be tailored to the needs of the project with respect to; job descriptions, procedures, work instructions and lines of communication.
Trade-off	The needs of the project and functional departments can be addressed by negotiation and trade-off. The project is mainly concerned with, **what** and **when** (scope and planning), while the functional department is concerned with, **who** and **how** (resources and technical).
Problem-Solving	Problem-solving can draw on a much wider base for ideas and options - brainstorming.
Experts	Teams of experts within the functional department are kept together even though the projects may come and go, therefore, technology, know-how, expertise and experience are not lost when the project is completed and the project team disbanded. Specialists like to work with other specialists in the same discipline thus increasing innovation, problem-solving ability and synergy.
Multi-Disciplinary	The multi-disciplinary environment exposes people to a wider range of considerations.
Career Path	By retaining their functional home, specialists keep their career path. If they work well in a multi-disciplined environment then a new career in the project office may open up.
Training	The matrix structure is a good training ground for project managers working in multi-functional and cross-functional environments.
Integrates	The matrix structure integrates the WBS with the OBS.

The following **disadvantages** are inherent with the matrix structure:

Complex	The organisation structure is complex and more difficult for the participants to understand than the simpler functional or pure project organisations.
Dual Responsibilities	Dual responsibility and authority leads to confusion, divided loyalties, unclear responsibilities, and conflicts over priorities and allocation of resources.
Conflict	The two boss situation is a recipe for conflict, between both managers and employees, and between managers over the allocation of employees.
Priorities	A company with a number of projects calling on the same resources faces real problems establishing priorities and resource allocation, as the project manager and functional manager will claim their work should have the highest priority. In this situation, the priority should be made at a senior management level.
Cost	The cost of running a matrix organisation is higher than a functional or pure project because of the increased number of managers involved in the administration and decision-making process.
Integration	Project integration between departments is more involved and complex than integrating people within one functional department. With functional projects and pure projects it is clear who has the power to make decisions, however, with the matrix structure the power may be balanced between departments. If this causes doubt and confusion then the productivity of the project may suffer.
Sharing	The sharing of scarce resources could lead to inter-departmental conflict.
No Desk	After a secondment of a several months personnel may find they either do not have a functional department to return to, or their position has been re-appointed - *"Someone is sitting at my desk!!"*
Complex	In the matrix structure the project manager controls the administration decisions, while the functional managers control the technical decisions. This division of power and responsibility could lead to an overly complex situation.
Conflict	Where the project and functional lines of influence cross there exists a two boss situation which is a recipe for conflict.
Personnel	Functional departments are unlikely to give their best personnel to the project.

For the matrix organisation structure to work successfully the functional departments will have to make major changes in the way they work. The matrix structure introduces new management interfaces and increases the potential for conflict. New management skills are required for the functional managers to accommodate conflicting goals, priorities and resource demands.

3. Job Description

The job description develops the organisation structure's position into a further level of detail. The job description should contain the job title, the supervisor, a job summary, duties, responsibilities and authority. A **framework** for a job description should include:

- Who the person reports to.
- Who reports to that person.
- What duties the person is responsible for.
- What authority the person has to issue instructions.

Using this basic framework consider an example of a project manager's job description - reporting to the general manager the project manager is assigned responsibility and authority to:

- Achieve all the targets set out in the baseline plan.
- Select and manage the project team.
- Set up the project office and management system to manage and control the project.
- Represent the company at the client meetings.
- Process all project related correspondence.
- Authorise all reimbursable procurement and services required by the project.
- Negotiate and award all the sub-contracts.
- Process all non-conformance reports (NCR's).
- Issue the necessary project procedures.
- Issue weekly / monthly progress reports and financial statements.
- Approve all changes on behalf of the company.
- During the development of the scope of work it is the project manager's responsibility to structure and co-ordinate the input and involve all interested parties (internal and external). This involvement is required to determine the technical and managerial requirements.
- Some of the qualities the project manager requires include: an ability to communicate, negotiate, deduce, quantify dreams, quantify wish lists and interpret the client's needs correctly.

As the project manager is responsible for selecting the project team it can be assumed that the project manager is also responsible for defining their job descriptions. These would normally include the following positions:

- Project Accountant
- Project Planner
- Project Engineer
- Project QA
- Project Procurement

The size of the project would determine the number of people in the team. On a small project one person might cover all these positions, while on a large project there could be a number of people per position. The bottom line is that the project manager is the single point of responsibility and, as such, has a blanket responsibility for the project. The project manager's authority however, might be limited. The key word here is to strive for authority commensurate with your responsibility.

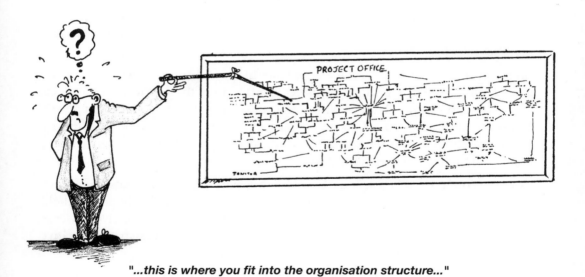

"...this is where you fit into the organisation structure..."

4. Responsibility - Authority Gap

A characteristic of the matrix organisation structure is that it relies on the functional departments for resources. Although the project and functional departments may appear to work autonomously, for project success they need strong communication bonds with each other. The project manager needs to cut across organisational lines to co-ordinate and integrate specific resources located in the functional departments. To achieve this the project manager must have both a fully integrated information and control system and the means of addressing the responsibility - authority gap.

Responsibility may be defined as feeling obliged to perform assigned work, while authority is the power to carry out the work. The authority gap is being assigned responsibility, but not having sufficient authority to make the work happen. It is often stated that authority should be commensurate with responsibility, but feedback suggests that general managers are often reluctant to assign sufficient formal power to project managers. In which case, the project managers need to address the authority gap in other ways.

Formal Authority: Or position power is automatically conferred on you with your appointment to the project. While position power can be exerted over subordinates, this type of power is very limited in its acceptance and often does little to influence behaviour particularly with the functional manager who own the resources the project manager needs.

Budget Authority: If the project manager holds the purse strings this will confer some financial power over the functional managers, particularly if the functional departments are run as cost centres. It is certainly powerful when dealing with outside suppliers and contractors who depend on the payments for their existence. Budget authority can lie with both the carrot and the stick - the promise of future business, incentive bonus and threats of withholding payment for poor work.

Coercive Power: Uses the fear and the avoidance of punishment and threats to influence behaviour. This may be seen as power not to reward, or threaten demotion, withhold overtime, limit salary increase, or transfer to another job. Use of coercive power is linked to organisation position, but tends to inhibit creativity and can have a negative impact on team morale.

Information Power: Expert knowledge and technical ability are effective if perceived valuable and shared appropriately with functional managers and project participants, however, it will erode trust and creates resentment if hoarded. As project manager you should be at the centre of the information and control system, and therefore in an ideal position to capture, process, file and disseminate useful information.

Reward Power: This is the ability to provide positive rewards for performance, and to be effective, it must properly correspond to participants' values and expectations. Since money is not always available, project managers must consider a variety of potentially satisfying sanctions especially those related to work challenge and recognition (see Herzberg's motivation and hygiene factors in the *Project Leadership* chapter in Burke 5ed).

Cognitive Persuasion: The logical (cognitive) approach includes the use of reasoned argument, evidence and logical consistency. This way you persuade the functional managers to contribute to your project and part with their best people for the success of the project, their department and the company. This approach works well on large projects.

Emotional Persuasion: Beg the functional managers for their assistance, requesting a favour, say "please", appeal to their better nature - go down on your knees!

Personal Power: Charismatic project managers can compel people to listen and follow them. They are natural leaders who can persuade and encourage others to follow a certain course of action. They have a sense of mission, a sense of purpose, a good sense of humour, are empathetic to staff needs, enthusiastic and self-confident.

Ideally, project managers should be competent in all areas of authority for continuing success. Charismatic project managers, for example, may have initial appeal, but as problems arise if they are not able to assist technically their power will be undermined. The project managers' leadership ability is usually expressed in terms of influencing the behaviour and attitudes of the project team, the effectiveness of leaders is therefore dependant to some extent on their power.

Exercises:

1. Discuss the application of an organisation structure found in a project management environment.
2. Discuss the difference between a matrix and functional organisation structure with examples of each.
3. Discuss how project managers can improve their level of influence and power in a project environment.

22

Project Teams

Learning Outcomes

After reading this chapter, you should be able to;

Explain the reason teams are used in the project environment

Outline the role of the project manager

Explain the individuals' purpose for project team membership

A project team may be defined as a number of people who work closely together to achieve shared common goals. Through interaction they strive to enhance their creativity, innovation, problem-solving, decision-making, morale and job performance. A team implies a number of people working together to achieve results, while a group of people implies a collection of individuals who, although they may be working on the same project, do not necessarily interact with each other. This is often the case when the project manager co-ordinates the people individually. Under such conditions, unity of purpose is a myth (see figure 22.1).

Management teams are not always associated with projects, but as companies move to a management-by-projects approach, so the link will become better recognised. The implementation of the project planning and control techniques is through people, therefore, to effectively implement the management system one must gain support and commitment from the project team and other stakeholders. Many projects fail to reach their optimum level of performance, not because of any lack of equipment or project systems, but purely because the human factors were not addressed.

The growth of new technology, increased complexity and competition, has generated a need for multi-disciplined teams to work closely together. Teamwork should aim to bring individuals together in such a way that they increase their effectiveness without losing their individuality - an orchestra is a good example of a team working harmoniously on this basis.

DEFINITION

The PMBOK defines team development [managerial and technical] as; *'... both enhancing the ability of stakeholders to contribute as individuals as well as enhancing the ability of the team to function as a team.'*

DEFINITION

The APM bok defines teamwork as; *'... effective teamwork is generally at the heart of effective project management.'*

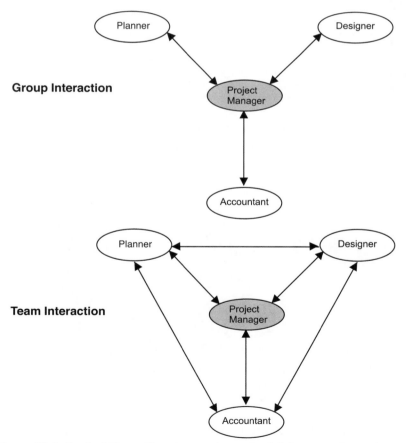

Figure 22.1: Project Team Structure – shows the link between the project manager and the other team members

1. Purpose of Project Teams

Project teams are an efficient and effective way of managing projects, where efficiency implies performing the work well, and effectiveness implies performing the right work. Consider the following points:

Volume of Work	To achieve the schedule the volume of work must be distributed (shared) amongst a number of people.
Range of Skills	The scope of the project may require a range of skills which any one person is unlikely to have. Consider the orchestra again - this is an excellent example of a set of complementary skills and talents (functional skills) which are required to produce the music.
Ideas	Brainstorming and discussions are a good example of interactive team work to generate creative ideas and solve problems.
Decisions	Once a project team has made a collective decision, the team will be committed to support their course of action.
Risk	Project teams generally take riskier decisions than an individual would on their own. There is a feeling of mutual support.
Motivation	Project teams enhance self-motivation - each members does not want to let the side down.
Support	Project teams support other team members when they need help both technically and emotionally.

Management tests show that teams repeatedly make better decisions than the team members would make individually with the same information. This has been attributed to the teams' wider range of skills and experiences.

"...ladies and gentlemen may I introduce you to the Harmonious Trio?!..."

2. Individual's Purpose for Team Membership

Why would an individual wish to be part of a project team? Consider the following:

Affiliation	It is a means of satisfying an individual's social or affiliation needs - to belong to something or be part of a team.
Risk	To share risk with other team members - spread the load.
Relationship	To be associated with a company is a means of establishing self-esteem.
Support	It is a means of gaining support and someone to bounce ideas off.
Home	The team provides a psychological home for the individual.

The previous table outlines why some people prefer to work in groups. It should be mentioned, however, that not everyone wants to work in a team - many people prefer to work on their own. And with the increasing use of email, the Internet and video-conferencing, working from home is becoming a feasible option.

3. Benefits of Teams

In the past, corporations have been preoccupied with the qualities of individual people. Any attempt to list the qualities of a good project manager would demonstrate abilities that are almost certainly mutually exclusive to any individual:

Intelligent	They must be highly intelligent but not a boffin.
Forceful	They must be forceful but also sensitive to people's feelings.
Dynamic	They must be dynamic but also patient.
Communication	They must be a fluent communicator but also a good listener.
Decisive	They must be decisive but also reflective.
Expert	They must be an expert on a wide range of different fields.

And if a project manager is found with the above attributes, what happens if the project manager is offered a better salary with a competitor and leaves? However, if no individual can combine all these qualities, a team of individuals certainly could. Consider:

Sustaining	It is not the individual but the team that is instrumental in sustaining and enduring management success.
Renew	A team can renew and regenerate itself through new recruitment as individual team members come and go.
Experiences	A team can also build up a store of shared and collectively owned experiences, information and judgement which can be passed on to new team members.
More Successful	Many people are more successful working within a team or partnership than working alone (for example, Mr Rolls and Mr Royce).
Synergy	Team synergy generates more output than the sum of the individual inputs.
Support	The team can offer a wide range of technical support.

Having established the need for a project team the to next step is to design the team and consider an appropriate team size.

4. Team Size

The appropriate team size depends on a number of factors. Consider the following:

Spread Load	How many people are required to perform the work? This is a trade-off between schedule and resource numbers.
Variety	What variety and range of technical expertise is required by the project to perform the work? If the team is too small it may not have the knowledge base and skills depth to meet the needs of the project.
Conflict	What is the appropriate level of conflict in a team? Mathematically, the odds of conflict increase with the number of people in the team.
Unwieldy	Large teams tend to be unwieldy and unable to reach agreement, or collect everyone's contribution to the discussion. If decisions are made by majority vote, an uneven number may prevent 'ties' (although some members could abstain).
Communication	Too large and the team may find communication and agreement difficult, the team may subdivide into cliques.
Personalities	The team needs a balance of personalities (see Belbin).

Table 22.1: Team Size - shows a number of considerations which influence team size.

The ideal team size depends very much on its application. Teams tend to grow in size until some magic number is reached - then they subdivide. The experts suggest the ideal size is between five and ten people.

Sporting teams provide us with some guidelines, consider a rugby team for example, which consists of fifteen players. This number is slightly higher than recommended, and sure enough there is subdivision into a pack of eight forwards and seven backs.

...the Cohorts marched in ten by ten!..

5. Why Teams Win

Research by Belbin at Henley Management College shows that some or all of the following characteristics are present in a successful team:

Management Style	The team leader has an appropriate management style for the project, and is not challenged by other team members.
Chairman	There is a chairman type person who encourages all the team members to contribute.
Ideas	At least one member of the team generates innovative ideas as a means to solve problems and identify new products and new markets.
Opportunities	At least one member is able to spot entrepreneurial opportunities.
Mental Ability	There is a spread of mental abilities.
Personalities	There is a spread of personalities which gives the team a balanced appearance.

The project manager or team leader will be successful if they gain and earn respect from the other team members. Generally, the chairman does not need to dominate the proceedings but should know how to pull matters together and integrate the team. In practice, Belbin's research found the leader always worked closely with the talented members of the team.

Innovation: In our changing world (market and technology), to solve problems and respond to change, innovation and creativity are essential for continuing project success. Ideas can be generated in many ways from people both inside and outside the team.

Flexibility: In flexible teams the team members play the role or support the role that is in demand or overloaded at the time. Successful teams exhibit flexibility where members are able to move around in the team to find the best match between people and jobs. They also realise that if they do not have a balanced distribution of team roles they will have to appoint members to play those missing roles.

Belbin (Management Teams); '... *the essence of a team is that its members form a co-operative association through a division of labour that best reflects the contribution that each can make towards the common objectives*.'

6. Why Teams Fail

Belbin states that the single factor evident in all unsuccessful teams is low mental ability. If this is compared with the innovation and creativity of winning teams, then it would imply that low mental ability teams are:

- Poor at **problem-solving**
- Unable to **change** with the market and respond to the competition
- Unable to take advantage of **opportunities**.

Negative Selection: The failure of companies to produce teams which have an adequate proportion of managers with good mental ability must surely not be due to any conscious search for such people, but rather the unintended by-product of negative selection. Negative selection refers to the recruitment process designed to filter out the type of people the company really needs. Consider the company which is looking for a good manager to reverse their present decline, but will not increase the current salary package offered. This low salary will unintentionally exclude the quality manager the company needs.

7. Role of the Project Manager

The project manager's position evolved in the 1950s as the single point of responsibility to co-ordinate multi-disciplined projects and make the best use of the company's resources. The role of the project manager is influenced by the size of the project - on a small project for example, the project manager may be expected to be a technical expert as well. Consider the following points in favour of the project manager being a **technical expert**:

Technical Expert	Companies prefer their managers to be technical experts in the field of the project as it enables the managers to confirm technical decisions themselves. This view is supported by the fact that most project management positions advertised require managers to be technically competent in the field of the project.
Judgment	If project managers know and understand the technical issues of their projects they will be in a better position to apply judgment and forecast problems.
Skills	Project management selection can be based on both the project manager's human compatibility and technical ability.
Feasibility Study	The project manager can effectively be involved up-front during the feasibility study, estimating and quotation stage of the project.
Respect	The project manager will be able to gain respect from the team by demonstrating not only good management but also technical expertise.

Now for the other side of the argument in favour of the project manager being a **generalist** in the field of the project:

Co-ordinating	As a project manager moves up the corporate ladder the project manager will be concerned more with people, costs and co-ordinating multi-disciplines and less concerned with technical issues.
Expertise	It could be undesirable to have the technical expert project manager leading the team, as innovation from the other team members could be suppressed, particularly in the project manager's area of expertise.
Non-Technical	Effective project management requires many non-technical skills such as human resource management, team building, financial accounting, negotiation, integration and co-ordination.

It would seem from commercial feedback that initially to embark on a career in project management you need experience in the field of the project, but once established you will slowly become more of a generalist in project management.

Exercises:

1. Discuss the reason teams are used in a project environment.
2. Discuss the role the project manager plays within the project team.
3. Discuss the reasons individuals join a project team.
4. Identify management teams in your company and discuss why you use them.
2. From your experience, discuss the ideal team size, taking into consideration the generation of innovative ideas and manageability.

Further Reading:

Belbin, M., *Management Teams,* Butterworth-Heinemann, 1996

23

Managing Small Projects

Learning Outcomes

After reading this chapter, you should be able to;

Understand the definition of small projects

Manage a small project

Understand the management skills required over the product lifecycle

Mention project management and most people will conjure up in their minds an image of large scale capital projects in the construction industry or defence procurement - but there is a wind of change happening – the prevalence and importance of small projects is being recognised. In the context of this book, new venture creation and the implementation of new products all have the characteristics of a small project, so it is appropriate, if not essential, to use project management techniques to implement them.

In recent years there has also been a trend towards proactive companies restructuring their work into a number of small projects to give them better planning and control. In this **management-by-projects** approach project management techniques are being used to plan and control these new enterprises, new ventures and outsourcing.

Projects can range in size, scope, cost and time from mega international capital projects costing millions of dollars over many years (building a power station or establishing a new mobile phone network), to small business projects or new ventures with a low budget taking just a few weeks to complete (setting-up a small business or servicing your car). It is the techniques and problems associated with these small projects that this chapter will focus on.

Although large capital projects catch our imagination in practice they only account for a few percent of project activity. At the other end of the scale, small projects account for a whopping 90% of project activity - making them by far the most pervasive type of projects. Therefore, it makes sense to focus on the tools and techniques that project managers and entrepreneurs can use to manage these small projects.

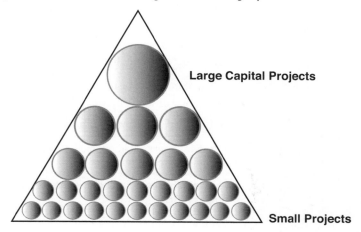

Figure 23.1: Pyramid of Projects – shows a few large projects at the top, but many small projects at the base of the pyramid

Many people think that project management techniques are only for managing large construction projects. This myth has developed because most of the project management methodologies and frameworks were originally designed for managing large projects. And using these frameworks and methodologies for small projects does not always work. In fact, they can be counter-productive. What most small projects need is a simple methodology to help guide them.

1. Define Small Project

It is common practice to quantify the size of a business by the number of employees and turnover. For example, SMEs (Small Medium size Enterprise) are defined as:

Micro firm	0 - 9 employees	Euro 2m turnover
Small firm	0 - 49 employees (includes micro)	Euro 10m turnover
Medium firm	50 - 249 employees	Euro 50m turnover
Large firm	over 250 employees	Euro <50m turnover

Using this structure and terminology we can define SMPs (Small Medium size Projects) as:

Micro project	0 - 9 employees	Euro 2m turnover
Small project	0 - 49 employees (includes micro),	Euro 10m turnover
Medium project	50 - 249 employees	Euro 50m turnover
Large project	over 250 employees	Euro <50m turnover

It should be noted that project size is relevant to industry sector, for example, a project of a few million dollars would be considered small in the oil industry; but a project of a few thousand dollars would be considered large in the fashion industry.

A project's perceived size may also relate to the type of work, type of industry, level of complexity and duration. Small projects would probably only have a few employees with a simple organisation structure making communication rapid and efficient. And because there are only a few people, each person may be responsible for a number of positions, for example, the planner becomes the accountant, and the procurement manager becomes the quality control inspector.

Define Small Project: A 'small project' may be defined, for the purpose of this chapter, as a simple project with a limited scope of work managed by one person (the entrepreneur / project manager), or a small project team. Consider the following points;

Simple	A simple project implies it is possible to visualize the whole project in your head, it is not complex.
Scope of Work	A small project implies a limited change with a limited scope of work with a simple WBS.
Small Team	The organization structure may consist of only the entrepreneur / project manager and a small project team. This should mean the lines of communication are short and reaction should be quick.
Short Duration	A small project implies a short duration, which means you may not have time to develop your systems and learn by your mistakes.
Small Budget	A small project implies a small budget which should be tight and visible, with no excess funds for mistakes.
Skills	A small project implies a limited range of skills, as small companies tend to focus on niche markets.
Risk	A small simple project implies limited risk, as small companies do not have capacity to accept risky projects.
Strategic	A small project implies limited strategic and political importance.
Decision-Making	A small project implies innovative problem-solving and fast decisive decision-making.
Information	A small project implies small volume of information and small computer systems. The sheer volume of data can make large projects complex.

Knowing the size of your project will enable you to determine the appropriate project management system that best suits the project. However, deciding whether your project is small or large may be an over simplification, as the real question should be whether the project is simple or **complex**. As projects become more complex so the project management style needs to change from intuitive and informal to organized and structured.

2. Managing Small Projects

Managing a small project is not necessarily a scaled down version of a large project, although small projects may appear to be simpler and more straight forward they often have their own unique problems. Small projects are often doomed to fail, or be self-limiting, because of the way they are set up which is generally far too informally. Consider the following points:

Scope of Work	The scope of work is inadequately and inaccurately defined - no drawings, no specifications and no contact.
Instructions	Instructions given verbally - nothing in writing to confirm agreements. This could lead to misunderstandings.
Standards	Minimum quality standards not established or adequately defined at the outset - making it difficult to enforce quality control to accept or reject the work.
Schedule	Schedule not discussed, although there may be a perception that the work will be done straight away once the order is given.
Payment	Method of payment not discussed, although price would usually be agreed.
Arbitration	No arbitration mechanisms - making it difficult to quickly and amicably sort out any disputes.
Exit	No exit strategies - making it difficult to terminate the contract.
Duration	Short duration - this does not give the project manager time to establish a management system and learn by mistakes.
One-off	Many projects are one offs, for example, building a house extension. Therefore, there will be limited knowledge to draw from previous experience.

The project manager has a multitude of challenges to face when implementing small projects and new ventures, so it is important to ensure innovative ideas and marketable opportunities are not handicapped at the outset by ineffective project management. Many creative ideas have floundered because of unrealistic expectations, poor estimating, communication breakdown within the team, poor co-ordination between the stakeholders and uncontrolled cashflow.

To over come these shortcomings project managers use a number of special project management techniques to plan and control the progress of their projects. These should form an important part of the project management entrepreneur's portfolio of project management skills.

3. Product Lifecycle (management skills)

The product lifecycle or new venture lifecycle is an excellent model for clearly showing the different phases or stages a product or company passes through from the cradle to the grave, or more realistically from new venture opportunity to its eventual disposal or replacement.

The interaction between the phases has been developed and discussed in detail in the *Product Lifecycle* chapter. This chapter will outline how the different management skills are integrated and relate to each other on small projects.

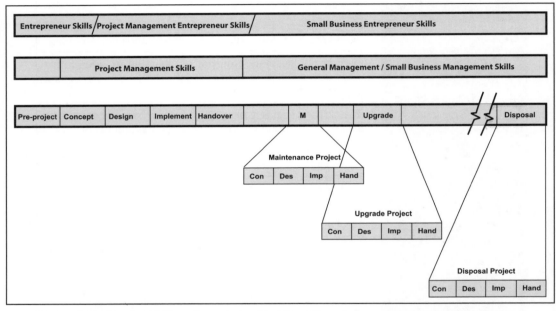

Figure 23.2: Product Lifecycle – shows how the different management skills relate to the product lifecycle phases

Entrepreneur Skills: It is the Entrepreneur or entrepreneurial skills which start the ball rolling. Entrepreneurs are experts at inventing new products, spotting innovative opportunities, solving challenging problems and making the decision to initiate new ventures or projects. Once the new venture has been identified it is handed over to the project manager for implementation.

Project Management Skills: It is the project manager who uses project management skills to implement or set-up a new venture. Project managers are experts at planning and controlling the scope of work to implement the new venture using a portfolio of special project management tools and techniques.

Project Management Entrepreneur Skills: During the implementation of the project or new facility, the entrepreneurial project manager will be continually looking for better opportunities. This effectively delays the design freeze and keeps the door open to the latest technology, responding to competitors products and responding to changing market fashions. The entrepreneurial project manager will also be continually looking for ways to speed up production to beat the competition to market – this may involve shortening lead times and running activities in parallel. All these fast tracking skills rely on a quick response to better information as the project moves forward. However, it can also greatly increase risks. As the implementation or project phase is completed so the new venture or facility is handed over to the small business manager for the operational phase to make the product or service.

Small Business Management Skills: When the new venture is up and running or created the new facility is now complete and the venture moves into the next phase - the operational phase to manufacture the product or provide the service. This is when the product is made and distributed to the market and sold. This is the acid test of the marketing plan – can you sell the product?

It is the small business management skills which run the new venture, facility or company on a day-to-day basis. Small business management skills are essentially inward looking trying to continually improve efficiency and productivity.

Small Business Entrepreneur Skills: Where the small business manager is inward looking at efficiency and productivity, the small business entrepreneur is outward looking at the market and competition. It is a natural trait to continually monitor;

- Their competition's products
- Their pricing strategy
- The market (latest fashion trends)
- Ways to incorporate the latest cutting edge technology to maintain competitive advantage.

This is when you need small business entrepreneurial skills to be aware of changes in the market, incorporate new technology and respond to competition and, like links in a chain, they all rely on each other to ensure continuing success. This brief overview of the product lifecycle clearly outlines the different management skills that are required as the new venture moves through the growth phases.

4. Small Business Management

Entrepreneurs and small business managers are often thought of as being one and the same. But in practice entrepreneurship is the management of change, particularly when starting a new venture or introducing a new product or service. Whereas, small business management is the management of the company on a day-to-day basis - particularly with respect to repetitive jobs. Some of the key small business management functions include:

- marketing the company and the products
- accounts, budgets, book-keeping and cash flow
- paying wages, invoices and debtors
- complying with rules, regulations and taxes
- buying or renting premises
- buying, leasing or hiring plant and equipment
- procurement of material and services
- warehousing and stock control (JIT)
- distribution
- labour relations, recruitment and hiring
- supervision and leadership
- manufacturing the product (technical), and scheduling the workflow
- quality control
- customer service.

Entrepreneurship and small business management obviously go hand-in-hand, and may be seen as two sides of the same coin. Small businesses swing in and out of periods of entrepreneurial change as the small business responds to new technology, competitors and the latest market fashions.

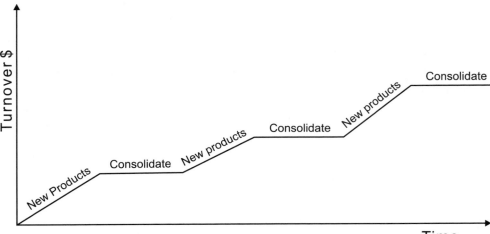

Figure 23.3: Entrepreneur / Small Business Manager Cycles - showing periods of entrepreneurship followed by periods of consolidation

Exercise:

1. Outline the difference between large and small projects.
2. Discuss why entrepreneurs need project management skills to set up new ventures.
3. Discuss the potential problems of managing small projects intuitively.

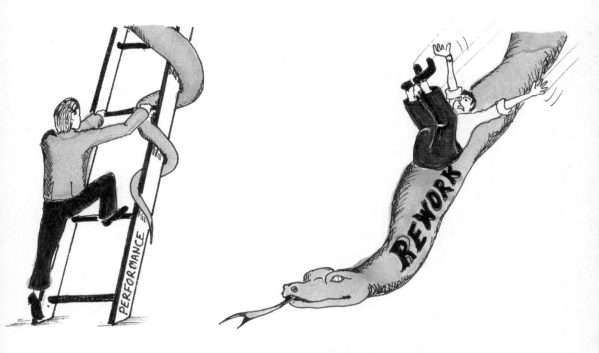

"...I was doing really well until the quality inspector rejected my work!   "

24

Project Management Office

Learning Outcomes

After reading this chapter, you should be able to;

Understand the principles behind the project management office

Understand the benefits of a project management centre of excellence

Set up a project office to offer a management-by-projects approach

Understand the benefits of a mobile office in a project environment

The project management office (PMO) or project office enshrines the project management approach as a central point for managing a company's projects. Companies have design offices and IT departments as centres of excellence, so it also makes sense to have a project management office as a centre for project management excellence.

DEFINITION

The PMBOK defines the project management office (PMO) as; '....an organisational body or entity assigned various responsibilities related to the centralised and co-ordinated management of those projects under its domain. The responsibilities of a PMO can range from project management support functions to actually being responsible for the direct management of a project....'

1. Site Office

To understand the purpose and workings of the project office it is interesting to look at how it evolved and developed. Historically the site office on a construction project was probably the first example of a project office. Out of necessity the site office was located on site at the work face close to the action. This enabled the site manager (project manager) to monitor the progress directly and make quick on the spot decisions as required.

"... Hey Fred ..... get me a chisel from the site office..."

2. Matrix Organisation Structure

Multi-disciplined projects were another motivator to create a project office. Multi-disciplined projects were originally passed from one functional department to another as the work progressed. The OBS chapter has already discussed the problems associated with this arrangement. The outcome was to manage these multi-disciplined projects using a matrix organisation structure, where the project manager would manage the project as it passed through the functional departments.

As the benefits of this type of management approach were realised so the project manager(s) needed a more permanent home – and this home became the project office. Once the home had been established so other benefits followed particularly those associated with the project management office as a centre of excellence, and ultimately channelling all the company's work through the project office using a management-by-projects approach.

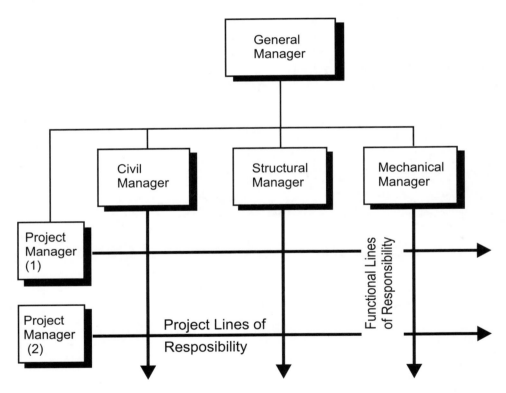

Figure 24.1: Matrix Organisation Structure – shows the project office driving the project through the functional departments

3. Centre of Excellence

One of the benefits of having a project management office is to create a centre of excellence for all aspects of project management. By grouping the project managers and the project team members in the same office, you create a pool of project expertise to draw from and a data base of project information they can use. Consider subdividing the project management office into the following subheadings:

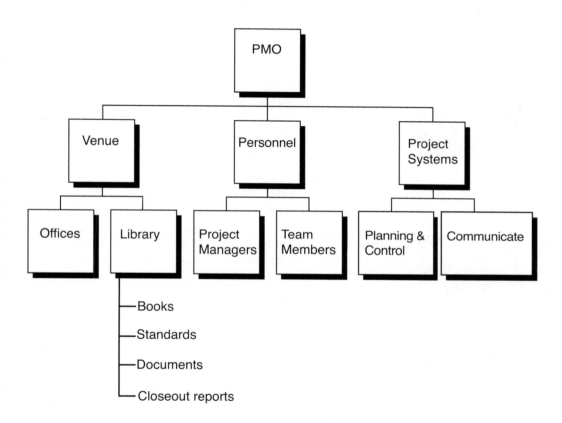

Figure 24.2: Project Management Office – shows subdivision into Venue, Personnel and Project Systems

Venue: The project management office (PMO) as a physical venue offers the following type of facilities;

Offices	The PMO gives the project managers and project team workers office space and a home. For convenience, they could be grouped per project in the same area (so they can shout across to each other).
War Room	The PMO provides a central *'war room'* to manage projects where all the information, people and communication facilities are available.
Central Point	The PMO offers a central point for the company to network with stakeholders and potential clients.
Meetings	The PMO has meeting rooms with audio-visual facilities.
Communicate	The PMO provides a front door for the project and the company. If you need to communicate with someone on any project, you will find them in the PMO.
Equipment	The PMO offers an economy of scale by grouping all the company's project activities. This means they can warrant buying and installing the latest project management software and hardware, together with trained people to run and maintain them.

Library: The project management office as a library offers a central place to file, store and retrieve project information.

Central Point	The PMO offers a central point to collect, file, store and retrieve project information which can be accessed both in hard copy and electronically.
Standards	The PMO is the ideal place to keep the latest information on project management standards.
Books	The PMO library is a central place containing a range of project management literature and technical journals, together with a broad selection of relevant books and videos.
Document Control	The PMO is a central place to store controlled drawings, specifications and contract documents in a secure environment.
Closeout Reports	Once the project is over many may wish to forget the experience. However, the library is the ideal place to house the closeout reports.

Personnel: The project management office offers a team of project experts. As projects are run by people the project team members are a key resource.

Resource Pool	The PMO offers a flexible resource pool of project managers and project team members.
Matrix OBS	The PMO offers the option to use a range of organisation structures. A matrix structure is often used as a temporary organisation structure which overlays the other departments and enables the PMO to share and co-ordinate resources across a number of projects.
Problem-Solving	The PMO offers a cross-section of experienced team members which enhances brainstorming workshops and problem-solving.
Home	The PMO offers the project managers a home to go to between projects. This may be the ideal time to update their skills and prepare for next project – perhaps becoming part of the bidding team.

Systems and Methodologies: The project management office offers a central place in the company to set up project management systems, methodologies and information formats.

Systems	The PMO offers a central point to design and develop project management systems appropriate for the type of projects the company runs.
Standards	The PMO has the expertise to identify the latest information on project management standards so they can comply with the latest standards.
Software	The PMO offers a central point to install project management software and associated hardware. This can be used for both projects managed by the project office and other projects managed by other departments within the company.
Project Quality Plan	The PMO often supplements the company's quality plan with a project quality plan which is tailored to the needs of the project.
Quality Control Plan	The PMO offers the expertise to develop the quality control plan (QCP). The quality control plan links the scope of work (WBS) with the project quality plan. The QCP identifies what needs to be inspected, the level of inspection and the hold points.
Audits	The PMO can carry out project management audits (internal and external) to confirm the project management systems are conforming to the project quality plan.
Administration	The PMO has admin staff to support the project managers. This enables the project managers to spend more time managing their projects and less time on processing data and admin chores (Research indicates that project managers spend 50% of their time on admin).

Project Communication: Information is the life blood of projects. The PMO is in an ideal position to control all the lines of project communication.

Lines of Communication	The PMO is responsible for identifying the project's lines of communication.
Directory	The PMO is the keeper of the project directories, of clients, stakeholders, suppliers, contractors and team members, etc.
Communication	The PMO can communicate project information to the project team, the client, contractor, suppliers and other stakeholders.
Document Control	The PMO provides a documentation control centre to manage the collection, storage and distribution of project documents. Controlling the flow of documents is often a weak link on small projects. The hub and spoke arrangement enables prompt expediting and follow up, with signed transmittals to confirm delivery.
Website	The PMO can set-up a website to present the status on all their projects - there is a trend towards real time reporting.

Tendering: The project management office provides the facilities to tender for new work.

Marketing	The PMO is an ideal place to advertise (design brochures) and promote the company's capabilities and qualities.
Networking	The PMO should excel in network skills to open the doors of business opportunities.
Quotation	The PMO quotations are based on an empirical data base of past performance built-up over time from experience and documented in closeout reports. This ensures a respectable level of accuracy.
Legal	The PMO offers a central point to co-ordinate quotations. This would include legal support with the company's standard terms and conditions of contract.

Planning and Control: The project management office provides the facilities, project systems and personnel to plan and control the company's projects.

Baseline Plan	The PMO integrates all the components to produce a coherent baseline plan.
Instructions	The PMO issues work instructions and job cards to authorize and execute the scope of work.
Monitoring	The PMO measures progress through a structured data capture process.
Meetings	The PMO manages project progress meetings with the client, project team, contractors and suppliers.
Scope Changes	The PMO manages the scope change process, revising plans and issuing instructions.
Multi-Projects	The project office team is able to support several projects simultaneously from their pool of resources.

Training: The project management office offers a centre of project management expertise which can be used to train and mentor project team members.

Project Training	The PMO is the ideal place to design, setup and run project focused training courses.
Training	The PMO offers project management training courses for the whole company which can be run in conjunction with the HR and training manager.
Fast Tracking	The PMO is able to run fast track training sessions in project management for newly formed project management teams.
Mentoring	The PMO has experienced project managers who can mentor, coach and support apprentices with on the job training this will ensure the development of future leaders.

4. Management-by-Projects

The PMO is an ideal venue for controlling the management-by-projects approach. The benefit of the management-by-projects approach was discussed in the introduction chapter. To recap, the management-by-projects approach, is schedule focused and not resource focused. This means the workforce is scaled up or down to suit the workload and schedule. Clients can now plan ahead with some certainty knowing when their work will be completed.

5. Mobile Project Office

Mobile phones, portable notebook computers and wi-fi communication networks are making the mobile project office a feasible reality. These mobile facilities are not only enabling project managers to stay in touch with the project office while on site trips, but actually enable project managers to take their office with them.

Mobile facilities enable communication with the head office, clients, suppliers and contractors while on the move. The mobile office could be a site office, an Internet cafe, an airport lounge (or any wi-fi hotspot), the project manager's car, their campervan or even their yacht. Consider the following points:

- The mobile office frees the project manager from their corporate desk so they can actually spend more time on site visiting clients, contractors and suppliers.
- Mobile conferencing enables project managers to attend virtual meetings with their project team and clients. Regular virtual meetings should keep a scattered team linked and working together.

Project managers can even benefit from mobile office facilities while they are on an extended business trip or a holiday. They are able to relax knowing everything is okay back at the PMO, and if there is a problem they have the opportunity to nip it in the bud. They can also keep on top of their emails while they are away to avoid being greeted by several hundred emails on their first day back at work. Holidays in the bush, on a tropical island and flying time no longer need to be vacuum periods without any business contact.

It is expensive to keep office space and a desk for project managers who are working away from the office for long periods of time. A more cost effective option is to **hot desk!** This means a returning project manager would use any desk that is available and hook into the PMO's wireless network from their laptop. If the project manager has files, reference material and books which cannot be electronically stored, these can be kept safely in a locked cabinet.

Exercise:

1. Discuss the benefits for your company using a PMO approach.
2. Discuss the benefits of the mobile PMO and discuss how this facility can be used on your projects.
3. Discuss the problems associated with hot desking in the PMO.

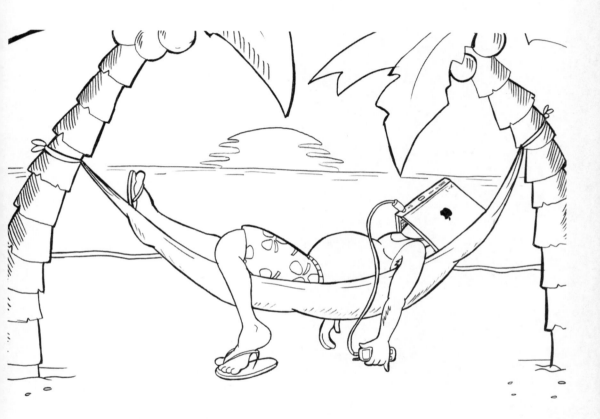

"...tell the client I'm working on his project!..."

25

Event Management

Learning Outcomes

After reading this chapter, you should be able to;

Understand how event management can benefit from using project management techniques

Understand the different types of events

Understand that events are the ultimate in time-limited scheduling

Event Management has all the characteristics of a project, which is why project management techniques are a core subject within the event management body of knowledge.

This chapter will outline how a range of special project management tools and techniques can be used to structure, plan and control an event.

Event management, also called event co-ordination, must be the ultimate in time-limited scheduling – because if you are only one day late, or even only one hour late you have just missed the whole event.

1. What is an Event?

An event has already been defined in the *CPM* and *Gantt Chart* chapters as an activity with zero duration. At the activity level an event is only a minor part of a WBS work package. But in the context of this chapter an event is the whole purpose of the project – so it has a completely different meaning.

An event may be defined as a special occasion such as, a wedding, a show, a business conference, or a sports match. Events range in size from a meeting of a few people to a mega event such as, the Olympic Games which involves thousands of people and costs billions of dollars even though it only lasts a couple of weeks.

Events can be subdivided into a number of different types which have different purposes, different venues and a different way of interacting;

Exhibition	Exhibition events, such as, a Boat Show or a Book Fair are typical of events where a number of companies come together under one roof to present their products on stands/booths while the visitors walk around the venue.
Fashion Show	A fashion show is a typical example of a dynamic type of event where the buyers and clients sit and watch, and the models walk down the catwalk wearing the products.
Conference	A conference is a typical example of an event where the experts come to present their papers or opinions (product) and the audience sits and listens. These types of events are particularly popular with education and politics. And, at a conference, if you are the key note speaker at 9.00 am you have a precise deadline.
Sports Match	Sports matches are usually short intense competitions – often held in specially built stadiums (tennis court, ice rink, bowling alley).
Music Concert	Music concert events can attract huge crowds, where the artists come to perform a gig on stage and the audience sits, stands or even dances. Venues can range from theatres and football stadiums to old air bases.
Wine Tasting	Wine tasting is a popular social and cultural event where vine growers and wine makers come to present their products and the guests sample the products.
Yacht Building	Building projects often include a number of distinct events – launching a yacht would be one, others would include; laying the foundation of a house and the roof wetting celebrations.
Team Building	Team building events use a range of innovative locations to improve management teams' interaction - locations and situations would include; mountaineering, sailing and African safaris.
Holiday	A two week holiday in the sun is an annual event most people look forward to. These events are characterized by at least one precise deadline - the flight - and a number of prerequisites (passport and visas).
Wedding	A wedding is probably the largest private event / function people have, others would include; christening, 21st, graduation, retirement leaving party and a funeral / wake.

2. Project Management Techniques

The project lifecycle technique offers an overview of an event from the embryo of an idea, to the preparation, to the event, and, finally, to the closeout. Events have a distinctive lifecycle profile which is characterized by a long preparation phase followed by a very short implementation phase.

The event lifecycle can be represented by the product lifecycle where the project phase is the preparation of the event and the operation phase is the running of the actual event (see figure 25.1 and table 25.1).

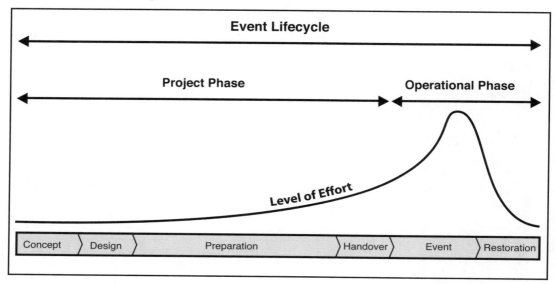

Figure 25.1: Lifecycle of an Event – shows the long preparation phase, followed by a very short implementation phase

Concept Phase	Includes feasibility study and build-method.
Planning phase	Includes detailed planning, booking venue, organising the exhibitors, designing the layout of the exhibition, marketing and promotion.
Implementation	Implementation of the preparation phase.
Commission	Handover to run and coordinate the event.
Operation	Set-up the event, run and coordinate the event, then remove the props.
Disposal	Restore the venue, and compile the event closeout report.

Table 25.1: Event Lifecycle - shows the phases of the event lifecycle

An extreme case of an event would be the Olympic Games which has an eight year preparation phase, followed by a very short, two week competition phase. With such long lead times event managers need to beware they do not fall into the trap of delaying planning design decisions because the event is many years away, and then end up with panic decisions and a rushed building programme. This is probably what happened to the Greek Olympics which was touch and go whether they would finish on time.

The Football World Cup, which is the biggest sporting event in the world, has addressed this problem by staging the Confederations Cup one year before the World Cup. This is in effect a dress rehearsal for the main event, but it also ensures everything is up and running well in advance.

Strategy: The starting point of event management is to determine the purpose of the event – it may be in response to an opportunity for a new exhibition, or it may be an annual event such a Motor Show.

Feasibility Study: The feasibility study technique can be used by event coordinators to identify the stakeholders and determine their needs and expectations. This exercise encourages the event coordinators to cast the net wider than just over the people attending the event and the companies represented. The feasibility study outlines the build-method and confirms the event is feasible, commercial and making the best use of the company's financial resources. The feasibility study should also consider the best time and venue to hold the event, considering availability of venue and potential clashing with other events.

"...come back!! I'm only a few minutes late!!..."

Event WBS: The WBS techniques can be used by event coordinators to subdivide the scope of work into manageable work packages and/or a checklist. The work packages and checklist of tasks become the backbone of the project to setup the event. Consider the WBS for a wedding event, which most of us have experienced.

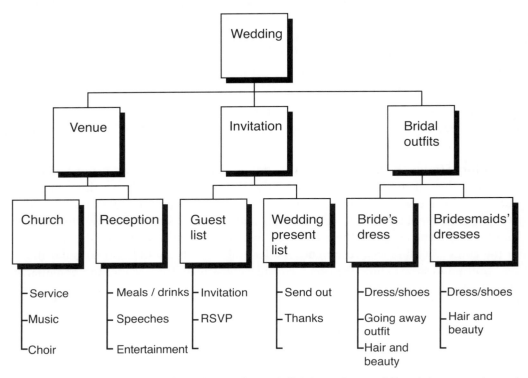

Figure 25.2: Event WBS – shows the subdivision of a wedding into a number of components

WBS Checklist	Description	Responsibility	Budget	Procure	Resource	Risk
100	Reception	Family	$30,000	Catering	Waiters	Rain
200	Bride's dress	Maid of Honour	$10,000	Dress	Bridesmaids	Dress Gets damaged
300	Groom	Best Man	$5,000	Ring	Hotel	Loses the ring

Table 25.2: WBS Spreadsheet – shows a wedding checklist which links the responsibility, budget, procurement, resources and risk to the WBS

CPM: The CPM techniques can be used by event organisers to establish the logical sequence of activities leading up to the event, together with the start and finish dates of all the activities and the critical path.

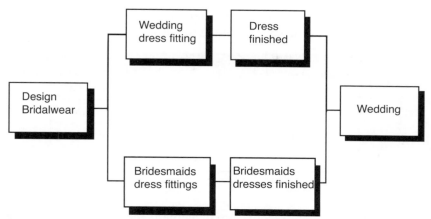

Figure 25.3: Event CPM – shows how the network diagram presents the logical sequence of the activities

Gantt Chart: The Gantt chart techniques can be used by event coordinators to present the scheduling of the activities and the keydates. Events by definition are time-limited projects, so the management of the event has to focus on achieving a number of keydates.

For the wedding event the marriage proposal initiates the project and, once the couple have come to terms with the reality of their commitment, they need to start planning. One of the first decisions is the trade-off between the budget, number of guests, venue, and date, as each one influences the others.

Description	Jan	Feb	Mar	Apr	May	Jun	Jul	Aug	Sep
Marriage Proposal	◆								
Wedding Plan		▬▬▬							
Book Venues			▬						
Guest List				▬▬▬					
Bridalwear						▬▬▬			
Wedding									◆

Figure 25.4: Event Gantt Chart – shows how the Gantt chart presents the key milestones and activities

Procurement Schedule: The procurement scheduling techniques can be used by event coordinators to compile a procurement list and a procurement schedule. The procurement list is developed from the WBS work packages and checklists. The long lead items need to be identified early on so they can be actioned to prevent any delays. In the case of a wedding the booking of the venues (the church and reception - probably in that order), determine the actual date of the wedding.

Procurement List	Date Required (from Gantt chart)	Lead Time	Order By Date
Bridal Dresses	Two weeks before wedding	3 months	
Flowers	Two hours before the wedding	1 month	
Car	One hour before the wedding ceremony	2 months	
Reception	Immediately after the wedding ceremony	6 months	

Table 25.3: Procurement Schedule

Resource Management: The resource management techniques can be used by event coordinators to determine the manpower requirements. Typically, during the preparation phase the manpower requirement is low (even working part-time), but the numbers dramatically increase during the set-up and running of the event.

Description	Mon 1	Tue 2	Wed 3	Thu 4	Fri 5	Sat 6	Sun 7	Mon 8	Tue 9	Wed 10	Thu 11
Preparation	2	2	2								
Set Up Event				20	20						
Wedding						50					
Dismantal Event							10				
Restore								5	5		
Total	2	2	2	20	20	50	10	5	5		

Figure 25.5: Event Resource Histogram – shows how you need to increase resources to set up and run the event

Risk Management: The risk management techniques can be used by event coordinators to identify the risks that will stop them from achieving their objectives, and develop responses to remove or reduce the impact.

Scope	Objective	Identify Risk	Quantify	Respond
Ceremony	3.00 pm	Bride late – get me to the church on time	Massive impact	Maid of honour to help bride
Ceremony	As per programme	Lose wedding ring	High impact	Give the ring to best man
Venue (garden)	Sociable and Comfortable	Rain	High impact	Marquee

Table 25.4: Event Risk Management Table – shows how risks can be identified and managed

Exercises:

1. Discuss how Event Coordinators can use project management techniques.
2. Discuss the different types of events.
3. Events are usually time-limited occasions – you have to get it right on the day. Discuss the importance of planning and how parts of the event can be practised before the event so you hit the ground running.

"...I've got to get to the church on time!..."

Appendix 1

This appendix contains the solutions to exercises in the book.

The solutions are presented in chapter sequence.

Chapter 2: History of Project Management

Exercise 2: Calculate the PERT exercise from section 2.

Using the PERT equation, Expected Time = (o + 4m + p) / 6

o = 12 days

m = 15 days

p = 24 days

What is T (expected)?

Expected Time = (12 + 4 x 15 + 24) / 6

$\qquad\qquad$ = 16 days

Chapter 8: Work Breakdown Structure (WBS)

Exercise 4: Carry out the WBS exercise from section 7.

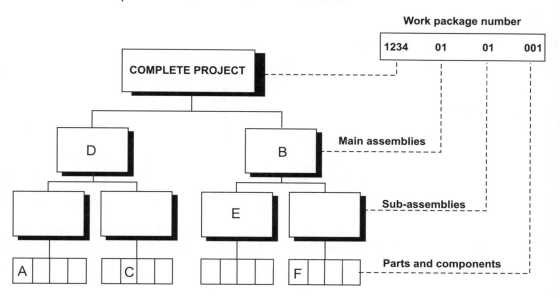

Solutions for chapter 8, exercise 4:

D = 1234   01   00   00

E = 1234   02   01   00

F = 1234   02   02   01

Chapter 11: Critical Path Method (CPM)

Exercise 2: Calculate the following network diagram.

Activity	Duration	Logic
100	1	Start
200	2	100
300	4	100
400	3	200
500	2	300
600	2	400, 500

Table 11.4: Activity Table, Exercise 2

Solution for chapter 11, exercise 2:

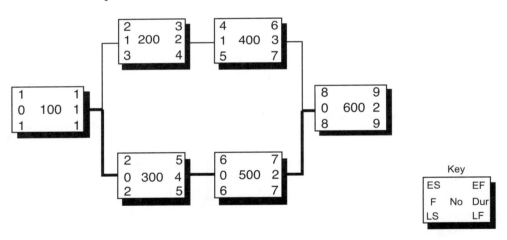

Figure 11.12: Critical Path Method, exercise 2 - shows the solution to Chapter 11, exercise 2

Chapter 11: Critical Path Method (CPM)

Exercise 3: Calculate the following network diagram

Activity	Duration	Logic
100	2	Start
200	6	100
300	2	100
400	2	300
500	3	200, 400

Table 11.5: Activity Table, Exercise 3

Solution for chapter 11, exercise 3:

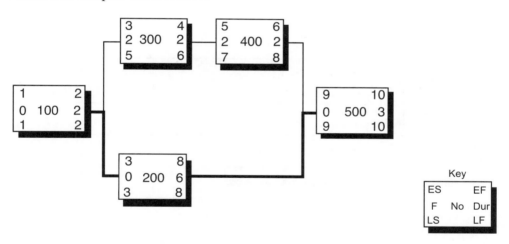

Figure 11.3: Critical Path Method, exercise 3 - shows the solution to chapter 11, exercise 3

Chapter 12: Gantt Chart

Exercise 2: Go back to Chapter 11, exercise 2 and transpose the network diagram into a Gantt chart.

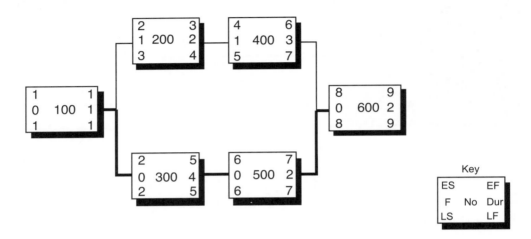

Solution for chapter 12, exercise 2:

Activity Number	Mon 1	Tue 2	Wed 3	Thu 4	Fri 5	Sat 6	Sun 7	Mon 8	Tue 9	Wed 10
100	▬									
200		▬▬	▬---◆							
300		▬▬▬▬▬▬▬								
400				▬▬▬	▬---◆					
500						▬▬				
600								▬▬		

Gantt Chart, chapter 12, exercise 2

Chapter 12: Gantt Chart

Exercise 3: Go back to Chapter 11, exercise 3 and transpose the network diagram into a Gantt chart.

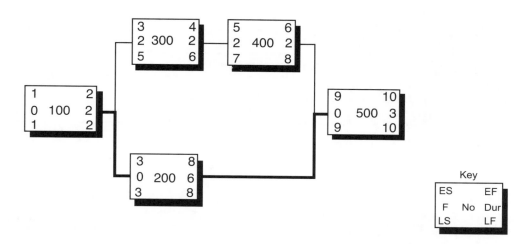

Solution for chapter 12, exercise 2:

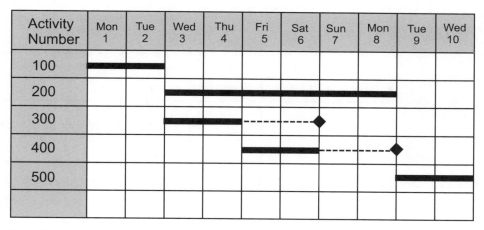

Activity Number	Mon 1	Tue 2	Wed 3	Thu 4	Fri 5	Sat 6	Sun 7	Mon 8	Tue 9	Wed 10
100										
200										
300										
400										
500										

Gantt Chart, chapter 12, exercise 3

Chapter 15: Project Accounts

Exercise 1: Continuing with cashflow example 2 produce the cashflow statement using the information below.

Brought Forward	January $500
Income	$8,000 per month from February to June
Equipment	$2,000 per month from January to April
Labour	$4,000 per month from February to June
Materials	$1,000 per month from February to June

Table 15.3: Cashflow, exercise 1

Solution for chapter 15, exercise 1:

	Jan	Feb	Mar	Apr	May	Jun
B/F	$500	($1,500)	($500)	$500	$1,500	$4,500
Income		$8,000	$8,000	$8,000	$8,000	$8,000
Total Income	$500	$6,500	$7,500	$8500	$9,500	$12,500
Equipment	$2,000	$2,000	$2,000	$2,000		
Labour		$4,000	$4,000	$4,000	$4,000	$4,000
Material		$1,000	$1,000	$1,000	$1,000	$1,000
Total	$2,000	$7,000	$7,000	$7,000	$5,000	$5,000
Closing Amount	($1,500)	($500)	$500	$1,500	$4,500	$7,500

Table 15.4: Cashflow statement, exercise 1 - shows the solution to chapter 15 exercise 1

Chapter 17: Earned Value

Exercise 1: Continue with the painting example and produce the earned value table similar to table 17.6 for timenow 2 and timenow 3.

Solution for chapter 17, earned value exercise for timenow 2 and 3:

WBS Activity	BAC Budget	PV	PC	EV Earned	AV Actual	SV	CV	EAC
100	16 hrs	16 hrs	100%	16 hrs	16 hrs	0	0	16 hrs
200	16 hrs	16 hrs	50%	8 hrs	20 hrs	(8 hrs)	(12 hrs)	40 hrs
300	16 hrs	0						16 hrs
400	16 hrs	0						16 hrs
500	16 hrs	0						16 hrs
Totals	80 hrs	32 hrs 40%	30%	24 hrs	36 hrs	(8 hrs)	(12 hrs)	104 hrs

Earned Value Table at timenow 2 **(end of Tuesday)** - late, over manhours

WBS Activity	BAC Budget	PV	PC	EV	AV Actual	SV	CV	EAC
100	16 hrs	16 hrs	100%	16 hrs	16 hrs	0	0	16 hrs
200	16 hrs	16 hrs	100%	16 hrs	24 hrs	0	(8 hrs)	24 hrs
300	16 hrs	16 hrs	100%	16 hrs	8 hrs	0	8 hrs	8 hrs
400	16 hrs	0	50%	8 hrs	4 hrs	8 hrs	4 hrs	8 hrs
500	16 hrs	0						16 hrs
Totals	80 hrs	48 hrs 60%	70 %	56 hrs	52 hrs	8 hrs	4 hrs	72 hrs

Earned Value Table at timenow 3 **(end of Wednesday)** - ahead, under budget

Bibliography

Association of Project Managers (APM)., *Body of Knowledge (BOK)*

Belbin, M., *Management Teams,* Butterworth-Heinemann, 1996
Benedetto, R., *Matrix Management Theory in Practice*, Kendall Hunt
Bentley, C., *Configuration Management Within Prince,* 1993
BS 5750 (1979), *Quality Management*
Burke, Rory, *Entrepreneurs Toolkit,* Burke Publishing, 2006
Burke, Rory, *Small Business, Entrepreneur,* Burke Publishing, 2006
Burleson, C., *Effective Meetings*, Wiley

Chapman, C., and **Ward**, Stephen, *Project Risk Management: Processes, Techniques and Insights,* Wiley, 1996
Charland, T., *Advanced Project Management Techniques Handbook*, 1990
Clark, C., *Brainstorming*, Wilshire
Cleland, D., *Project Management Field Guide*, Van Nostrand Reinhold, 1997
Crosby, P.B., *Quality is Free*, McGraw-Hill, 1987
Crosby, P.B., *Quality Without Tears*, McGraw-Hill, 1995

Davidson Frame, J., *The Project Office (Best Management Practices)*, Crisp, 1998
Dinsmore, P., *Human Factors in Project Management*, Amacom

Fewings, Peter, *Construction Project Management*, Taylor & Francis
Field, M., and **Keller,** L., *Project Management,* Thomson
Frank, M., *How to Run a Successful Meeting in Half the Time*, Corgi
Frigenti, Enzo, and **Comninos**, D., *The Practice of Project Management: a guide to the business - focused approach,* Kogan Page, 2002.

Gido, J., and **Clements**, J., *Successful Project Management,* South Western College Pub, 1999
Gray, C., and **Larson**, E., *Project Management (the Managerial Process),* McGraw-Hill Irwin

Haynes, Marion, *Project Management (Fifty Minute Book),* Elaine Fritz, 1997
Jones, Peter, *Handbook of Team Design: A Practitioner's Guide to Team Systems Development,* McGraw-Hill, 1997

Kerzner, H., *Project Management A Systems Approach to Planning, Scheduling and Controlling,* Van Nostrand Reinhold, 1997
Kimbler, D., and **William**, Ferrell, *TQM-Based Project Planning,* 1997

Lewis, James, *Project Planning, Scheduling & Control: A Hands-On Guide to Bringing Projects in on Time and on Budget,* McGraw-Hill, 1995
Lock, D., *Project Management*, Gower, 1996
Lockyer, Keith, *Production Management*, Financial Times Pitman, 1992

Lockyer, Keith, and **Gordon**, James, *Project Management and Project Network Techniques,* Financial Times Pitman, 1996
Lysons, C., *Purchasing*, Financial Times Pitman, 1998

Meredith, J., and **Samuel**, J., *Project Management A Managerial Approach*, Wiley, 1995
Morris, Peter, *The Anatomy of Projects*, Thomas Telford, 1997
Morris, Peter, *The Management of Projects,* Thomas Telford, 1994

Obeng, Eddie, *All Change: Project Manager's Secret Handbook,* Financial Times Management, 1996
O'Connell, Fergus, *How to Run Successful Projects II: The Silver Bullet,* Prentice Hall, 1996
Oosthuizen, Pieter, *Goodbye MBA*, International Thomson, 1998

Pennypacker, James, *Project Management Forms*, Cambridge University Press, 1997
Pokras, Sandy, *Rapid Team Deployment: Building High-Performance Project Teams (Fifty-Minute Series)*, 1995
Project Management Institute (PMI)., *A Guide to the Project Management Body of Knowledge (PMBOK), 1996*

Raftery, John, *Risk Analysis in Project Management,* Routledge, 1993
Rosenau, M., *Successful Project Management*, Van Nostrand Reinhold, 1998

Schuyler, John, *Decision Analysis in Projects*, Cambridge University Press, 1996
Stuckenbruck, L., *The Implementation of Project Management: The Professional Handbook*, PMI

Turner, R., *Handbook of Project-Based Management*, McGraw-Hill, 1993

Walker, Anthony, *Project Management in Construction*, Blackwell Science, 1996
Westney, Richard, *Computerized Management of Multiple Small Projects,* Marcel Dekker
Wideman., *A Framework for Project and Program Management Integration*, PMBOK Handbook Series - volume 1, 1991

Van Der Waldt, Andre, *Project Management For Strategic Change and Upliftment*, International Thomson, 1998

Glossary

Activity: Item of work, task or job. A list of activities is required for the CPM calculation.

APM: Association of Project Managers (UK).

Audit: An investigation to compare actual performance with planned work, or compare actual management system with planned management system.

Backward Pass: After completing the CPM's forward pass, the backward pass calculates the late start and late finish dates.

Barchart: see Gantt chart.

Baseline Plan: The original plan to implement the project, or latest updated plan which progress is tracked against.

Body of Knowledge (bok): The body of knowledge (of a profession) identifies and describes the generally accepted practices for which there is widespread consensus of the value and usefulness, and also establishes a common lexicon of terms and expressions used within the profession.

Brainstorming: A group method of generating a flood of creative ideas and novel solutions.

Breakeven Point: This is the number of products the company needs to sell to cover the set up costs – after this point the company starts to make a profit.

Brief: The project brief is a statement of the situation. It should outline what product or facility may be required, or what problem is to be solved.

Budget: Planned allocation of funds to perform a fixed amount of work.

Build-Method: Outlines how to make the product.

Calendar: Outlines the days work can be scheduled.

Cashflow: The flow of cash in and out of the project's account – typically presented as a monthly snap shot.

Charter: (Also called Project Charter), formally acknowledges the start of a project.

Client: The client is the key customer (the employer) who initiates the project, accepts the project and will pay for the project.

Closeout Report: The closeout report progressively signs off the completed work, (as-built drawings) and identifies experiences - what went right and what went wrong; useful information for the rest of the project and future projects.

Communications: A process through which information is exchanged.

Contingency: An additional amount (say 10%) or plan of action to cover unforeseen problems.

Contract: Legal agreement between two parties.

Control: The process of determining progress, comparing planned with actual, and making changes to keep the project on track.

Critical Path Method (CPM): The CPM calculates the start and finish dates of all the activities to calculate the float and identify the critical path.

Data Capture: The process of gathering information on the project's progress.

Document Control: The process of managing the movement of project documents to the people identified in the lines of communication. This process may also include the storing of documents and signing of transmittals.

Duration: Total time to complete an activity from start to finish.

Earned Value: The integration of cost and time (or manhours and time) to determine the projects progress.

Entrepreneur: A person who spots an opportunity and co-ordinates resources to make-it-happen.

Estimate: Prediction of what will happen in the future.

Event: A point in time with no duration, for example the award of contract.

Event Management: Coordinates the preparation, setup, run and restore of an event or occasion, such as, an exhibition, conference, sports match etc.

Execution Strategy: The buy-or-make decision.

Expediting: Is the project support function to anticipate problems before they arise and offer solutions before delays are encountered. This includes: periodic visits to vendor's premises, frequent telephone calls to check on vendor's progress control, materials, resources, workload, progress, quality control, manuals, and delivery.

Fast Track: Start the following activity before the current activity has completely finished, or change logic to run activities in parallel to reduce the duration of the project.

Feasibility Study: A process usually conducted in the concept phase to quantify if the project can be performed, meet company requirements and make the best use of resources.

Float: The amount of time an activity can be delayed without delaying the total project.

Forward Pass: To calculate all the activities early start and early finish dates.

Gantt Chart: A scheduling tool where the time of each activity is represented as a horizontal bar. The length of the bar is proportional to the duration of the activity.

Hammock: A group of related activities that are shown as one aggregate activity and reported at a summary level.

Impact Statement: The impact proposed changes will have on other activities.

Job Description: Outlines duties, responsibilities and authority.

Key Date: See milestone.

Management-by-Projects: Packaging a company's work into many small projects to improve focus and accountability.
Matrix OBS: An organization structure where the project manager shares responsibility with the functional managers who supply the resources.
Milestone: A significant event which acts as a progress marker of achievement.
Monitoring: Data capture, establishing what is happening on the project, its status.

Network Diagram: A graphic presentation of the logical sequence of activities.

Parallel Activities: Activities which can be carried out at the same time.
Payback Period: The time the income takes to payback the original investment.
Percentage Complete: A measure of the work done.
PMBOK: Project Management Body of Knowledge (USA).
PMI: Project Management Institute (USA).
Procedures: Methods, practices, instructions and policies which explain how work should be carried out.
Process: A set of activities which will produce the required product.
Procurement: The buying into the company or project of goods and services.
Product Lifecycle: Expands the project lifecycle to include: operation, maintenance, upgrade and disposal.
Project Lifecycle: Usually presented as four. sequential phases: concept, design, implementation and commissioning.
Project Management: The management of a project using the project management principles, and the special planning and control tools and techniques.
Project Manager: The person appointed with single point responsibility to manage and achieve the project's objectives.

Resource: The machine or person who performs the work.
Resource Management: Forecasting manpower loading, smoothing resources to match supply and demand.
Risk Management: The process of identifying risk, quantifying risk, responding to risk, and controlling the risk management.
Rolling Wave Horizon: Focusing on the activities happening in the immediate future.

S-Curve: Graphic display of cumulative costs, labour hours or other quantities, plotted against time. The curve is flat at the beginning and end, steep in the middle, as it follows an S shape. It generally describes a project that starts slowly, accelerates and then tapers off.

Scope Management: Concerned with identifying what is included and what is not included in the project scope to achieve the stated objectives.

Scope of Work: The work content of the project, usually subdivided into work packages and checklists by a WBS.

Single Point of Responsibility: The one person who is responsible for the completion of the project (the project manager).

Stakeholder: An individual or group whose interest in the project must be recognised if the project is to be successful. In particular, the stakeholders who may be positively or negatively impacted during or after the project.

Task: see activity.

Team Building: Activities designed to increase the performance of the team.

Teams: Project teams are formed to carry out a specific task.

Timenow: The date up to which the progress is measured.

Work Breakdown Structure (WBS): A subdivision of the work into work packages and checklists which can be more easily planned and controlled, and responsibility assigned.

Index

accounts, 168-175
- financial, 169
- management, 169
- project, 169
activity, 134
- float, 147
- in parallel, 135
- in series, 135
- list (WBS), 103
- on-Arrow (AOA), 36
- on-Node (AON), 37
ACWP, 185
APM bok, 41
Apple, 83
audits, 193
authorise work, 77
authority, 230
AV (ACWP), 185

barchart, (see Gantt Charts)
baseline plan, 75
BCWS, 185
Belbin, 236-239
benefits of project management, 27
body of knowledge (bok), 39
bond (performance), 128
brainstorming, 220
breakeven point, 56
budget, 75
build-method, 65, 72

calendar, 133
cashflow statement, 168-175
certification (PMP), 42
change control, 86
change management (control), 78, 86
change request (template), 89
charter, 84
checklists, 97, 104
client's needs, 62
closeout report, 93-95
code of ethics, 42
cognitive persuasion, 231
commissioning phase, 46
communications, 75, 89, 198-211,
Comninos, Dennis, 19
computing, 36
concept phase, 46
configuration management, 83
construction phase, 46
contingencies, 114
contract, 72
control cycle, 77
control project, 176-183
costing, 109
critical path method (CPM), 72, 128-139

data capture, 180
decision-making, 78
decommissioning phase, 46
design and development phase, 46
direct costs, 109
document control, 208-211

earned value (EV), 184-19
emotional persuasion, 231
entrepreneur projects, 22, 246
environment, 27
estimating, 72, 108-115
ethics, 42
events, 133, 145
event management, 258-265
execution strategy, 72
expediting, 78, 156

failure (project), 120, 238
fashion examples, 84, 118
fast tracking, 50
feasibility study, 58-69, 71
financial accounting, 169
fixed costs, 110
float, 138, 143
Frigenti, Enzo, 19
functional OBS, 223

Gantt, Henry (chart), 30, 75, 140-149
general management, 22
global project management forum, 43

half-life refit, 56
hammocks, 144
handover meeting, 217
history of project management, 30-37
hub and spoke, 91
human resource management, 40

impact statement, 90
implementation phase, 46
indirect costs, 110
information power, 230
instructions, 77
insurance, 128
International Project Management
Association (IPMA), 43

job description, 228

keydates, 145

labour costs, 111
level of effort, 45
library, 93
lifecycle (cashflow), 56
lifecycle costing, 56
lines of communication, 203

management accounting, 169
management-by-projects, 21, 256
matrix (OBS), 34, 225, 250
meetings, 212-221

Microsoft Project (software), 27
milestones, 145
mission statement, 84
mobile project office, 256
model testing, 65, 127
monitoring progress, 77
monthly reports, 206

needs analyses, 62
network diagram, 129
non conformance report (NCR), 88
non-verbal communication, 201

Obeng, 19
OBS, 34, 72, 222-231

payback period, 56
percentage complete (PC), 180
performance bond, 124
personal power, 231
PERT, 32-33
planned value (PV), 185
planning and control cycle, 70-81
planning software, 27
PMBOK, 40
PMI, 39
PMO, 248-257
PMP, 42
portfolio management, 22
power (authority), 230
problem-solving, 78
procedures, 24
process management, 23
procurement, 150-157
    - control, 154
    - costs, 112
    - cycle, 152
    - schedule, 150-157
product lifecycle, 53, 244
production management, 22
programme management, 21
progress meeting, 219
progress report, 206

project
- accounts, 169
- brief, 71, 83
- charter, 71, 84
- closeout report, 93-95
- communication, 198-211
- control, 176-183
- control cycle, 77
- definition, 16
- environment, 35, 27
- estimating, 108-115
- information and control system, 205
- initiation, 83
- integration, 40
- interfaces, 40
- lifecycle, 25, 44-57
- lifecycle cashflow, 56
- Management Associations, 38-43
- management (definition), 18
- Management Institute (PMI), 38-43
- management office (PMO), 248-257
- management process, 24
- Management Professional (PMP), 42
- management standards, 38-43
- management triangle, 35
- office, 248-257
- organisation structures (matrix), 34, 222-231
- procurement management, 150-157
- quality management, 192-197
- quality plan, 193
- risk management, 116-127
- scope management, 82-95
- teams, 232-239
- time management, 140-149
- types, 19
proposal, 71, 83
purchase order, 153

quality 192-197
- assurance, 193
- audit, 193
- control, 195
- control plan (QCP), 196
- definitions, 203
- management, 75, 192-197

reporting, 206
- exception, 207
- frequency, 79
- trends, 207
resource, 158-167
- availability, 161
- estimating, 159
- forecasting, 161
- histogram, 75, 160
- limited resource scheduling, 165
- loading, 161
- management, 158-167
- planning, 158-167
- planning and control, 75
- smoothing, 162
responsibility, 230
- authority gap, 230
- matrix, 225
retention, 124
revised barchart, 157-151
reward power, 230
risk, 116-127
- contracting, 124
- control, 118
- deflection, 124
- elimination, 124
- failure, 120
- management, 72, 116-127
- mitigating, 124
- objectives, 117
- quantify, 117
- response, 123
role of the project manager, 26, 238
rolling horizon barchart, 148

S Curve (how to draw), 174
schedule barchart, 140-149
schedule variance (SV), 186
scheduling (definition), 75
scope, 82-95
   - change control, 86
   - control, 86
   - creep, 77
   - definition, 85
   - management, 72, 82-95
   - planning, 85
   - verification, 85
single point of responsibility, 26
site office, 249
small business management, 246
small projects, 240-247
software, 27
spiral (planning and control cycle), 79
Solent University (model testing), 65
stakeholders, 59-61
standards, 38
systems breakdown structure, 102

task, (see activity)
team building, 232-239
team roles, 26
teams, 232-239
technical management, 22
templates (WBS), 105
time,
   - cost, quality triangle, 35
   - limited resource scheduling, 164
   - management, 140-149
timenow, 185
top-down estimating, 114
total quality management (TQM), 194
tracking progress, 78
training (computer skills), 255
transmittal note, 210
trend reports, 207
triangle of forces (time, cost, quality), 35

unit rates, 113
unit standards, 42
upgrade, 55

variable costs, 110

WBS, 72, 96-107
   - event, 262
   - numbering system, 106
   - roll-up, 107
   - templates, 105
work
   - authorisation, 77
   - package (see WBS), 97
   - pattern, 133
workshop (brainstorming), 220

This bluewater trilogy by Rory and Sandra Burke includes a preparation guide, a travelogue and a checklist. Bluewater cruising has all the features of a complex project, requiring effective budgeting, procurement, scope management and time planning. Most importantly it requires effective risk management and disaster recovery for the safety of the crew and integrity of the yacht.

Managing Your Bluewater Cruise

ISBN: 0-473-03822-6

352 pages, 200+ photographs, UK: £9.95

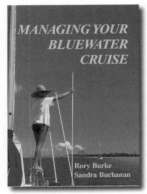

This preparation guide discusses a range of pertinent issues from establishing budgets and buying equipment to preventative maintenance and heavy weather sailing. The text works closely with the ORC category 1 requirements and includes many comments from other cruisers who are *'out there doing it'*. This book also outlines what training courses to attend before leaving, what gear to take, provisioning strategy and, equally important, how to stow it all. If you wish to bridge the gap between fantasy and reality then your bluewater cruise must be effectively managed.

Greenwich to the Dateline

ISBN: 0-620-16557-x

352 pages, 200+ photographs, UK: £9.95

This is a travelogue of our bluewater cruising adventure from the Greenwich Meridian to the International Dateline – sit back with a sundowner and be inspired to cruise to the Caribbean and Pacific islands. In this catalogue of rewarding experiences we describe how we converted our travelling dreams into a bluewater cruising reality.

Bluewater Checklist

ISBN: 0-9582 391-0-x

96 pages, UK: £4.95

Checklists provide an effective management tool to confirm everything is on board, and all tasks are completed. Why try to remember everything in your head when checklists never forget!!! This book provides a comprehensive portfolio of checklists covering every aspect of bluewater cruising. To ensure your bluewater cruise will be successful, it must be effectively managed. Checklists provide an excellent tool for this purpose - even NASA uses them!!!

cosmic mba series

This *Fashion Design Series* by *Sandra Burke* promotes fashion design skills and techniques which can be effectively applied in the world of fashion. In a competitive market it is important to produce designs that are not only stylish and pleasing to the eye, but also commercially viable.

Fashion Artist - *Drawing Techniques to Portfolio Presentation*
ISBN 0-9582 391-7-7, Sandra Burke

Fashion drawing is an essential part of the fashion designer's portfolio of skills, enabling them to develop ideas and visually communicate design concepts on paper. This book is set out as a self-learning programme to teach you how to draw fashion figures and clothing, and present them in a portfolio. The text is supported with explanatory drawings and photographs.

Fashion Computing – *Design Techniques and CAD*
ISBN 0-9582 391-3-4, Sandra Burke

This book introduces you to the computer drawing and design skills used by the fashion industry. Through visuals and easy steps, you learn creative fashion computing design techniques. It includes, flats/working drawings, illustrations, fabrics, presentation and the digital fashion portfolio. Specific software includes: Photoshop, Illustrator, CorelDRAW, Freehand, PowerPoint, Gerber and Lectra Systems.

Fashion Designer – *Design Techniques, Catwalk to Street*
ISBN 0-9582 391-2-6, Sandra Burke

This book will help you develop your portfolio of fashion design skills while guiding you through the fashion design process in today's fashion industry. It explains how to analyse and forecast fashion trends, interpret a design brief, choose fabrics and colour ways, develop designs, create design presentations and develop collections for specific target markets.

Fashion Entrepreneur
ISBN 0-9582 733-0-8, Sandra Burke

With your head buzzing with innovative and creative ideas – welcome to the Fashion Entrepreneurs' world of glamour, style and wealth. This book outlines the traits and techniques fashion designers use to spot opportunities and set up small businesses. These topics include: writing business plans, raising finance, sales and marketing, and the small business management skills required to run a fashion companies on a day-to-day basis.

Project Management - *Planning and Control Techniques (5ed)*
Rory Burke
ISBN 0-9582 733-1-6
384 pages

PM 5ed presents the latest planning and control techniques, particularly those used by the project management software and the body of knowledge (APM bok and PMI's PMBOK). This book has established itself internationally as the standard text for Project Management programs.

Introduction to Project Management
Rory Burke
ISBN: 0-9582 733-3-2
288 pages

This book is a broad based introduction to the field of Project Management which explains all the special planning and control techniques needed to manage projects successfully. This book is ideal for managers entering project management and team members in the project management office (PMO).

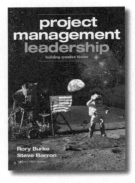

Project Management Leadership - *building creative teams*
Rory Burke and Steve Baron
ISBN 0-9582 733-5-9
384 pages

This book is a comprehensive guide outlining the essential leadership skills to manage the human side of managing projects. Key topics include: leadership styles, delegation, motivation, negotiation, conflict resolution, and team building.

Project Management Entrepreneur - *creating new ventures*
Rory Burke
ISBN 0-9582 733-2-4
384 pages

This is the first book to integrate the three management skills of Entrepreneurship, Project Management, and Small Business Management. Entrepreneur skills are required to spot opportunities, project management skills are required to implement the new venture and small business management skills are required to run the business on a day-to-day basis.

German translation of:

Project Management - *Planning and Control Techniques*
Rory Burke
ISBN: 3-8266-1443-7

Project management techniques are perfect for a country renowned for its precise time keeping and production quality.

Greek translation of:

Project Management - *Planning and Control Techniques*
Rory Burke
ISBN: 960-218-289-X

The 2004 Olympic Games clearly showed how project management techniques can be used to control an event to meet a fixed end date.

Chinese translation of:

Project Management - *Planning and Control Techniques*
Rory Burke
ISBN: 0-471-98762-X

With the boom in demand for Chinese manufacturing, so there is an associated boom in Chinese infrastructure projects and the need for project management techniques.

Entrepreneurs Toolkit

Rory Burke
ISBN: 0-9582 391-4-2
160 pages

Entrepreneurs Toolkit is a comprehensive guide outlining the essential entrepreneur skills to spot a marketable opportunity, the essential business skills to start a new venture and the essential management skills to make-it-happen.

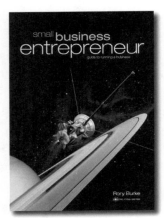

Small Business Entrepreneur

Rory Burke
ISBN: 0-9582 391-6-9
160 pages

Small Business Entrepreneur is a comprehensive guide outlining the essential management skills to run a small business on a day-to-day basis. This includes developing a business plan and sources of finance.

BBC interview

Rory Burke was educated at Wicklow and Oswestry. He has an MSc in Project Management (Henley) and degrees in Naval Architecture (Southampton) and Computer Aided Engineering (Coventry). After working internationally on marine and offshore projects, Rory set-up a publishing business to strike a work-life balance between sailing and writing. Rory is a visiting lecturer to universities in Britain, America, Canada, HK, New Zealand, Australia and South Africa.